Visit classzone.com and get connected

Online resources for students and parents

ClassZone resources provide instruction, practice, and learning support.

eEdition Plus ONLINE

This interactive version of the text encourages students to explore science.

Content Review Online

Interactive review reinforces the big idea and key concepts of each chapter.

SciLinks

NSTA-selected links provide relevant Web resources correlated to the text.

Chapter-Based Support

Math tutorials, news, resources, test practice, and a misconceptions database help students succeed.

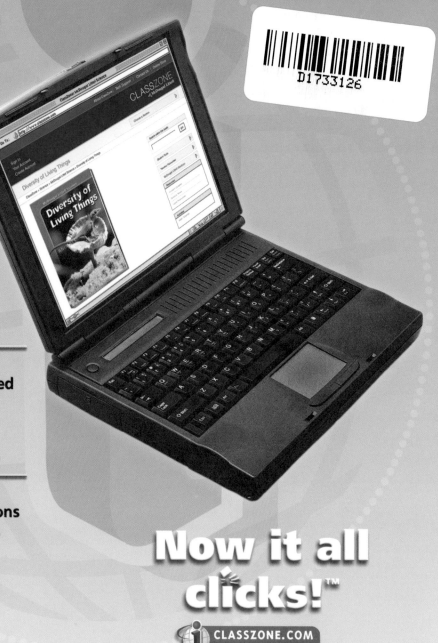

Now it all clicks!™

CLASSZONE.COM

McDougal Littell

Diversity of Living Things

ANIMALS

fungi

adaptations

PLANTS

LIFE SCIENCE

A ▶ Cells and Heredity
B ▶ Life Over Time
C ▶ Diversity of Living Things
D ▶ Ecology
E ▶ Human Biology

EARTH SCIENCE

A ▶ Earth's Surface
B ▶ The Changing Earth
C ▶ Earth's Waters
D ▶ Earth's Atmosphere
E ▶ Space Science

PHYSICAL SCIENCE

A ▶ Matter and Energy
B ▶ Chemical Interactions
C ▶ Motion and Forces
D ▶ Waves, Sound, and Light
E ▶ Electricity and Magnetism

Acknowledgments: Excerpts and adaptations from *National Science Education Standards* by the National Academy of Sciences. Copyright © 1996 by the National Academy of Sciences. Reprinted with permission from the National Academies Press, Washington, D.C.

Excerpts and adaptations from *Benchmarks for Science Literacy: Project 2061*. Copyright © 1993 by the American Association for the Advancement of Science. Reprinted with permission.

ISBN 13: 978-0-618-84219-3

ISBN 10 : 0-618-84219-5   2 3 4 5 VJM 10 09 08 07

Internet Web Site: http://www.mcdougallittell.com

Science Consultants

Chief Science Consultant

James Trefil, Ph.D. is the Clarence J. Robinson Professor of Physics at George Mason University. He is the author or co-author of more than 25 books, including *Science Matters* and *The Nature of Science.* Dr. Trefil is a member of the American Association for the Advancement of Science's Committee on the Public Understanding of Science and Technology. He is also a fellow of the World Economic Forum and a frequent contributor to *Smithsonian* magazine.

Rita Ann Calvo, Ph.D. is Senior Lecturer in Molecular Biology and Genetics at Cornell University, where for 12 years she also directed the Cornell Institute for Biology Teachers. Dr. Calvo is the 1999 recipient of the College and University Teaching Award from the National Association of Biology Teachers.

Kenneth Cutler, M.S. is the Education Coordinator for the Julius L. Chambers Biomedical Biotechnology Research Institute at North Carolina Central University. A former middle school and high school science teacher, he received a 1999 Presidential Award for Excellence in Science Teaching.

Instructional Design Consultants

Douglas Carnine, Ph.D. is Professor of Education and Director of the National Center for Improving the Tools of Educators at the University of Oregon. He is the author of seven books and over 100 other scholarly publications, primarily in the areas of instructional design and effective instructional strategies and tools for diverse learners. Dr. Carnine also serves as a member of the National Institute for Literacy Advisory Board.

Linda Carnine, Ph.D. consults with school districts on curriculum development and effective instruction for students struggling academically. A former teacher and school administrator, Dr. Carnine also co-authored a popular remedial reading program.

Donald Steely, Ph.D. serves as principal investigator at the Oregon Center for Applied Science (ORCAS) on federal grants for science and language arts programs. His background also includes teaching and authoring of print and multimedia programs in science, mathematics, history, and spelling.

Sam Miller, Ph.D. is a middle school science teacher and the Teacher Development Liaison for the Eugene, Oregon, Public Schools. He is the author of curricula for teaching science, mathematics, computer skills, and language arts.

Vicky Vachon, Ph.D. consults with school districts throughout the United States and Canada on improving overall academic achievement with a focus on literacy. She is also co-author of a widely used program for remedial readers.

Content Reviewers

John Beaver, Ph.D.
Ecology
Professor, Director of Science Education Center
College of Education and Human Services
Western Illinois University
Macomb, IL

Donald J. DeCoste, Ph.D.
Matter and Energy, Chemical Interactions
Chemistry Instructor
University of Illinois
Urbana-Champaign, IL

Dorothy Ann Fallows, Ph.D., MSc
Diversity of Living Things, Microbiology
Partners in Health
Boston, MA

Michael Foote, Ph.D.
The Changing Earth, Life Over Time
Associate Professor
Department of the Geophysical Sciences
The University of Chicago
Chicago, IL

Lucy Fortson, Ph.D.
Space Science
Director of Astronomy
Adler Planetarium and Astronomy Museum
Chicago, IL

Elizabeth Godrick, Ph.D.
Human Biology
Professor, CAS Biology
Boston University
Boston, MA

Isabelle Sacramento Grilo, M.S.
The Changing Earth
Lecturer, Department of the Geological Sciences
San Diego State University
San Diego, CA

David Harbster, MSc
Diversity of Living Things
Professor of Biology
Paradise Valley Community College
Phoenix, AZ

Richard D. Norris, Ph.D.
Earth's Waters
Professor of Paleobiology
Scripps Institution of Oceanography
University of California, San Diego
La Jolla, CA

Donald B. Peck, M.S.
Motion and Forces; Waves, Sound, and Light;
 Electricity and Magnetism
Director of the Center for Science Education (retired)
Fairleigh Dickinson University
Madison, NJ

Javier Penalosa, Ph.D.
Diversity of Living Things, Plants
Associate Professor, Biology Department
Buffalo State College
Buffalo, NY

Raymond T. Pierrehumbert, Ph.D.
Earth's Atmosphere
Professor in Geophysical Sciences (Atmospheric Science)
The University of Chicago
Chicago, IL

Brian J. Skinner, Ph.D.
Earth's Surface
Eugene Higgins Professor of Geology and Geophysics
Yale University
New Haven, CT

Nancy E. Spaulding, M.S.
Earth's Surface, The Changing Earth, Earth's Waters
Earth Science Teacher (retired)
Elmira Free Academy
Elmira, NY

Steven S. Zumdahl, Ph.D.
Matter and Energy, Chemical Interactions
Professor Emeritus of Chemistry
University of Illinois
Urbana-Champaign, IL

Susan L. Zumdahl, M.S.
Matter and Energy, Chemical Interactions
Chemistry Education Specialist
University of Illinois
Urbana-Champaign, IL

Safety Consultant

Juliana Texley, Ph.D.
Former K–12 Science Teacher and School Superintendent
Boca Raton, FL

English Language Advisor

Judy Lewis, M.A.
Director, State and Federal Programs for reading proficiency
and high risk populations
Rancho Cordova, CA

Teacher Panel Members

Carol Arbour
Tallmadge Middle School,
Tallmadge, OH

Patty Belcher
Goodrich Middle School,
Akron, OH

Gwen Broestl
Luis Munoz Marin Middle School,
Cleveland, OH

Al Brofman
Tehipite Middle School,
Fresno, CA

John Cockrell
Clinton Middle School,
Columbus, OH

Jenifer Cox
Sylvan Middle School,
Citrus Heights, CA

Linda Culpepper
Martin Middle School,
Charlotte, NC

Kathleen Ann DeMatteo
Margate Middle School,
Margate, FL

Melvin Figueroa
New River Middle School,
Ft. Lauderdale, FL

Doretha Grier
Kannapolis Middle School,
Kannapolis, NC

Robert Hood
Alexander Hamilton Middle School,
Cleveland, OH

Scott Hudson
Covedale Elementary School,
Cincinnati, OH

Loretta Langdon
Princeton Middle School,
Princeton, NC

Carlyn Little
Glades Middle School,
Miami, FL

Ann Marie Lynn
Amelia Earhart Middle School,
Riverside, CA

James Minogue
Lowe's Grove Middle School,
Durham, NC

Joann Myers
Buchanan Middle School,
Tampa, FL

Barbara Newell
Charles Evans Hughes Middle School,
Long Beach, CA

Anita Parker
Kannapolis Middle School,
Kannapolis, NC

Greg Pirolo
Golden Valley Middle School,
San Bernardino, CA

Laura Pottmyer
Apex Middle School,
Apex, NC

Lynn Prichard
Booker T. Washington Middle Magnet
School, Tampa, FL

Jacque Quick
Walter Williams High School,
Burlington, NC

Robert Glenn Reynolds
Hillman Middle School,
Youngstown, OH

Stacy Rinehart
Lufkin Road Middle School,
Apex, NC

Theresa Short
Abbott Middle School,
Fayetteville, NC

Rita Slivka
Alexander Hamilton Middle School,
Cleveland, OH

Marie Sofsak
B F Stanton Middle School,
Alliance, OH

Nancy Stubbs
Sweetwater Union Unified School District,
Chula Vista, CA

Sharon Stull
Quail Hollow Middle School,
Charlotte, NC

Donna Taylor
Okeeheelee Middle School,
West Palm Beach, FL

Sandi Thompson
Harding Middle School,
Lakewood, OH

Lori Walker
Audubon Middle School & Magnet Center,
Los Angeles, CA

Teacher Lab Evaluators

Andrew Boy
W.E.B. DuBois Academy,
Cincinnati, OH

Jill Brimm-Byrne
Albany Park Academy,
Chicago, IL

Gwen Broestl
Luis Munoz Marin Middle School,
Cleveland, OH

Al Brofman
Tehipite Middle School,
Fresno, CA

Michael A. Burstein
The Rashi School,
Newton, MA

Trudi Coutts
Madison Middle School,
Naperville, IL

Jenifer Cox
Sylvan Middle School,
Citrus Heights, CA

Larry Cwik
Madison Middle School,
Naperville, IL

Jennifer Donatelli
Kennedy Junior High School,
Lisle, IL

Melissa Dupree
Lakeside Middle School,
Evans, GA

Carl Fechko
Luis Munoz Marin Middle School,
Cleveland, OH

Paige Fullhart
Highland Middle School,
Libertyville, IL

Sue Hood
Glen Crest Middle School,
Glen Ellyn, IL

William Luzader
Plymouth Community Intermediate School,
Plymouth, MA

Ann Min
Beardsley Middle School,
Crystal Lake, IL

Aileen Mueller
Kennedy Junior High School,
Lisle, IL

Nancy Nega
Churchville Middle School,
Elmhurst, IL

Oscar Newman
Sumner Math and Science Academy,
Chicago, IL

Lynn Prichard
Booker T. Washington Middle Magnet
School, Tampa, FL

Jacque Quick
Walter Williams High School,
Burlington, NC

Stacy Rinehart
Lufkin Road Middle School,
Apex, NC

Seth Robey
Gwendolyn Brooks Middle School,
Oak Park, IL

Kevin Steele
Grissom Middle School,
Tinley Park, IL

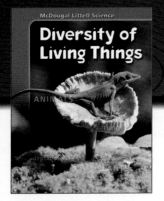

Diversity of Living Things

eEdition

Unit Features

1 Single-Celled Organisms and Viruses   6

the BIG idea

Bacteria and protists have the characteristics of living things, while viruses are not alive.

2 Introduction to Multicellular Organisms   40

the BIG idea

Multicellular organisms live in and get energy from a variety of environments.

How does an organism get energy and materials from its environment?

Features

Visual Highlights

Internet Resources @ ClassZone.com

INVESTIGATIONS AND ACTIVITIES

Standards and Benchmarks

Each chapter in **Diversity of Life** covers some of the learning goals that are described in the *National Science Education Standards* (NSES) and the Project 2061 *Benchmarks for Science Literacy.* Selected content and skill standards are shown below in shortened form. The following National Science Education Standards are covered on pages xii-xvii, in Frontiers in Science, and in Timelines in Science, as well as in chapter features and laboratory investigations: Understandings About Scientific Inquiry (A.9), Science and Technology in Society (F.5), Understandings About Science and Technology (E.6), Science as a Human Endeavor (G.1), Nature of Science (G.2), and History of Science (G.3)

Content Standards

1 Single-Celled Organisms and Viruses

National Science Education Standards

C.1.b	All organisms are composed of cells—the fundamental unit of life. Most organisms are single cells; other organisms are multicellular.
C.1.c	Cells carry on the many functions needed to sustain life.
C.1.f	Some diseases are the result of damage by infection by other organisms.
C.2.a	Reproduction is a characteristic of all living systems.
C.3.a	All organisms must be able to obtain and use resources, grow, reproduce, and maintain stable internal conditions.

Project 2061 Benchmarks

5.C.1	All living things are composed of cells, from just one to many millions, whose details usually are visible only through a microscope.
5.C.3	Many of the basic functions of organisms—such as extracting energy from food and getting rid of waste—are carried out within cells.
6.E.3	Viruses, bacteria, fungi, and parasites may infect the human body and interfere with normal body functions.

2 Introduction to Multicellular Organisms

National Science Education Standards

C.1.a	Important levels of organization for structure and function include cells, organs, tissues, organ systems, whole organisms, and ecosystems.
C.3.c	Behavior is one kind of response an organism makes to an internal or external stimulus.
F.1.e	Food provides energy and nutrients for growth and development.

Project 2061 Benchmarks

5.A.1	One of the most general distinctions among organisms is between plants, which use sunlight to make their own food, and animals, which consume energy-rich foods.
5.B.2	In sexual reproduction, a single specialized cell from a female merges with a specialized cell from a male.
5.C.2	Various organs and tissues serve the needs of cells for food, air, and waste removal.
5.D.2	Organisms may interact with one another as producer/consumer, predator/prey, or one organism may scavenge or decompose another.
5.E.3	Energy can change from one form to another in living things. Animals get energy from oxidizing their food, releasing some of its energy as heat.
6.C.1	Organs and organ systems are composed of cells and help provide cells with basic needs.
6.C.2	For the body to use food for energy and building materials, the food must first be digested into molecules that are absorbed and transported to cells.

3 Plants

National Science Education Standards

C.2.b | Plants can reproduce sexually—the egg and sperm are produced in the flowers of flowering plants.

C.4.c | Energy in the form of sunlight is transferred by producers into chemical energy through photosynthesis.

Project 2061 Benchmarks

4.C.6 | The composition of soil is greatly influenced by plant roots and debris, bacteria, fungi, worms, insects, rodents, and other organisms.

5.A.5 | All organisms are part of global food webs. One web includes land plants, the animals that feed on them, and so forth.

5.E.1 | Plants use the energy in light to make sugars out of carbon dioxide and water. This food can be used immediately for fuel or materials or it may be stored for later use.

4 Invertebrate Animals

National Science Education Standards

C.1.d | Specialized cells perform specialized functions in multicellular organisms.

C.5.a | Although different species might look dissimilar, the unity among organisms becomes apparent from an analysis of internal structures.

Project 2061 Benchmarks

5.A.2 | Animals have a great variety of body plans and internal structures that contribute to their being able to find food and reproduce.

5.A.3 | Similarities among organisms are found in internal anatomical features.

5 Vertebrate Animals

National Science Education Standards

C.3.b | Regulation of an organism's internal environment keeps conditions within the range required to survive.

C.5.b | Biological adaptations include changes in structures, behaviors, or physiology that enhance survival in a particular environment.

Project 2061 Benchmarks

5.F.2 | Changes in environmental conditions affect survival of organisms and entire species.

6.B.3 | Patterns of human development are similar to those of other vertebrates.

6.C.3 | Lungs take in oxygen for combustion of food, they eliminate the carbon dioxide produced.

Process and Skill Standards

National Science Education Standards

A.1 | Identify questions that can be answered through scientific methods.

A.2 | Design and conduct a scientific investigation.

A.3 | Use appropriate tools and techniques to gather and analyze data.

A.4 | Use evidence to describe, predict, explain, and model.

A.5 | Think critically to find relationships between results and interpretations.

A.6 | Give alternative explanations and predictions.

A.7 | Communicate procedures, results, and conclusions.

A.8 | Use mathematics in all aspects of scientific inquiry.

Project 2061 Benchmarks

9.A.3 | Write numbers in different forms.

9.A.4 | Use the operations addition and subtraction as inverses of each other—one undoing what the other does; likewise multiplication and division.

9.B.2 | Use mathematics to describe change.

9.B.3 | Use graphs to show relationships.

9.C.4 | Use a graphic display of numbers to show patterns such as trends, varying rates of change, gaps, or clusters.

11.A.2 | Think about things as systems.

11.A.3 | See how systems are interconnected.

11.C.5 | Understand how symmetry (or the lack of it) can determine properties of many objects, including organisms.

12.A.2 | Investigate, using hypotheses.

12.A.3 | See multiple ways to interpret results.

12.B.7 | Determine units for answers.

12.D.2 | Read and interpret tables and graphs.

12.D.3 | Research books, periodicals, databases.

12.D.4 | Understand charts, graphs and tables.

12.E.5 | Criticize faulty reasoning.

Introducing Life Science

Scientists are curious. Since ancient times, they have been asking and answering questions about the world around them. Scientists are also very suspicious of the answers they get. They carefully collect evidence and test their answers many times before accepting an idea as correct.

In this book you will see how scientific knowledge keeps growing and changing as scientists ask new questions and rethink what was known before. The following sections will help get you started.

What Is Life Science?

Life science is the study of living things. As you study life science, you will observe and read about a variety of organisms, from huge redwood trees to the tiny bacteria that cause sore throats. Because Earth is home to such a great variety of living things, the study of life science is rich and exciting.

But life science doesn't simply include learning the names of millions of organisms. It includes big ideas that help us to understand how all these living things interact with their environment. Life science is the study of characteristics and needs that all living things have in common. It's also a study of changes—both daily changes as well as changes that take place over millions of years. Probably most important, in studying life science, you will explore the many ways that all living things—including you—depend upon Earth and its resources.

The text and visuals in this book will invite you into the world of living things and provide you with the key concepts you'll need in your study. Activities offer a chance for you to investigate some aspects of life science on your own. The four unifying principles listed below provide a way for you to connect the information and ideas in this program.

- **All living things share common characteristics.**

- **All living things share common needs.**

- **Living things meet their needs through interactions with the environment.**

- **The types and numbers of living things change over time.**

the **BIG** idea

Each chapter begins with a big idea. Keep in mind that each big idea relates to one or more of the unifying principles.

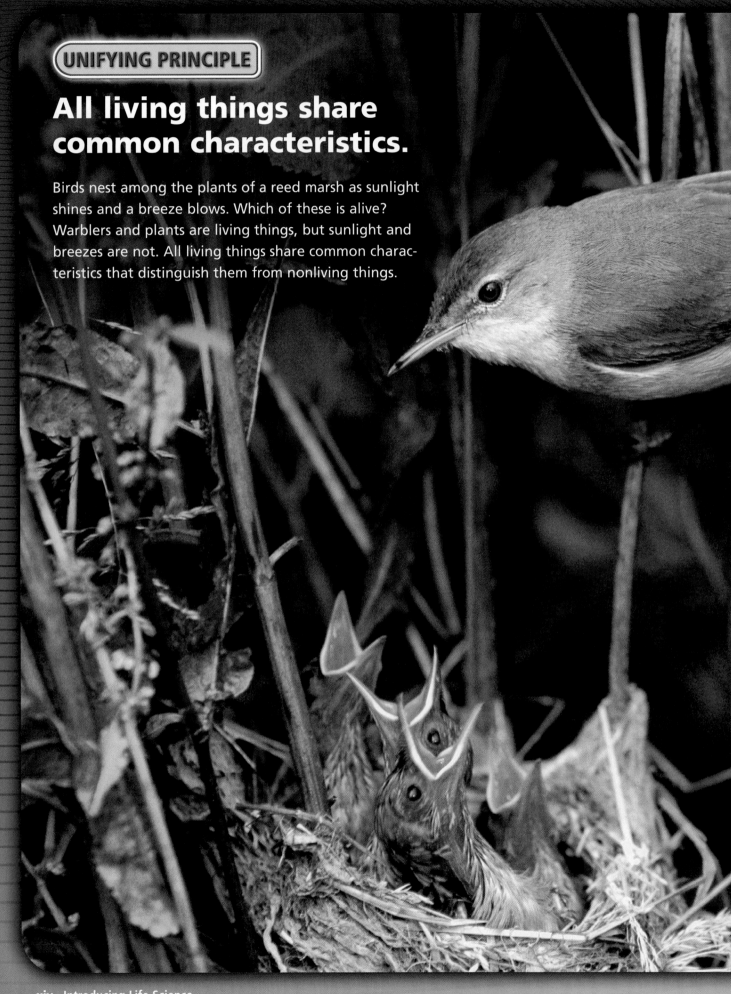

All living things share common characteristics.

Birds nest among the plants of a reed marsh as sunlight shines and a breeze blows. Which of these is alive? Warblers and plants are living things, but sunlight and breezes are not. All living things share common characteristics that distinguish them from nonliving things.

What It Means

This unifying principle helps you explore one of the biggest questions in science, "What is life?" Let's take a look at four characteristics that distinguish living things from nonliving things: organization, growth, reproduction, and response.

Organization

If you stand a short distance from a reed warbler's nest, you can observe the largest level of organization in a living thing—the **organism** itself. Each bird is an organism. If you look at a leaf under a microscope, you can observe the smallest level of organization capable of performing all the activities of life, a **cell.** All living things are made of cells.

Growth

Most living things grow and develop. Growth often involves not only an increase in size, but also an increase in complexity, such as a tadpole growing into a frog. If all goes well, the small warblers in the picture will grow to the size of their parent.

Reproduction

Most living things produce offspring like themselves. Those offspring are also able to reproduce. That means that reed warblers produce reed warblers, which in turn produce more reed warblers.

Response

You've probably noticed that your body adjusts to changes in your surroundings. If you are exploring outside on a hot day, you may notice that you sweat. On a cold day, you may shiver. Sweating and shivering are examples of response.

Why It's Important

People of all ages experience the urge to explore and understand the living world. Understanding the characteristics of living things is a good way to start this exploration of life. In addition, knowing about the characteristics of living things helps you identify

• similarities and differences among various organisms
• key questions to ask about any organism you study

All living things share common needs.

What do you need to stay alive? What does an animal like a fish or a coral need to stay alive? All living things have common needs.

What It Means

Inside every living thing, chemical reactions constantly change materials into new materials. For these reactions to occur, an organism needs energy, water and other materials, and living space.

Energy

You use energy all the time. Movement, growth, and sleep all require energy, which you get from food. Plants use the energy of sunlight to make sugar for energy. Almost all animals get their energy by eating either plants or other animals that eat plants.

Water and Other Materials

Water is an important material in the cells of all living things. The chemical reactions inside cells take place in water, and water plays a part in moving materials around within organisms.

Other materials are also essential for life. For example, plants must have carbon dioxide from the air to make sugar. Plants and animals both use oxygen to release the energy stored in sugar. You and other animals that live on land get oxygen when you breathe in air. The fish swimming around the coral reef in the picture have gills, which allow them to get oxygen that is dissolved in the water.

Living Space

You can think of living space as a home—a space that protects you from external conditions and a place where you can get materials such as water and air. The ocean provides living space for the coral that makes up this coral reef. The coral itself provides living space for many other organisms.

Why It's Important

Understanding the needs of living things helps people make wise decisions about resources. This knowledge can also help you think carefully about

- the different ways in which various organisms meet their needs for energy and materials
- the effects of adding chemicals to the water and air around us
- the reasons why some types of plants or animals may disappear from an area

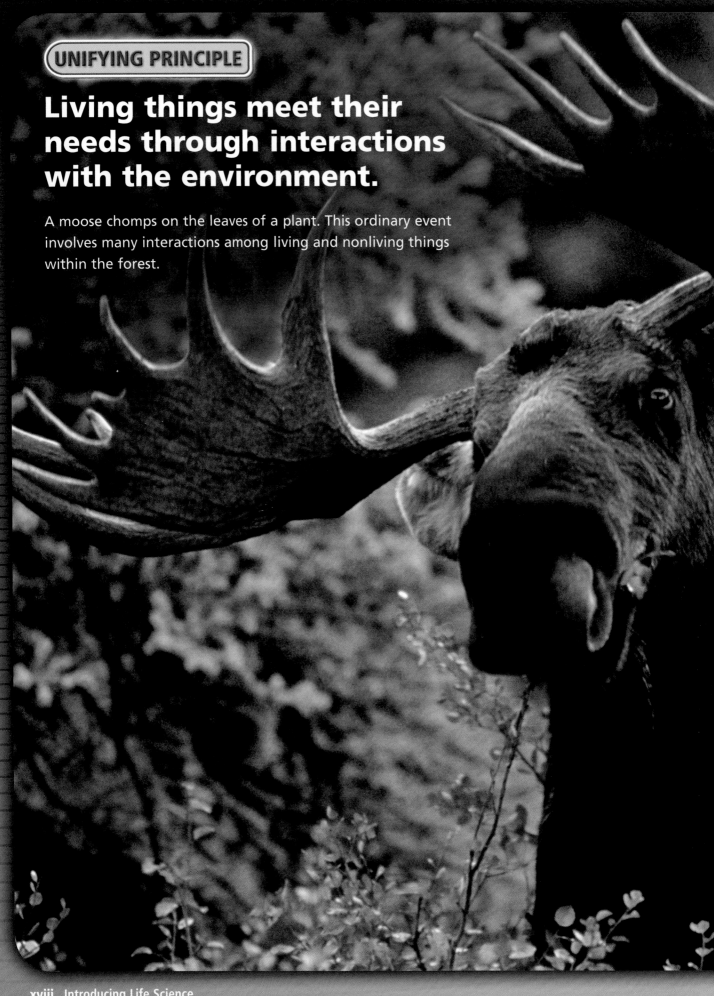

Living things meet their needs through interactions with the environment.

A moose chomps on the leaves of a plant. This ordinary event involves many interactions among living and nonliving things within the forest.

What It Means

To understand this unifying principle, take a closer look at the words *environment* and *interactions*.

Environment

The **environment** is everything that surrounds a living thing. An environment is made up of both living and nonliving factors. For example, the environment in this forest includes rainfall, rocks, and soil as well as the moose, the evergreen trees, and the birch trees. In fact, the soil in these forests is called "moose and spruce" soil because it contains materials provided by the animals and evergreens in the area.

Interaction

All living things in an environment meet their needs through interactions. An **interaction** occurs when two or more things act in ways that affect one another. For example, trees and other forest plants can meet their need for energy and materials through interactions with materials in soil and with air and light from the Sun. New plants get living space as birds, wind, and other factors carry seeds from one location to another.

Animals like this moose meet their need for food through interactions with other living things. The moose gets food by eating leaves off trees and other plants. In turn, the moose becomes food for wolves.

Why It's Important

Learning about living things and their environment helps scientists and decision makers address issues such as

- predicting how a change in the moose population would affect the soil in the forest
- determining the ways in which animals harm or benefit the trees in a forest
- developing land for human use without damaging the environment

The types and numbers of living things change over time.

The story of life on Earth is a story of changes. Some changes take place over millions of years. At one time, animals similar to modern fish swam in the area where this lizard now runs.

What It Means

To understand how living things change over time, let's look closely at the terms *diversity* and *adaptation*.

Diversity

You are surrounded by an astonishing variety of living things. This variety is called **biodiversity.** Today, scientists have described and named an estimated 1.75 million species. There are even more species that haven't been named. Scientists use the term *species* to describe a group of closely related living things. Members of a **species** are so similar that they can reproduce offspring that are able to reproduce. Lizards, such as the one you see in the photograph, are so diverse that they make up many different species.

Over the millions of years that life has existed on Earth, new species have originated and others have disappeared. The disappearance of a species is called **extinction.** Fossils, like the one in the photograph, provide evidence that some types of organisms that lived millions of years ago became extinct.

Adaptation

Scientists use the term **adaptation** to mean a characteristic of a species that allows members of that species to survive in a particular environment. Adaptations are related to needs. A salamander's legs are an adaptation that allows it to move on land.

Over time, species either develop adaptations to changing environments or they become extinct. The history of living things on Earth is related to the history of the changing Earth. The presence of a fish-like fossil indicates that the area shown in this photograph was once covered by water.

Why It's Important

By learning how living things change over time, you will gain a better understanding of the life that surrounds you and how it survives. Discovering more about the history of life helps scientists to

• identify patterns of relationships among various species
• predict how changes in the environment may affect species in the future

The Nature of Science

You may think of science as a body of knowledge or a collection of facts. More important, however, science is an active process that involves certain ways of looking at the world.

Scientific Habits of Mind

Scientists are curious. They are always asking questions. A scientist who observes that the number of plants in a forest preserve has decreased might ask questions such as, "Are more animals eating the plants?" or "Has the way the land is used affected the numbers of plants?" Scientists around the world investigate these and other important questions.

Scientists are observant. They are always looking closely at the world around them. A scientist who studies plants often sees details such as the height of a plant, its flowers, and how many plants live in a particular area.

Scientists are creative. They draw on what they know to form a possible explanation for a pattern, an event, or a behavior that they have observed. Then scientists create a plan for testing their ideas.

Scientists are skeptical. Scientists don't accept an explanation or answer unless it is based on evidence and logical reasoning. They continually question their own conclusions as well as conclusions suggested by other scientists. Scientists trust only evidence that is confirmed by other people or methods.

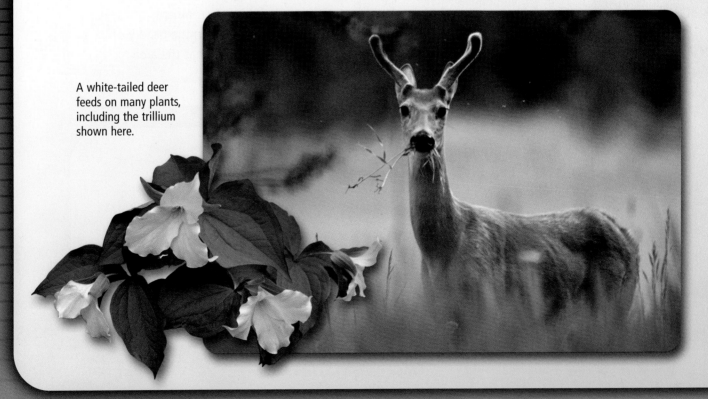

A white-tailed deer feeds on many plants, including the trillium shown here.

By measuring the growth of this tree, a scientist can study interactions in the ecosystem.

Science Processes at Work

You can think of science as a continuous cycle of asking and seeking answers to questions about the world. Although there are many processes that scientists use, scientists typically do each of the following:

• Observe and ask a question
• Determine what is known
• Investigate
• Interpret results
• Share results

Observe and Ask a Question

It may surprise you that asking questions is an important skill. A scientific investigation may start when a scientist asks a question. Perhaps scientists observe an event or a process that they don't understand, or perhaps answering one question leads to another.

Determine What Is Known

When beginning an inquiry, scientists find out what is already known about a question. They study results from other scientific investigations, read journals, and talk with other scientists. A biologist who is trying to understand how the change in the number of deer in an area affects plants will study reports of censuses taken for both plants and animals.

Investigate

Investigating is the process of collecting evidence. Two important ways of collecting evidence are observing and experimenting.

Observing is the act of noting and recording an event, a characteristic, a behavior, or anything else detected with an instrument or with the senses. For example, a scientist notices that plants in one part of the forest are not thriving. She sees broken plants and compares the height of the plants in one area with the height of those in another.

An **experiment** is an organized procedure during which all factors but the one being studied are controlled. For example, the scientist thinks the reason some plants in the forest are not thriving may be that deer are eating the flowers off the plants. An experiment she might try is to mark two similar parts of an area where the plants grow and then build a fence around one part so the deer can't get to the plants there. The fence must be constructed so the same amounts of light, air, and water reach the plants. The only factor that changes is contact between plants and the deer.

Close observation of the Colorado potato beetle led scientists to a biological pesticide that can help farmers control this insect pest.

Forming hypotheses and making predictions are two other skills involved in scientific investigations. A **hypothesis** is a tentative explanation for an observation or a scientific problem that can be tested by further investigation. For example, since at least 1900, Colorado potato beetles were known to be resistant to chemical insecticides. Yet the numbers of beetles were not as large as expected. It was hypothesized that bacteria living in the beetles' environment were killing many beetles. A **prediction** is an expectation of what will be observed or what will happen and can be used to test a hypothesis. It was predicted that certain bacteria would kill Colorado potato beetles. This prediction was confirmed when a bacterium called *Bt* was discovered to kill Colorado potato beetles and other insect pests.

Interpret Results

As scientists investigate, they analyze their evidence, or data, and begin to draw conclusions. **Analyzing data** involves looking at the evidence gathered through observations or experiments and trying to identify any patterns that might exist in the data. Often scientists need to make additional observations or perform more experiments before they are sure of their conclusions. Many times scientists make new predictions or revise their hypotheses.

Computers help scientists analyze the sequence of base pairs in the DNA molecule.

Share Results

An important part of scientific investigation is sharing results of experiments. Scientists read and publish in journals and attend conferences to communicate with other scientists around the world. Sharing data and procedures gives them a way to test one another's results. They also share results with the public through newspapers, television, and other media.

Living things contain complex molecules such as RNA and DNA. To study them, scientists often use models like the one shown here.

The Nature of Technology

Imagine what life would be like without cars, computers, and cell phones. Imagine having no refrigerator or radio. It's difficult to think of a world without these items we call technology. Technology, however, is more than just machines that make our daily activities easier. Like science, technology is also a process. The process of technology uses scientific knowledge to design solutions to real-world problems.

Science and Technology

Science and technology go hand in hand. Each depends upon the other. Even designing a device as simple as a toaster requires knowledge of how heat flows and which materials are the best conductors of heat. Scientists also use a number of devices to help them collect data. Microscopes, telescopes, spectrographs, and computers are just a few of the tools that help scientists learn more about the world. The more information these tools provide, the more devices can be developed to aid scientific research and to improve modern lives.

The Process of Technological Design

Heart disease is among the leading causes of death today. Doctors have successfully replaced damaged hearts with hearts from donors. Medical engineers have developed pacemakers that improve the ability of a damaged heart to pump blood. But none of these solutions is perfect. Although it is very complex, the heart is really a pump for blood; thus, using technology to build a better replacement pump should be possible. The process of technological design involves many choices. In the case of an artificial heart, choices about how and what to develop involve cost, safety, and patient preference. What kind of technology will result in the best quality of life for the patient?

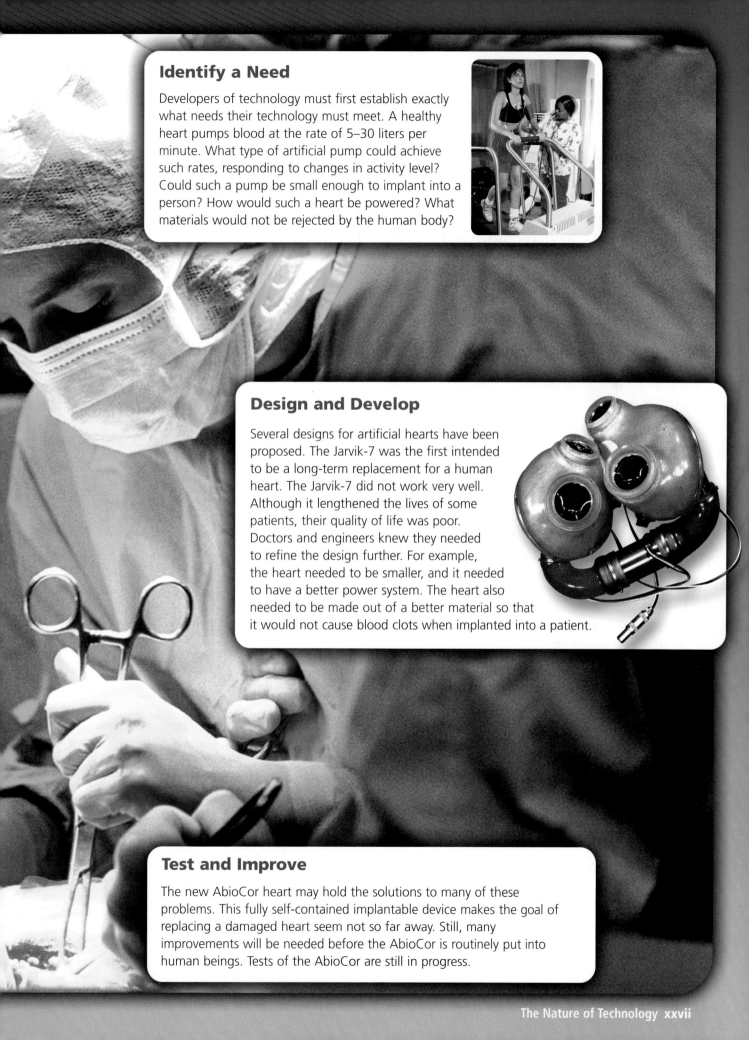

Identify a Need

Developers of technology must first establish exactly what needs their technology must meet. A healthy heart pumps blood at the rate of 5–30 liters per minute. What type of artificial pump could achieve such rates, responding to changes in activity level? Could such a pump be small enough to implant into a person? How would such a heart be powered? What materials would not be rejected by the human body?

Design and Develop

Several designs for artificial hearts have been proposed. The Jarvik-7 was the first intended to be a long-term replacement for a human heart. The Jarvik-7 did not work very well. Although it lengthened the lives of some patients, their quality of life was poor. Doctors and engineers knew they needed to refine the design further. For example, the heart needed to be smaller, and it needed to have a better power system. The heart also needed to be made out of a better material so that it would not cause blood clots when implanted into a patient.

Test and Improve

The new AbioCor heart may hold the solutions to many of these problems. This fully self-contained implantable device makes the goal of replacing a damaged heart seem not so far away. Still, many improvements will be needed before the AbioCor is routinely put into human beings. Tests of the AbioCor are still in progress.

Using McDougal Littell Science

Reading Text and Visuals

This book is organized to help you learn. Use these boxed pointers as a path to help you learn and remember the **Big Ideas** and **Key Concepts**.

Take notes.

Use the strategies on the **Getting Ready to Learn** page.

Read the Big Idea.

As you read **Key Concepts** for the chapter, relate them to **the Big Idea**.

CHAPTER 5
Getting Ready to Learn

CHAPTER

5 Verteb Animal

the **BIG** idea

Vertebrate animals live in most of Earth's environments.

Key Concepts

SECTION 5.1 Vertebrates are animals with endoskeletons. Learn how most of the vertebrates on Earth are fish.

SECTION 5.2 Amphibians and reptiles are adapted for life on land. Learn how most amphibians hatch in water and most reptiles hatch on land.

SECTION 5.3 Birds meet their needs on land, in water, and in the air. Learn how adaptations for flight affect how birds meet their needs.

SECTION 5.4 Mammals live in many environments. Learn about mammals' many adaptations.

 Internet Preview
CLASSZONE.COM
Chapter 5 online resources: Content Review, two Visualizations, four Resource Centers, Math Tutorial, Test Practice.

C 154 Unit: Diversity of Living Things

CONCEPTS REVIEW

- All living things have common needs.
- Plants and some invertebrates have adaptations for life on land.
- Most multicellular organisms can reproduce sexually.

VOCABULARY REVIEW

migration p. 64
embryo p. 98
gill p. 137
lung p. 137
exoskeleton p. 143

CONTENT REVIEW
CLASSZONE.COM
Review concepts and vocabulary.

TAKING NOTES

CHOOSE YOUR OWN STRATEGY

Take notes using one or more of the strategies from earlier chapters – **main idea webs**, **main idea and details**, **mind maps**, or **combination notes**. You can also use other note-taking strategies that you may already know.

VOCABULARY STRATEGY

Think about a vocabulary term as a **magnet word** diagram. Write other terms and ideas related to that term around it.

See the Note-Taking Handbook on pages R45–R51.

SCIENCE NOTEBOOK

Main Idea Web   Main Idea and Details

Mind Map

bird   ENDOTHERM   hair, feather blubber

mammal   shivers, swea pants

transforms food   active in co
into heat   environment

C 156 Unit: Diversity of Living Things

KEY CONCEPT

5.1 Vertebrates are animals with endoskeletons.

◀ **BEFORE, you learned**

- Most animals are invertebrates
- Animals have adaptations that suit their environment
- Animals get energy by consuming food

▶ **NOW, you will learn**

- About the skeletons of vertebrate animals
- About the characteristics of fish
- About three groups of fish

VOCABULARY

vertebrate p. 157
endoskeleton p. 157
scale p. 161

EXPLORE Streamlined Shapes

How does a fish's shape help it move?

PROCEDURE

① Place your hand straight up and down in a tub of water. Keep your fingers together and your palm flat.

② Move your hand from one side of the tub to the other, using your palm to push the water.

③ Move your hand across the tub again, this time using the edge of your hand as if you were cutting the water.

MATERIALS
tub of water

WHAT DO YOU THINK?

- In which position was the shape of your hand most like the shape of a fish's body?
- How might the shape of a fish's body affect its ability to move through water?

Vertebrate animals have backbones.

If you asked someone to name an animal, he or she would probably name a vertebrate. Fish, frogs, snakes, birds, dogs, and humans are all **vertebrates,** or animals with backbones. Even though only about 5 percent of animal species are vertebrates, they are among the most familiar and thoroughly studied organisms on Earth.

Vertebrate animals have muscles, a digestive system, a respiratory system, a circulatory system, and a nervous system with sensory organs. The characteristic that distinguishes vertebrates from other animals is the **endoskeleton,** an internal support system that grows along with the animal. Endoskeletons allow more flexibility and ways of moving than exoskeletons do.

VOCABULARY
Add magnet word diagrams for *vertebrate* and *endoskeleton* to your notebook.

Chapter 5: **Vertebrate Animals** 157 **C**

Reading Text and Visuals

RESOURCE CENTER
CLASSZONE.COM

Learn more about the
many types of worms.

Most worms have complex body systems.

Some worms have simple bodies. Others have well-developed body systems. Worms have a tube-shaped body, with bilateral symmetry. In many worms, food enters at one end and is processed as it moves through a digestive tract. Worms take in oxygen, dissolved in water, through their skin. Because of this, worms must live moist environments. Many live in water.

Segmented Worms

Segmented worms have bodies that are divided into individual compartments, or segments. These worms are referred to as annelids (AN-uh-lihdz), which means "ringed animals." One annelid you might be familiar with is the earthworm. As the diagram below shows, an earthworm's segments can be seen on the outside of its body.

An earthworm has organs that are organized into body systems. The digestive system of an earthworm includes organs for digestion and food storage. It connects to the excretory system, which removes waste. Earthworms pass soil through their digestive system. They digest decayed pieces of plant and animal matter from the soil and excrete what's left over. A worm's feeding and burrowing activity adds nutrients and oxygen to the soil.

CHECK YOUR READING Name two body systems found in earthworms.

Read one paragraph at a time.

Look for a topic sentence that explains the main idea of the paragraph. Figure out how the details relate to that idea. One paragraph might have several important ideas; you may have to reread to understand.

Answer the questions.

Check Your Reading questions will help you remember what you read.

Study the visuals.

- Read the title.
- Read all labels and captions.
- Figure out what the picture is showing. Notice the information in the captions.

Inside an Earthworm

An earthworm has organs and body systems.

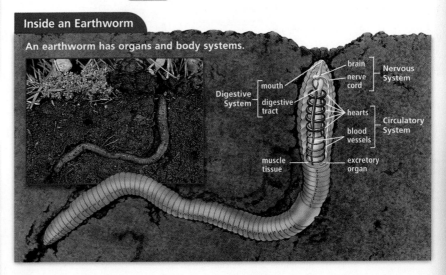

Digestive System — mouth, digestive tract

Nervous System — brain, nerve cord

Circulatory System — hearts, blood vessels

muscle tissue

excretory organ

132 Unit: Diversity of Living Things

Doing Labs

To understand science, you have to see it in action. Doing labs helps you understand how things really work.

① Read the entire lab first.

② Form a hypothesis.

③ Follow the procedure.

④ Record the data.

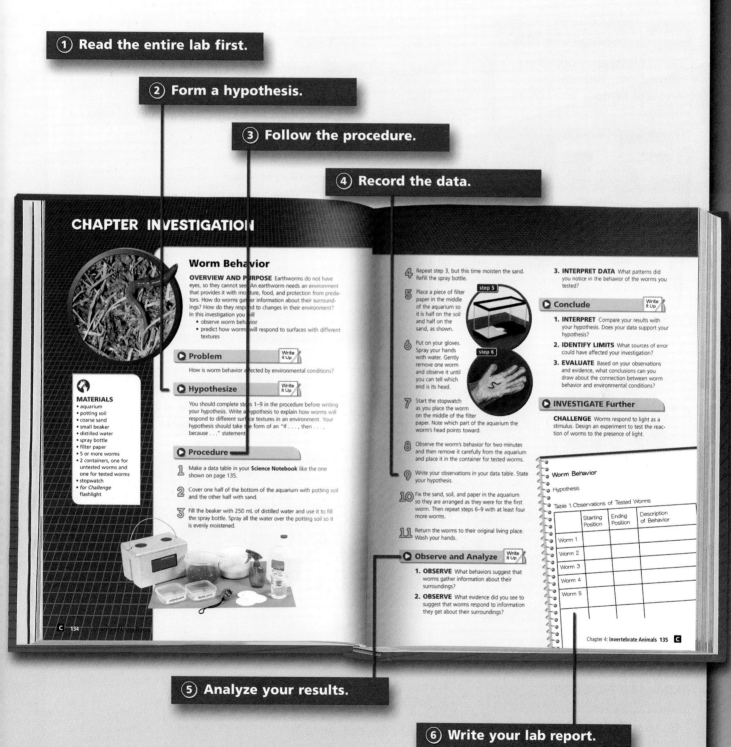

CHAPTER INVESTIGATION

Worm Behavior

OVERVIEW AND PURPOSE Earthworms do not have eyes, so they cannot see. An earthworm needs an environment that provides it with moisture, food, and protection from predators. How do worms gather information about their surroundings? How do they respond to changes in their environment? In this investigation you will
- observe worm behavior
- predict how worms will respond to surfaces with different textures

▶ **Problem**   Write It Up

How is worm behavior affected by environmental conditions?

▶ **Hypothesize**   Write It Up

You should complete steps 1–9 in the procedure before writing your hypothesis. Write a hypothesis to explain how worms will respond to different surface textures in an environment. Your hypothesis should take the form of an "If . . . , then . . . . because . . ." statement.

▶ **Procedure**

1 Make a data table in your **Science Notebook** like the one shown on page 135.

2 Cover one half of the bottom of the aquarium with potting soil and the other half with sand.

3 Fill the beaker with 250 mL of distilled water and use it to fill the spray bottle. Spray all the water over the potting soil so it is evenly moistened.

MATERIALS
- aquarium
- potting soil
- coarse sand
- small beaker
- distilled water
- spray bottle
- filter paper
- 5 or more worms
- 2 containers, one for untested worms and one for tested worms
- stopwatch
- *for Challenge* flashlight

4 Repeat step 3, but this time moisten the sand. Refill the spray bottle.

5 Place a piece of filter paper in the middle of the aquarium so it is half on the soil and half on the sand, as shown.

step 5

6 Put on your gloves. Spray your hands with water. Gently remove one worm and observe it until you can tell which end is its head.

step 6

7 Start the stopwatch as you place the worm on the middle of the filter paper. Note which part of the aquarium the worm's head points toward.

8 Observe the worm's behavior for two minutes and then remove it carefully from the aquarium and place it in the container for tested worms.

9 Write your observations in your data table. State your hypothesis.

10 Fix the sand, soil, and paper in the aquarium so they are arranged as they were for the first worm. Then repeat steps 6–9 with at least four more worms.

11 Return the worms to their original living place. Wash your hands.

▶ **Observe and Analyze**   Write It Up

1. **OBSERVE** What behaviors suggest that worms gather information about their surroundings?

2. **OBSERVE** What evidence did you see to suggest that worms respond to information they get about their surroundings?

3. **INTERPRET DATA** What patterns did you notice in the behavior of the worms you tested?

▶ **Conclude**   Write It Up

1. **INTERPRET** Compare your results with your hypothesis. Does your data support your hypothesis?

2. **IDENTIFY LIMITS** What sources of error could have affected your investigation?

3. **EVALUATE** Based on your observations and evidence, what conclusions can you draw about the connection between worm behavior and environmental conditions?

▶ **INVESTIGATE Further**

CHALLENGE Worms respond to light as a stimulus. Design an experiment to test the reaction of worms to the presence of light.

Worm Behavior

Hypothesis

Table 1. Observations of Tested Worms

	Starting Position	Ending Position	Description of Behavior
Worm 1			
Worm 2			
Worm 3			
Worm 4			
Worm 5			

Chapter 4: Invertebrate Animals **135** **C**

C 134

⑤ Analyze your results.

⑥ Write your lab report.

Using Technology

The Internet is a great source of information about up-to-date science. The ClassZone Web site and NSTA SciLinks have exciting sites for you to explore. Video clips and simulations can make science come alive.

Look for red banners.

Go to **ClassZone.com** to see simulations, visualizations, resource centers, and content review.

Watch the video.

See science at work in the **Scientific American Frontiers** video.

Look up SciLinks.

Go to **scilinks.org** to explore the topic.

NSTA scilinks.org **SCILINKS**

Animal Behavior **Code: MDL040**

Diversity of Living Things
Contents Overview

Unit Features

1 Single-Celled Organisms and Viruses   6

the **BIG** idea

Bacteria and protists have the characteristics of living things, while viruses are not alive.

2 Introduction to Multicellular Organisms   40

the **BIG** idea

Multicellular organisms live in and get energy from a variety of environments.

3 Plants   82

the **BIG** idea

Plants are a diverse group of organisms that live in many land environments.

4 Invertebrate Animals   120

the **BIG** idea

Invertebrate animals have a variety of body plans and adaptations.

5 Vertebrate Animals   154

the **BIG** idea

Vertebrate animals live in most of Earth's environments.

Chilling Changes

How do organisms survive in this chilly Arctic landscape? Scientists are studying how organisms have adapted to the extreme cold of Earth's northern climates.

SCIENTIFIC AMERICAN FRONTIERS

Learn more about how living things respond to freezing temperatures in the video "Frozen Alive."

Caribou search for lichen and small plants to eat in northern Alaska.

Lichen find materials and living space on rocks in frozen environments.

When Life Chills Out

When faced with the approach of winter, some animals hurry up, and some slow down. You may have seen animals getting a move on, migrating to warmer places. Other animals stay alive at home by hibernating, or entering a sleep-like state. Hibernation conserves energy until spring by slowing down many body processes. But what happens when an organism's body temperature dips below freezing?

Ice formation inside an organism's body is one of the most serious, and potentially damaging, threats to winter survival. If ice forms inside cells, it can damage the cell's operation and tear holes in the cell membrane, almost certainly leading to death.

An arctic ground squirrel peers above snow-covered ground in Alaska.

Some animals and plants take cold weather survival to an extreme. Some frogs and insects can allow their bodies to freeze solid. Some fish have fluids in their bodies that can *cool* below the freezing point of water and still flow. How do they do it?

Scientists studying survivors of extreme cold are not just learning about the ways organisms respond in the wild. Research on cold weather survival helps scientists understand problems faced by human society. Growing crops year-round and using bacteria to clean up pollution in a frozen environment are two examples. There are two main responses that allow living things to live in a sub-freezing world.

Arctic woolly bear caterpillars may take many years to grow to full size.

When the caterpillar reaches full size, it forms a cocoon and changes into a moth.

Avoid Ice, or Tolerate It

Organisms can either avoid the forming of ice or tolerate it. Some animals, like a fish called a flounder, produce antifreeze proteins in their bodies. The proteins keep ice from forming in the blood and other fluids. The fluids thicken but still flow. They never turn to ice crystals. Scientists call this response freeze-avoidance.

Other organisms—including some frogs, many types of insects, and some trees—do allow ice to form inside their bodies. In these organisms, ice forms, but only in the spaces outside the cells. Freeze-tolerant organisms pump fluid out of their cells. Specialized proteins located outside of the cells encourage ice to form there, rather than inside the cells.

Perhaps the champion of freeze tolerance is a small Arctic insect called the Arctic woolly bear caterpillar. It is only active for a few weeks out of the year, during the brief Arctic summer. It can take this caterpillar up to fifteen years to mature into a moth!

Temperatures during Arctic winters often fall as low as −70°C. Because the ground is frozen year-round, the caterpillars cannot burrow. Instead, their bodies freeze solid in winter, shutting down nearly all of their cellular activity and

SCIENTIFIC AMERICAN FRONTIERS

View the "Frozen Alive" segment of your Scientific American Frontiers video to see how scientists studying fish and frogs have begun to solve the mysteries of life surviving a freeze.

IN THIS SCENE FROM THE VIDEO ▶
How do the frog's systems start up again, after being shut down during freezing?

WHAT BRINGS ON THE THAW? Ken Storey collects wood frogs. The frogs have an automatic response to cold temperatures, which allows Ken and his team to keep them in a freezer without killing them. Storey and his team know the "what" of freeze tolerance. They want to learn the "how." How does the frog stay alive during and after shutdown? Storey expects that the thawing process works in the usual way, that the frogs will begin to warm from the outside in. Instead he finds that internal organs begin the thaw. The liver is the first organ to activate. It produces glucose or sugar, which then gets other cells, those in the heart, to begin their work.

expending almost no energy. Scientists have known for centuries that some insects can freeze over the winter, but only recently have they begun to understand exactly how insects' bodies change to allow them to freeze and thaw.

Scientist Ken Storey has discovered a set of genes that turn on, like a switch, in response to freezing temperatures. These genes are called master control genes, because they have the ability to turn other genes in the body on or off. In the case of freeze-tolerant animals, master control genes first turn off nearly all the genes in the body. Arctic woolly bear caterpillars have many thousands of genes, but during the winter most of those genes are turned off. Keeping genes turned off is an adaptation that helps the caterpillar conserve energy throughout the winter.

Is It Really Extreme?

Organisms have adapted to a wide variety of environments. The Arctic woolly bear caterpillar is suited to life near the Arctic Circle. Some organisms must be able to survive in the exact opposite—the extreme heat of deserts. Others thrive in extremely salty conditions. Some plants and bacteria can even live in places with dangerously high levels of poisonous chemicals.

An environment doesn't have to be extreme to present challenges to the organisms that live there. Animals in a forest or meadow still need to find food and shelter, avoid predators, and respond to changes. The organisms living in any environment face a unique set of challenges.

UNANSWERED Questions

As scientists learn more about how animals survive in extremely cold climates, they also uncover additional questions:

- Do animals respond to temperature or a lack of light?
- How do cellular processes that halt during the winter get started up again?
- Can scientists grow freeze resistant crops?

UNIT PROJECTS

As you study this unit, work alone or in a group on one of the projects listed below. Use the bulleted steps to guide your project.

Museum Exhibit

Plan a museum exhibit showing different ways in which animals respond to extreme environments.

- Research three to five types of organisms and find out what kind of environmental changes these organisms face.
- Design, make visuals, and write text to accompany your exhibit.

Grow a Fast Plant

Observe the entire life cycle of a plant in less than six weeks. Record your observations in a journal.

- Gather information and any materials necessary to grow and care for fast plants. Obtain fast plant seeds and plant them.
- Observe the plant for a few minutes every day. Make notes in your journal, and write weekly summaries.

Local Field Study

Report on organisms that live in your local area.

- Identify three organisms you see on a regular basis and learn more about how they survive throughout the year.
- Pick one plant or animal and observe it for a few minutes once a week in the morning and in the late afternoon. How does it change over time?

CAREER CENTER
CLASSZONE.COM

Learn more about careers in zoology.

Single-Celled Organisms and Viruses

the BIG idea

Bacteria and protists have the characteristics of living things, while viruses are not alive.

How can you tell if these structures, magnified 2800×, are alive?

Key Concepts

SECTION
1.1 **Single-celled organisms have all the characteristics of living things.**
Learn about characteristics shared by all living things.

SECTION
1.2 **Bacteria are single-celled organisms without nuclei.**
Learn about the characteristics of bacteria and archaea.

SECTION
1.3 **Viruses are not alive but affect living things.**
Learn about the structure of viruses and how they affect cells.

SECTION
1.4 **Protists are a diverse group of organisms.**
Learn about protists and how they affect the environment.

Internet Preview

CLASSZONE.COM

Chapter 1 online resources: Content Review, two Visualizations, three Resource Centers, Math Tutorial, Test Practice.

EXPLORE (the BIG idea)

Where Can You Find Microscopic Life?

Make a list of places where you might find living things that are too small to be seen by your unaided eye. Then use a hand lens, magnifying glass, or microscope, to investigate some of the places on your list.

Observe and Think What do you think microscopic organisms look like? Why can microscopic life be found in so many places?

How Quickly Do Bacteria Multiply?

Tape a funnel to the top of a two-liter bottle. Place one bean in the funnel. After one minute, drop two more beans into the funnel. Continue adding beans to the bottle every minute, adding twice as many beans as you did before. When it is time to add 64 beans, use 1/8 of a cup, and then continue to double the amounts.

Observe and Think How long did it take to fill the bottle?

Internet Activity: Microscopic Life and You

Go to **ClassZone.com** to learn about the single-celled organisms.

Observe and Think What types of organisms live in the human body?

Kingdom Protista **Code: MDL039**

Getting Ready to Learn

◀ CONCEPT REVIEW

- All living things interact with their environment to meet their needs.
- The cell is the fundamental unit of life.

◀ VOCABULARY REVIEW

See Glossary for definitions.

cell
matter
molecule
organism
species

 CONTENT REVIEW
CLASSZONE.COM
Review concepts and vocabulary.

▶ TAKING NOTES

MAIN IDEA WEB

Write each new blue heading in a box. Then write notes in boxes around the center box that give important terms and details about that blue heading.

VOCABULARY STRATEGY

Place each vocabulary term at the center of a **description wheel diagram.** Write some words describing it on the spokes.

See the Note-Taking Handbook on pages R45–R51.

SCIENCE NOTEBOOK

They are organized, with an outside and an inside.

They increase in size.

Living things share common characteristics.

They reproduce and form other organisms like themselves.

They respond to changes in the environment.

MICROORGANISM

some just one cell

need microscope

very small

most living things

Single-celled organisms have all the characteristics of living things.

◀ **BEFORE, you learned**

- All living things are made of cells
- Organisms respond to their environment
- Species change over time

▶ **NOW, you will learn**

- About the various sizes of organisms
- About characteristics that are shared by all living things
- About needs shared by all organisms

VOCABULARY

microorganism p. 10
kingdom p. 11
binary fission p. 12
virus p. 14

EXPLORE Organisms

What living things are in the room with you?

PROCEDURE

1. Make a list of all the living things that are in your classroom.

2. Compare your list with the lists of your classmates. Make one list containing all the living things your class has identified.

MATERIALS
- paper
- pencil

WHAT DO YOU THINK?
- How did you identify something as living?
- Were you and your classmates able to see all the living things on your list?

Living things come in many shapes and sizes.

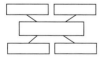

MAIN IDEA WEB
Make a web of the important terms and details about the main idea: *Living things come in many shapes and sizes.*

You can spot mushrooms in many places while walking through a forest. Scientists have discovered mushrooms that come from the same individual fungus more than 5 kilometers (3 miles) apart in an Oregon forest. Most of this honey mushroom fungus is below ground, stretching over an area covering more than 1600 football fields. This mushroom is one of the largest known living things on Earth.

Many other living things share the soil in the Oregon forest. Earthworms, insects, and many other organisms that are too small to be seen with a naked eye, also live there. For every living thing that is large enough to be seen, there are often countless numbers of smaller living things that share the same living space.

The honey mushroom fungus is one example of an organism. You, too, are an organism, and tiny bacteria living inside your body are also organisms. In fact, any living thing can be called an organism.

When you think of living things, you probably begin with those you can observe—plants, animals, and fungi such as mushrooms. However, most living things are too small to observe without a microscope. Even the tiniest organisms are made of cells. Very small organisms are called **microorganisms.** Many microorganisms are made of just one cell.

⬆ CHECK YOUR READING Compare and contrast the words *microorganism* and *organism.*

A visitor to a mangrove swamp forest can find an amazing variety of organisms. The mangrove trees themselves are the most obvious organisms. Roots from these trees grow above and below the muddy bottom of the forest. Other organisms live in almost every part of the mangrove tree.

READING TiP

The prefix *micro-* means "very small." Therefore, *microscope* means "very small scope" and *microorganism* means "very small organism."

Six Kingdoms of Life

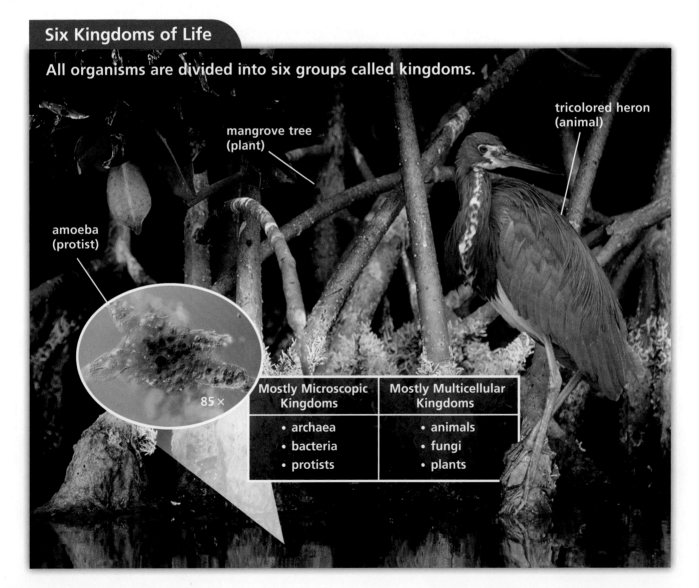

All organisms are divided into six groups called kingdoms.

tricolored heron (animal)

mangrove tree (plant)

amoeba (protist)

85 ×

Mostly Microscopic Kingdoms	Mostly Multicellular Kingdoms
• archaea • bacteria • protists	• animals • fungi • plants

A single drop of water from a mangrove swamp may be living space for many microorganisms. The circled photograph on page 10 was taken using a microscope, and shows an amoeba that may be found in the water of the swamp. Larger organisms, such as manatees and fish, swim around the roots of mangrove trees. Birds, such as tri-colored herons and roseate spoonbills, use the branches.

Scientists divide the organisms they identify into groups called **kingdoms.** This unit will cover all of the kingdoms of life, listed in the table on page 10. You are already familiar with plants and animals. Fungi are another kingdom. Fungi include mushrooms found in a forest. The other three kingdoms are composed of mostly microscopic life. You will learn more about microscopic organisms later in this chapter.

VOCABULARY
Add a description wheel for *kingdom* to your notebook. The spokes of your wheel should include examples from the six kingdoms.

Living things share common characteristics.

All living things—from the microorganisms living in a mangrove swamp to the giant organisms living in the open ocean—share similar characteristics. Living things are organized, grow, reproduce, and respond to the environment.

READING TiP
As you read about the four characteristics of all living things, note the examples of how single-celled organisms meet these four standards.

Organization

Cells are the basic unit of all living things. Cells, like all living things, have an inside and an outside. The boundary separating the inside from the outside of an individual cell is called the cell membrane. Within some cells, another structure called the nucleus is also sur-rounded by a membrane.

In this chapter, you will read about organisms made of a single cell. Some types of single-celled organisms contain a nucleus and some do not. All single-celled organisms contain everything they need to survive within their one cell. These cells are able to get energy from complex molecules, to move, and to sense their environment. The ability to perform these and other functions is part of their organization.

Growth

Living things increase in size. Organisms made of one cell do not grow as large as organisms made of many cells. But all living things need to get energy. All living things also need to obtain materials to build new structures inside cells or replace worn-out cell parts. As a result, individual cells grow larger over time.

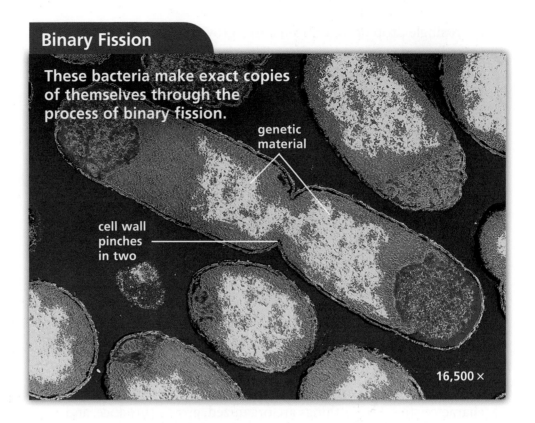

Binary Fission

These bacteria make exact copies of themselves through the process of binary fission.

genetic material

cell wall pinches in two

16,500 ×

Reproduction

Living things reproduce, forming other organisms like themselves. Every organism contains genetic material, which is a code contained in a special molecule called DNA. The code contains characteristics of the individual organism. In order to reproduce, an organism must make a copy of this material, which is passed on to its offspring.

Some single-celled organisms reproduce by a process called **binary fission.** In binary fission, material from one cell separates into two cells. The genetic material of the original cell first doubles so that each daughter cell has an exact copy of the DNA of the original cell. You might say that single-celled organisms multiply by dividing. One cell divides into 2 cells, 2 cells divide into 4, 4 into 8, 16, 32, 64, and so on. In some cells, binary fission can take place as often as every 20 minutes.

 CHECK YOUR READING   Describe how a single-celled organism is organized, grows, and reproduces.

VISUALIZATION
CLASSZONE.COM

Observe the process of binary fission.

Response

Organisms respond to changes in the environment. Even microscopic organisms respond to conditions such as light, temperature, and touch. The ability to respond allows organisms to find food, avoid being eaten, or perform other tasks necessary to survive.

INVESTIGATE Microorganisms

How do these organisms respond to their environment?

PROCEDURE

1. Place a drop of the hydra culture on a microscope slide. Using the microscope, find a hydra under medium power and sketch what you see.

2. Add a drop of warm water to the culture on the slide. How does the hydra respond? Record your observations.

3. Add a drop of the daphnia culture. Record your observations.

WHAT DO YOU THINK?

- Which observations, if any, indicate that hydras respond to their environment?
- Daphnia are organisms. What is the relationship between hydra and daphnia?

CHALLENGE What other experiments could you do to observe the responses of hydra or daphnia to their environment?

SKILL FOCUS
Observing

MATERIALS
- microscope
- slide
- hydra culture
- daphnia culture
- water

TIME
30 minutes

Living things need energy, materials, and living space.

Have you ever wondered why you need to eat food, breathe air, and drink water? All living things need energy and materials. For most organisms, water and air are materials necessary for life.

Food supplies you with energy. You—like all living things—need energy to move, grow, and develop. All animals have systems for breaking down food into usable forms of energy and materials. Plants have structures that enable them to transform sunlight into usable energy. Some microorganisms transform sunlight, while others need to use other organisms as sources of energy.

Most of the activities of living things take place in water. Water is also an ingredient for many of the reactions that take place in cells. In addition, water helps support an organism's body. If you add water to the soil around a wilted plant, you will probably see the plant straighten up as water moves into its cells.

Materials in the air include gases such as carbon dioxide and oxygen. Many of the processes that capture and release energy involve these gases. Some organisms—such as those found around hydrothermal vents—use other chemicals to capture and release energy.

Viruses are not alive.

Sometimes it's not easy to tell the difference between a living and a nonliving thing. A **virus** has genetic material enclosed in a protein shell. Viruses have many of the characteristics of living things, including genetic material. However, a virus is not nearly as complex as a cell and is not considered a living thing.

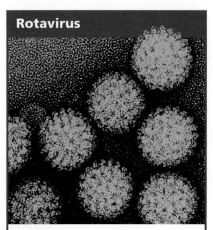

Rotavirus

These viruses contain DNA but do not grow or respond to their environment. 570,000×

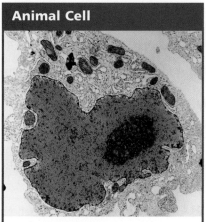

Animal Cell

Animal cells grow, reproduce, and respond to external conditions. 4800×

For example, animal cells have structures that allow them to get materials or energy from their environment. Virus particles do not grow once they have formed, and they do not take in any energy. Animal cells can make copies of their genetic material and reproduce by dividing in two. Viruses are able to reproduce only by "taking over" a cell and using that cell to make new viruses. Animal cells also have many more internal structures than viruses. Viruses usually contain nothing more than their genetic material and a protein coat.

1.1 Review

KEY CONCEPTS

1. Give examples of organisms that are very large and organisms that are very small.

2. Name four characteristics that all living things share.

3. Name three things that living things must obtain to survive.

CRITICAL THINKING

4. **Synthesize** Give examples of how a common animal, such as a dog, is organized, grows, responds, and reproduces.

5. **Predict** In a certain lake, would you expect there to be more organisms that are large enough to see or more organisms that are too small for you to see? Why?

⬥ CHALLENGE

6. **Design** Try to imagine the different structures that a single-celled organism needs to survive in pond water. Then use your ideas to design your own single-celled organism.

MATH TUTORIAL

Click on Math Tutorial for more help with interpreting line graphs.

Graphing Growth

If you hold marbles in your hand and drop them into a bowl one at a time, each drop into the bowl adds the same amount. If you plot this growth on a line graph, you will have a straight line.

By contrast, a bacterial colony's growth expands exponentially as it grows. All the bacteria divide in two. Every time all the bacteria divide, the colony doubles in size.

EXAMPLE

Compare the two types of growth on a graph.

Graph 1. Suppose the marble collection begins with one marble, and after every hour, one marble is added.

The graph shows: $x + 1 = y$
The slope of the line stays the same at each interval.

Graph 2. Suppose a bacterial colony begins with one bacterium, and every hour, a bacterial cell divides, forming two bacteria.

The graph shows: $2^x = y$
The slope gets steeper at each interval.

Examine the graphs and answer the questions.

1. How many marbles are in the collection after 3 h? How many bacteria are in the colony after 3 h?

2. After 7 h, what number of marbles would show in graph 1? Name the coordinates for this point. What number of bacteria would be shown in graph 2? Name the coordinates.

3. Copy the two graphs on graph paper. Extend each graph to 10 h. Plot the growth according to the pattern or formula given.

CHALLENGE Suppose each bacterium lives for 10 h. How many bacteria will be in the colony after 20 h?

Bacteria are single-celled organisms without nuclei.

 BEFORE, you learned

- Organisms come in all shapes and sizes
- All living things share common characteristics
- Living things may be divided into six kingdoms

 NOW, you will learn

- About the simplest living things
- About bacteria and archaea
- That bacteria may help or harm other organisms

VOCABULARY

bacteria p. 16
archaea p. 18
producer p. 19
decomposer p. 19
parasite p. 19

THINK ABOUT

Where are bacteria?

Bacteria are the simplest form of life. But that doesn't mean they're not important or numerous. As you look about the room you're sitting in, try to think of places where you might find bacteria. In fact, bacteria are on the walls, in the air, on the floor, and on your skin. It's hard to think of a place where you wouldn't find bacteria. The photograph shows a magnification of bacteria living on a sponge. The bacteria are magnified 580×. There are hundreds of millions of bacteria on your skin right now. There are trillions of bacteria that live inside your intestines and help you digest food.

Bacteria and archaea are the smallest living things.

MAIN IDEA WEB
Make a web of the important terms and details about the main idea: *Bacteria and archaea are the smallest living things.* Be sure to include how bacteria are classified.

The names of the organisms belonging in the kingdoms Archaea and Bacteria are probably unfamiliar. Yet you actually encounter these organisms every day. Bacteria are everywhere: on your skin, in the ground, in puddles and ponds, in the soil, and in the sea. About 300 species of bacteria are living in your mouth right now.

Bacteria are the simplest kind of life known on Earth. All bacteria are composed of just one cell without a nucleus. Their genetic material is contained in loops within the cell. A bacterium reproduces using binary fission.

Bacteria

All bacteria are single cells without nuclei.

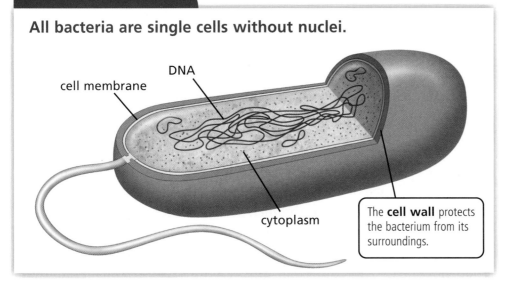

cell membrane
DNA
cytoplasm
The **cell wall** protects the bacterium from its surroundings.

Bacterial cells are different from the cells of other organisms. A bacterial cell is about 1/10 to 1/20 the size of a typical cell from organisms such as animals, plants, fungi, or protists. These four groups include organisms made up of cells with true nuclei. The nucleus is a structure that is enclosed by a membrane and that holds the genetic material.

Despite their small size, bacteria are simple only when compared with more complex cells. Bacteria are much more complex than viruses, because they have many internal structures that viruses do not have. For example, one important feature of most bacteria is a covering called a cell wall, which surrounds and protects the soft cell membrane like a rain jacket. Bacterial cells contain many large molecules and structures that are not found in viruses.

READING TiP

The plural of *bacterium* is *bacteria,* and the plural of *nucleus* is *nuclei.*

Spiral Bacteria

Rod Bacteria

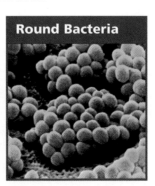
Round Bacteria

Scientists often classify bacteria by their external shapes.

- Spiral-shaped bacteria occur in single strands.
- Rod-shaped bacteria may occur singly or in chains.
- Round-shaped bacteria may occur singly or in pairs, chains, or clusters.

CHECK YOUR READING   Name two features that all bacteria share.

Archaea and bacteria are found in many environments.

RESOURCE CENTER
CLASSZONE.COM

Find out more about the many different types of bacteria.

Two types of single-celled organisms do not have nuclei. Bacteria are the most common and can be found in nearly every environment. Archaea are similar in size to bacteria, but share more characteristics with the cells of complex organisms like plants and animals.

Archaea

Archaea (AHR-kee-uh) are single-celled organisms that can survive in the largest range of environments. These environments may be very hot, very cold, or contain so much of a substance such as salt that most living things would be poisoned. As a result, scientists often group archaea according to where they live.

Methanogens take their name from methane, the natural gas they produce. These archaea die if they are exposed to oxygen. They may live in the dense mud of swamps and marshes, and in the guts of animals such as cows and termites.

READING TiP

The word halophile is formed using the root word *halo-* which means "salt," and the suffix *–phile* which means "love." Therefore, a *halophile* is a "salt lover."

Halophiles live in very salty lakes and ponds. Some halophiles die if their water is not salty enough. When a salty pond dries up, so do the halophiles. They can survive drying and begin dividing again when water returns to the pond.

Thermophiles are archaea that thrive in extreme heat or cold. They may live in hot environments such as hot springs, near hot vents deep under the sea, or buried many meters deep in the ice.

Archaea

Archaea are organisms that can live in extreme environments.

Methanogens

Methanogens may be found in a cow's stomach where they help with digestion.

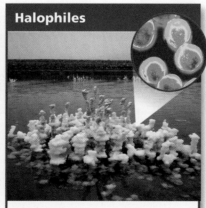

Halophiles

Halophiles can be found in extremely salty bodies of water such as the Dead Sea.

Thermophiles

Thermophiles may be found in hot geysers such as this one in Yellowstone National Park.

Bacteria

Most single-celled organisms without a nucleus are classified as bacteria. Bacteria are found in almost every environment and perform a variety of tasks. Some bacteria contain chlorophyll. Using sunlight for energy, these bacteria are an important food source in oceans. These bacteria also release oxygen gas, which animals need to breathe.

 CHECK YOUR READING What are some common traits of bacteria and archaea?

Bacteria without chlorophyll perform different tasks. Some bacteria break down parts of dead plants and animals to help recycle matter. Some bacteria release chemicals into the environment, providing a food source for other organisms. Scientists often group bacteria by the roles they play in the environment. Three of the most common roles are listed below.

Bacteria that transform energy from sunlight into energy that can be used by cells are called **producers.** These bacteria are a food source for organisms that cannot make their own food.

Decomposers get energy by breaking down materials in dead or decaying organisms. Decomposers help other organisms reuse materials found in decaying matter.

Some bacteria live in a very close relationship either inside or on the surface of other organisms. Some of these bacteria may have no effect on their host organisms or host cells. Some bacteria help their hosts. Other bacteria are **parasites,** organisms that harm their hosts.

VOCABULARY
Be sure to add description wheels for *producer, decomposer,* and *parasite* to your notebook.

Bacteria

Three roles bacteria play in the environment are shown below.

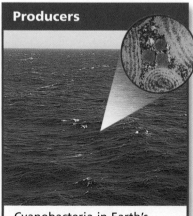
Producers
Cyanobacteria in Earth's oceans provide oxygen for animals to breathe.

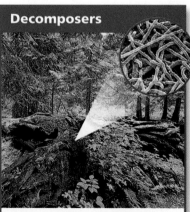
Decomposers
Some bacteria break down dead wood into materials used by other organisms.

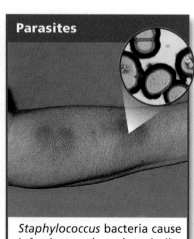
Parasites
Staphylococcus bacteria cause infections such as these boils in humans.

Bacteria may help or harm other organisms.

Some bacteria, such as producers and decomposers, are helpful to other organisms. But other bacteria can be harmful. These bacteria can cause diseases in animals and plants.

Helpful Bacteria

One shovelful of ordinary soil contains trillions of bacteria, and every fallen leaf or dead animal is covered with bacteria. These bacteria break down the matter in dead bodies and waste materials. These broken-down materials are then available for other organisms to build their bodies.

Cities use bacteria to break down sewage. Bacteria in sewage-treatment plants live on the material dissolved in liquid sewage. These bacteria help make the water clean enough to be released into rivers or oceans. Other bacteria are used to clean up oil spills by decomposing oil suspended on the ocean's surface.

Bacteria can also change materials that do not come from living things and make them available for other organisms. For example, some bacteria can convert nitrogen gas to nitrogen compounds. This process, called nitrogen fixation, makes nitrogen available to plants in a form that is useful to them. Plants use this nitrogen in making proteins, which are an important part of every cell.

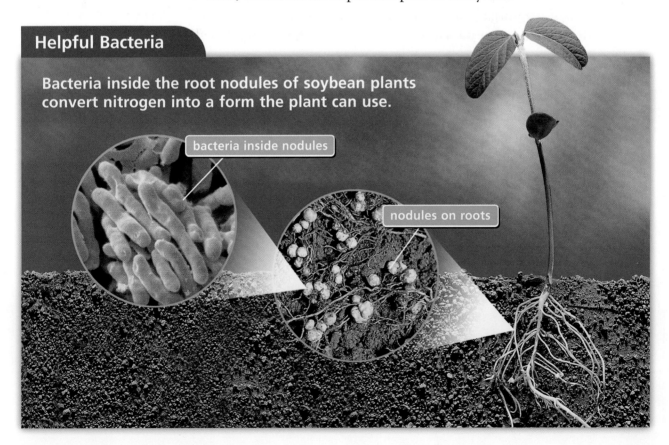

Helpful Bacteria

Bacteria inside the root nodules of soybean plants convert nitrogen into a form the plant can use.

bacteria inside nodules

nodules on roots

Like bacteria, certain types of archaea are helpful to other organisms. Animals that eat plants such as grass often depend on archaea. Methanogens help break down the cellulose in cell walls. Termites and cows are two examples of animals that can digest cellulose because of the archaea in their stomachs.

 CHECK YOUR READING Name two helpful roles that bacteria can play in the environment.

Harmful Bacteria

Not all bacteria are helpful to other organisms. Scientists first discovered that bacteria cause some diseases in the late 1800s. Much of the scientific research into harmful bacteria developed because bacteria cause disease in humans. Tuberculosis, cholera, and infant diarrhea are examples of disease caused by bacteria. Bacteria also may cause disease in many other animals and in plants.

Bacteria can cause the symptoms of disease in three ways.

- They can invade parts of the body, multiplying in body tissues and dissolving cells.
- They can poison the body with chemicals they produce and release.
- They can poison the body with chemicals that are part of the bacteria themselves.

One way to fight bacterial disease is with vaccinations. Vaccines help individual organisms prepare to fight diseases they might encounter in the future. Humans, as well as cats and dogs, get vaccinations for bacterial diseases.

Bacterial wilt caused disease in this pumpkin.

1.2 Review

KEY CONCEPTS

1. Explain why bacteria are classified as living cells but viruses are not.
2. Name two main groups of bacteria.
3. Describe three ways that bacteria affect other organisms.

CRITICAL THINKING

4. **Visualize** Draw a diagram of a bacterium. Label the parts of the cell.
5. **Predict** Where in your neighborhood would you find most of the bacteria that cause decomposition?

○ CHALLENGE

6. **Analyze** Parasitic bacteria do not usually kill their hosts, at least not quickly. For a parasite, why is it better not to kill the host?

CHAPTER INVESTIGATION

Bacteria

OVERVIEW AND PURPOSE People routinely wash themselves to keep clean. You probably take a bath or shower every day, and you also wash your hands. Your hands may appear to be perfectly clean, but appearances can be deceiving. Your hands pick up bacteria from the objects you touch. You cannot see or feel these microscopic organisms, but they are there, on your skin. In this activity you will

- sample bacteria in your environment
- sample bacteria on your hands

▶ Problem

Write It Up

Do you pick up bacteria from your environment?

▶ Hypothesize

Write It Up

Write a hypothesis about whether bacteria in your environment are transferred to your skin. Your hypothesis should take the form of an "If . . . , then . . . , because . . ." statement.

▶ Procedure

1. Make a data table in your **Science Notebook** like the one shown on page 23.

2. Obtain three agar petri dishes. Be careful not to accidentally open the dishes.

3. Remove the lid from one dish and gently press two fingers onto the surface of the agar. Close the lid immediately. Tape the dish closed. Mark the tape with the letter A. Include your initials and the date. Mark your hand as the source in Table 1. Wash your hands.

step 3

MATERIALS
- 3 covered petri dishes with sterile nutrient agar
- marker
- tape
- everyday object, like a coin or eraser
- sterile cotton swab
- hand lens

for Challenge:
- 1 covered petri dish with sterile nutrient agar
- sterile swab

4. Choose a small object you handle every day, such as a coin or an eraser. Remove the lid from the second petri dish and swipe the object across the agar. You can instead use a sterile swab to rub on the object, and then swipe the swab across the agar. Close the lid immediately. Tape and mark the dish B, as in step 3. Include the source in Table 1.

5. Choose an area of the classroom you have regular contact with, for example, the top of your desk or the classroom door. Use a clean swab to rub the area and then swipe the swab across the agar of the third petri dish. Tape and mark the dish as C, following the instructions in step 3. Dispose of the swab according to your teacher's instructions.

step 5

6. Place the agar plates upside down in a dark, warm place for two to three days. **CAUTION: Do not open the dishes. Wash your hands when you have finished.**

▶ Observe and Analyze

Write It Up

1. **OBSERVE** Observe the dishes with the hand lens. You may want to pull the tape aside, but do not remove the covers. Include a description of the bacteria in Table 1. Are the bacteria in one dish different from the others?

2. **OBSERVE** Observe the amounts of bacterial growth in each dish and record your observations in Table 1. Describe the amount of growth in relative terms, using words such as *most, least,* or *moderate.* Which dish has the most bacterial growth? the least growth?

3. Return the petri dishes to your teacher for disposal. **CAUTION: Do not open the dishes. Wash your hands thoroughly with warm water and soap when you have finished.**

▶ Conclude

Write It Up

1. **INFER** Why is it necessary for the agar to be sterile before you begin the experiment?

2. **INFER** What function does the agar serve?

3. **INTERPRET** Compare your results with your hypothesis. Do your observations support your hypothesis?

4. **IDENTIFY LIMITS** What limits are there in making a connection between the bacteria in dish A and those in dishes B and C?

5. **EVALUATE** Why is it important to keep the petri dishes covered?

6. **APPLY** Why is it important to use separate petri dishes for each sample?

▶ INVESTIGATE Further

CHALLENGE Contamination can be a problem in any experiment involving bacteria, because bacteria are everywhere. Obtain a petri dish from your teacher. Swipe a sterile swab on the agar and place the agar plate upside down in a dark, warm place for two to three days. Do the results of this test make you reevaluate your other lab results?

Bacteria

Table 1. Observations of Bacteria

Petri Dish	Source	Description of Bacteria	Amount of Bacteria
A	hand		
B			
C			

Viruses are not alive but affect living things.

BEFORE, you learned	NOW, you will learn
• Most organisms are made of a single cell • Living things share common characteristics • Viruses are not living things	• About the structure of viruses • How viruses use a cell's machinery to reproduce • How viruses affect host cells

VOCABULARY

host cell p. 26

EXPLORE Viruses

How were viruses discovered?

PROCEDURE

1. Fill a small container with mixed sesame seeds and salt.

2. Holding the sieve over the paper plate, pour the mixture into the sieve.

3. Gently shake the sieve until nothing more falls through.

4. Using a hand lens, examine the material that fell through the sieve and the material that stayed in the sieve.

MATERIALS
- small container
- sesame seeds
- table salt
- small kitchen sieve
- paper plate
- hand lens

WHAT DO YOU THINK?
- What is the most important difference between the particles that got through the sieve and the particles that remained behind?
- How could you change your sieve to make it not let through both kinds of particles?

Viruses share some characteristics with living things.

MAIN IDEA WEB
Remember to make a web of the important terms and details about the main idea: *Viruses share some characteristics with living things.*

In the late 1800s, scientists such as Louis Pasteur showed that some small organisms can spoil food and cause disease. Once the cause was found, scientists looked for ways to prevent spoilage and disease. One method of prevention they found was removing these harmful organisms from liquids.

Bacteria may be removed from liquids by pouring the liquid through a filter, like a coffee filter or a sieve. To remove bacteria, a filter must have holes smaller than one millionth of a meter in diameter.

INVESTIGATE Viruses

How do infections spread?

PROCEDURE

(1) Get a cup of sample liquid from your teacher. Pour half the liquid from your cup into the cup of a classmate, then pour the same amount back into the original cup. Your cup should then contain a mixture of the liquids from both cups.

(2) Repeat step 1 with at least two other classmates.

(3) Drop one drop of solution A into your paper cup. If it changes color, you are "infected." If you were "infected," add drops of solution B until your liquid turns clear again. Count how many drops it takes to "cure" you.

WHAT DO YOU THINK?

• If you were "infected," can you figure out who "infected" you?

• If you were not "infected," is it possible for anyone who poured liquid into your cup to be "infected"?

CHALLENGE Only one person in your class started out with an "infection." Try to figure out who it was.

SKILL FOCUS
Analyzing

MATERIALS
• paper cup
• sample liquid
• solution A
• solution B

TIME
30 minutes

When a filter had removed all of the harmful organisms from a liquid, the liquid no longer caused any illnesses. This method worked when there was only bacteria in the liquid. Sometimes filtering did not prevent disease. Something much smaller than bacteria was in the liquid. Scientists called these disease-causing particles viruses, from the Latin word for "slimy liquid" or "poison."

RESOURCE CENTER
CLASSZONE.COM

Learn more about viruses.

 CHECK YOUR READING How does the size of viruses compare with the size of bacteria?

Scientists have learned much about viruses, and can even make images of them with specialized microscopes. Viruses consist of genetic material contained inside a protective protein coat called a capsid. The protein coat may be a simple tube, such as the coat of an ebola virus, or have many layers, such as the smallpox virus shown on page 26.

Viruses may come in many shapes and sizes, but all viruses consist of a capsid and genetic material. Viruses are able to use living cells to get their DNA copied and so can produce new viruses, a characteristic that makes them similar to living things. Also the protein coat is similar to a cell's outer membrane. But viruses do not grow, and viruses do not respond to changes in their environment. Therefore, viruses are not living organisms.

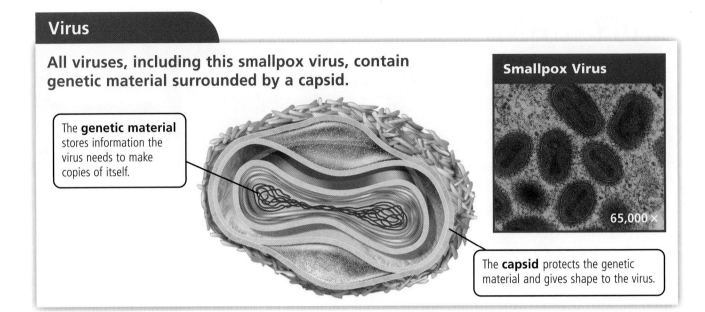

Virus

All viruses, including this smallpox virus, contain genetic material surrounded by a capsid.

The **genetic material** stores information the virus needs to make copies of itself.

Smallpox Virus

65,000 ×

The **capsid** protects the genetic material and gives shape to the virus.

Viruses multiply inside living cells.

VISUALIZATION
CLASSZONE.COM

See how viruses infect and multiply within bacteria.

Remember that all living things reproduce. Viruses cannot reproduce by themselves, which is one of the ways they are different from living things. However, viruses can use materials within living cells to make copies of themselves. The cells that viruses infect in order to make copies are called **host cells**. Despite their tiny size, viruses have the ability to cause a lot of damage to cells of other organisms.

One of the best studied viruses infects bacteria. It's called a bacteriophage (bak-TEER-ee-uh-FAYJ), which comes from the Latin for "bacteria eater." Some of the steps that a bacteriophage goes through to multiply are shown in the illustration on page 27.

❶ Attachment The virus attaches to the surface of a bacterium.

❷ Injection The virus injects its DNA into the bacterium.

❸ Production Using the same machinery used by the host cell for copying its own DNA, the host cell makes copies of the viral DNA.

❹ Assembly New viruses assemble from the parts that have been created.

❺ Release The cell bursts open, releasing 100 or more new viruses.

Viruses have proteins on their surfaces that look like the proteins that the host cell normally needs. The virus attaches itself to special sites on the host that are usually reserved for these proteins.

Not every virus makes copies in exactly the same way as the bacteriophage. Some viruses stay inside their host cells. Others use the host cell as a factory that produces new viruses one at a time. These viruses may not be as harmful to the infected organism because the host cell is not destroyed.

Making New Viruses

Viruses, such as this bacteriophage, use cells to make new viruses.

Virus (bacteriophage)
- head
- bacteriophage DNA
- tail

cell wall
cell membrane
bacterial DNA

Host cell (bacterium)

1 Attachment
The bacteriophage virus attaches to a bacterium.

injected DNA

bacterial DNA

2 Injection
The virus injects its DNA into the host cell.

empty virus
copies of viral DNA

bacterial DNA pieces

new virus parts

3 Production
The viral DNA uses the host cell's machinery to break down the host cell's DNA and produce the parts of new viruses.

new viruses

4 Assembly
The parts assemble into new viruses.

burst bacterium

5 Release
The host cell breaks apart and new viruses that are able to infect other host cells are released.

new viruses

Rows of hospital beds are filled with Massachusetts influenza patients in 1918.

Viruses may harm host cells.

A host cell does not often benefit from providing living space for a virus. The virus uses the cell's material, energy, and processes. In many cases, after a virus has made many copies of itself, the new viruses burst out of the host cell and destroy it.

Harmful viruses cause huge problems. Viruses that cause diseases such as polio, smallpox, diphtheria, or AIDS have had a major impact on human history. About 25 million people died of influenza in an outbreak that occurred just after World War I.

In the photograph, nurses work to ease the symptoms of infected patients. The most infectious patients were enclosed in tents. Others were made as comfortable as possible on beds outside. Since viruses such as influenza can spread quickly, the camp was isolated from the rest of the community.

Plant viruses can stunt plant growth and kill plants. When plant viruses invade crop plants, they can cause much economic damage, decreasing food production. Plants, animals, bacteria, and all other living things are capable of being infected by viruses.

Today, scientists are discovering ways to use viruses in a positive way. Scientists use viruses to insert certain pieces of genetic material into living cells. For example, the portion of genetic material that allows some marine organisms to produce a chemical that glows can be inserted into tissue samples to help scientists study the samples.

1.3 Review

KEY CONCEPTS

1. What are the two parts that every virus has?
2. Why are viruses not considered to be living things?
3. Explain how copies of viruses are produced.

CRITICAL THINKING

4. **Compare and Contrast** What features do viruses and cells have in common? How are they different?
5. **Explain** Summarize the steps by which a bacteriophage makes new viruses.

⬤ CHALLENGE

6. **Synthesize** What characteristics of viruses can make them so dangerous to humans and other living organisms?

The Virus and the Tulip

The people of Holland around the 1620s were trading fortunes and farmland for one beautiful flower. Tulips had arrived from Turkey by way of Vienna, and interest in the flower spread through Holland like a fever. In a frenzy called "tulipomania," collectors paid as much as 5400 guilders, the price of a city house, for just one tulip bulb—but not any ordinary tulip.

Broken Flower Bulbs

Tulip traders searched for tulips with patterns, stripes, or feathery petals. These plants were called broken bulbs. Within a field of colored tulips, suddenly an odd or patterned flower grew. Once a color break showed up, it stayed with that flower's line into each new generation, until the line died off. And die off it did. The patterned petals were caused by a virus inside the plant, and the virus caused the flowers to weaken. The blooms got smaller in each generation.

The Mystery Source

While the trade in tulips rose, growers tried many tricks to produce the crazy patterns. Still, the broken bulbs grew rarely and randomly, or so it seemed. Viruses weren't discovered until 300 years later. Scientists then figured out that a virus had caused the broken bulbs.

A small leaf-eating insect called an aphid had carried the virus from plant to plant.

© Dennis Kunkel/Dennis Kunkel Microscopy, Inc.

Back Down to the Ground

Like any goldrush, tulipomania crashed. People lost fortunes and fought over claims. In 1637, the government stopped all trading. Today, tulips with striped and feathery patterns grow around the world, but the patterns observed are not caused by viruses. Still, every now and then, a strange looking bulb appears. Instead of prizing it, growers remove it. They don't want a field of virus-infested, weakened plants.

EXPLORE

1. **OBSERVE** Look at tulips in a garden catalog, and find breeds with patterns. Observe the tulip closely. Draw or paint the modern flower and label its name.

2. **CHALLENGE** Viruses can produce sickness, but they have other effects too. Do research on viruses to list some effects of viruses that have value to scientists, doctors, or other people.

Patterns in these tulips are part of the genetic make-up of the flowers.

Protists are a diverse group of organisms.

BEFORE, you learned	NOW, you will learn
• Organisms are grouped into six kingdoms • Bacteria are single-celled organisms without a nucleus • Viruses are not living things	• About characteristics of protists • About the cell structure of protists • How protists get their energy

VOCABULARY

algae p. 31
plankton p. 33
protozoa p. 34

THINK ABOUT

Where can protists be found?

Protists include the most complex single-celled organisms found on Earth. Fifty million years ago, a spiral-shelled protist called a nummulitid was common in some oceans. Even though its shell was the size of a coin, the organism inside was microscopic and single celled. When the organism died, the shells accumulated on the ocean floor. Over millions of years, the shells were changed into the rock called limestone. This limestone was used to build the great pyramids of Egypt. Some of the most monumental structures on Earth would not exist without organisms made of just a single cell.

Most protists are single celled.

When Anton van Leeuwenhoek began using one of the world's first microscopes, he looked at pond water, among other things. He described, in his words, many "very little animalcules." Some of the organisms he saw probably were animals—microscopic but multicellular animals. However, many of the organisms Leeuwenhoek saw moving through the pond water had only a single cell. Today, more than 300 years later, scientists call these single-celled organisms protists.

Protists include all organisms with cells having nuclei and not belonging to the animal, plant, or fungi kingdoms. In other words, protists may be considered a collection of leftover organisms. As a result, protists are the most diverse of all the kingdoms.

INVESTIGATE Protists

What lives in pond water?

PROCEDURE

1. Using a dropper, place one small drop of pond water in the center of a slide. Try to include some of the material from the bottom of the container.

2. Gently place a cover slip on the drop of water.

3. Observe the slide with a hand lens first.

4. Starting with low power, observe the slide with a microscope. Be sure to follow microscope safety procedures as outlined by your teacher. Carefully focus up and down on the water. If you see moving organisms, try to follow them by gently moving the slide.

WHAT DO YOU THINK?

• Describe and draw what you could see with the hand lens.

• Describe and draw what you could see with the microscope.

• Compare your observations with those of other students.

CHALLENGE Choose one organism that moves and observe it for some time. Describe its behavior.

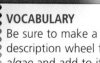

Most protists are single-celled, microscopic organisms that live in water. However, protists also include some organisms with many cells. These many-celled organisms have simpler structures than animals, plants, or fungi. They also have fewer types of cells in their bodies.

CHECK YOUR READING Why are protists considered the most diverse group of organisms?

The group of protists you're probably most familiar with is seaweeds. At first glance, seaweed looks like a plant. On closer inspection scientists see that it has a simpler structure. Some seaweeds called kelp can grow 100 meters long.

The name **algae** applies to both multicellular protists and single-celled protists that use sunlight as an energy source. Both seaweed and diatoms are types of algae. Slime molds are another type of multicellular protist.

VOCABULARY
Be sure to make a description wheel for *algae* and add to it as you read this section.

Given the many different types of organisms grouped together as protists, it is no surprise that protists play many roles in their environments. Algae are producers. They obtain energy from sunlight. Their cells provide food for many other organisms. These protists also produce oxygen, which is beneficial to many other organisms. Both of these roles are similar to those played by plants. Other protists act as parasites and can cause disease in many organisms, including humans.

Protists come in a variety of shapes and sizes.

Euglena

magnified 2800 ×

Diatoms

magnified 65 ×

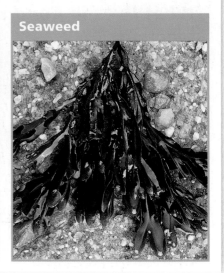

Seaweed

Protists live in any moist environment, including both freshwater and saltwater, and on the forest floor. Some protists move around in the water, some simply float in place, and some stick to surfaces. The photographs above show a small sample of the large variety of organisms that are called protists.

Seaweed is a multicellular protist that floats in the water and can be found washed up on beaches. Slime molds are organisms that attach to surfaces, absorbing nutrients from them. Diatoms are single-celled algae that float in water and are covered by hard shells. Euglena are single-celled organisms that can move like animals but also get energy from sunlight.

MAIN IDEA WEB
Remember to make a web of the important terms and details about the main idea: *Protists obtain their energy in three ways.* Include examples of each method of obtaining energy.

Protists obtain their energy in three ways.

Protists can be classified by their way of getting energy. Some protists capture sunlight and convert it to usable energy. Another group of protists gets its energy from eating other organisms. A third group gets energy by absorbing materials and nutrients from its environment.

Some protists, such as the euglena in the upper left photograph, can even switch from one mode of life to another. They swim rapidly through pond water like animals. If they receive enough sunlight, they look green and make their own food like plants. But if they are left in the dark long enough, they absorb nutrients from their environment like fungi.

 CHECK YOUR READING Explain how the organisms in the photographs above get their energy.

Algae

Plantlike protists, called algae, get energy from sunlight. Like plants, they use the Sun's energy, water, and carbon dioxide from the air or water. Algae contain chlorophyll, a green pigment that they use to capture the Sun's energy. In the process of transforming energy from sunlight, algae release oxygen gas into the air. This important process, which is called photosynthesis, also takes place in plants and some bacteria. Organisms that perform photosynthesis also supply much of the food for other organisms.

Diatoms are examples of single-celled algae. Like all algae, a diatom contains a nucleus which holds its genetic material. Diatoms also have chloroplasts, which are the energy-producing centers that contain chlorophyll.

Algae

Algae are plantlike protists. *Chlamydomonas* is an example of single-celled algae.

flagella

cell wall

nucleus

cell membrane

The **chloroplast** captures energy from sunlight.

mitochondrion

Chlamydomonas

1500×

Another type of algae, called volvox, are microscopic colonies of nearly identical cells. These cells, arranged in a hollow ball, look like some single-celled algae. Sometimes cells break off from the hollow ball to form new colonies. The new colonies will eventually escape the parent colony. Colonial organisms such as volvox are the simplest kind of multicellular organisms. Seaweed is another example of multicellular algae.

All organisms that drift in water are called **plankton.** Plankton include the young of many animals and some adult animals, as well as protists. Plankton that perform photosynthesis are called phytoplankton (plantlike plankton). Phytoplankton include algae and the cyanobacteria you learned about earlier. Phytoplankton live in all of the world's oceans and produce most of the oxygen animals breathe.

Protozoa, such as this *Paramecium*, are animal-like protists.

food vacuoles   large nucleus   cell membrane

Paramecium

40×

Cilia allow the *Paramecium* to move and to capture food.

Food is swept into the **oral groove.**

Protozoa

Protists that eat other organisms, or decaying parts of other organisms, are animal-like protists, or **protozoa.** They include many forms, all single-celled. Protozoa cannot use sunlight as a source of energy and they must move around to obtain the energy they need to survive. Certain chemicals in protozoa can recognize when a particle of food is nearby. The food particle is usually another organism or a part of one. The protozoan ingests the food and breaks it down to obtain energy.

Some animal-like protists swim rapidly, sweeping bacteria or other protists into a groove that looks like a mouth. One example, called a paramecium, is shown above. A paramecium moves about using thousands of short wavy strands called cilia.

Another group of protozoa swim with one or more long whiplike structures called flagella. A third group of protozoa has very flexible cells. Organisms such as the amoeba oozes along surfaces. When it encounters prey, the amoeba spreads out and wraps around its food.

A number of protists live as parasites, some of which cause disease in animals, including humans. One of the world's most significant human diseases, malaria, is caused by a protist. A mosquito carries the parasite from human to human. When the mosquito bites an infected human, it sucks up some of the parasite in the blood. When that same mosquito bites another human, it passes on some of the parasite. Within a human host, the parasite goes through a complex life cycle, eventually destroying red blood cells.

▼ REMINDER

A parasite is an organism that lives inside or on another organism and causes the organism harm.

△ CHECK YOUR READING   How do protozoa and algae differ in the way they obtain energy?

Decomposers

Protists that absorb food from their environment can be called funguslike protists. These protists take in materials from the soil or from other organisms and break materials down in order to obtain energy. They are called decomposers.

The term *mold* refers to many organisms that produce a fuzzy-looking growth. Most of the molds you might be familiar with, like bread mold, are fungi. But three groups of protists are also called molds. These molds have structures that are too simple to be called fungi, and they are single celled for a portion of their lives. One example of a funguslike protist is water mold, which forms a fuzzy growth on food. This food may be decaying animal or plant tissue or living organisms. Water molds live mainly in fresh water.

Slime molds live on decaying plants on the forest floor. One kind of slime mold consists of microscopic single cells that ooze around, eating bacteria. When their food is scarce, however, many of the cells group together to produce a multicellular colony. The colony eventually produces a reproductive structure to release spores. Wind can carry spores about, and they sprout where they land.

A walk in a moist forest might give you a chance to see a third kind of mold. This organism looks like a fine net, like lace, several centimeters across, on rotting logs. These slime molds are not multicellular, but instead one giant cell with many nuclei. They are the plasmodial slime molds.

Plasmodial slime mold may grow on decaying wood after a period of rainy weather.

 CHECK YOUR READING How do funguslike protists get energy?

1.4 Review

KEY CONCEPTS

1. What are two characteristics of protists?
2. What feature do all protists have in common?
3. What are the three different types of protists?

CRITICAL THINKING

4. **Provide Examples** Some protists are dependent on other organisms and cannot live independently. Other protists are independent and have organisms that depend on them. Give an example of each.

⬤ CHALLENGE

5. **Hypothesize** Scientists are considering reclassifying protists into many kingdoms. How might they decide how many kingdoms to use and how to place organisms within these kingdoms?

Chapter Review

the BIG idea

Bacteria and protists have the characteristics of living things, while viruses are not alive.

CONTENT REVIEW
CLASSZONE.COM

KEY CONCEPTS SUMMARY

1.1 Single-celled organisms have all the characteristics of living things.

Scientists divide organisms into six **kingdoms.** All living things, including **microorganisms,** are organized, grow, reproduce, and respond to the environment.

Plants   Animals   Protists   Fungi   Archaea   Bacteria

VOCABULARY
microorganism p. 10
kingdom p. 11
binary fission p. 12
virus p. 14

1.2 Bacteria are single-celled organisms without nuclei.

- Bacteria and archaea are the smallest living things.
- Archaea and bacteria are found in many environments.
- Bacteria may help or harm other organisms.

DNA

cell wall

VOCABULARY
bacteria p. 16
archaea p. 18
producer p. 19
decomposer p. 19
parasite p. 19

1.3 Viruses are not alive but affect living things.

A virus consists of genetic material enclosed in a protein coat. Viruses cannot reproduce on their own, but they use materials within living cells to make copies of themselves.

capsid

DNA

VOCABULARY
host cell p. 26

1.4 Protists are a diverse group of organisms.

Plantlike **algae** get energy from sunlight.

Funguslike protists are decomposers.

Protozoa, or animal-like protists, eat other organisms.

VOCABULARY
algae p. 31
plankton p. 33
protozoa p. 34

Reviewing Vocabulary

Draw a triangle for each of the terms listed below. Define the term, use it in a sentence, and draw a picture to help you remember the term. An example is completed for you.

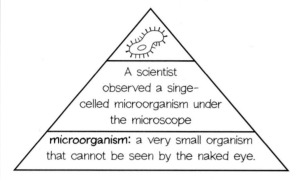

A scientist observed a singe-celled microorganism under the microscope

microorganism: a very small organism that cannot be seen by the naked eye.

1. binary fission

2. producer

3. virus

4. host cell

Describe how the vocabulary terms in the following pairs of words are related to each other. Explain the relationship in a one- or two-sentence answer. Underline each vocabulary term in your answers.

5. archaea, bacteria

6. microorganism, organism

7. decomposers, parasite

8. protists, algae

Reviewing Key Concepts

Multiple Choice *Choose the letter of the best answer.*

9. Which group is *not* a microscopic kingdom?
  a. fungi
  b. bacteria
  c. archaea
  d. protists

10. What happens in binary fission?
  a. DNA is combined into one cell.
  b. The daughter cells differ from the parent cell.
  c. Material from one cell is divided into two cells.
  d. One cell divides into four exact cells.

11. Which is a characteristic of a virus?
  a. obtains energy from sunlight
  b. responds to light and temperature
  c. doesn't contain DNA
  d. reproduces only within cells

12. Which is the simplest type of organism on Earth?
  a. protists
  b. bacteria
  c. viruses
  d. parasites

13. Which statement about bacteria is *not* true?
  a. Bacteria reproduce using binary fission.
  b. Bacteria do not have a nucleus.
  c. Bacteria do not contain genetic material.
  d. Bacteria are either rod-, round-, or spiral-shaped.

14. Archaea that can survive only in extreme temperatures are the
  a. methanogens
  b. halophiles
  c. thermophiles
  d. bacteria

15. A fluid containing weakened disease-causing viruses or bacteria is
  a. a filter
  b. a diatom
  c. a bacteriophage
  d. a vaccine

16. Which group of protists are decomposers?
  a. diatoms
  b. molds
  c. protozoa
  d. plankton

17. Which obtains energy by feeding on other organisms?

   a. amoeba   **c.** phytoplankton

   b. algae   **d.** mushroom

Short Answer *Write a short answer to each question.*

18. Briefly describe the characteristics that all living things share.

19. How are some bacteria harmful to humans?

20. What are plankton?

Thinking Critically

21. **APPLY** Imagine you are a scientist on location in a rain forest in Brazil. You discover what you think might be a living organism. How would you be able to tell if the discovery is a living thing?

22. **COMMUNICATE** What process is shown in this photograph? Describe the sequence of events in the process shown.

23. **CLASSIFY** Why are archaea classified in a separate kingdom from bacteria?

24. **ANALYZE** Why are some bacteria considered "nature's recyclers"? Explain the role that these bacteria play in the environment.

25. **CALCULATE** A bacterium reproduces every hour. Assuming the bacteria continue to reproduce at that rate, how many bacteria will there be after 10 hours? Explain how you know.

26. **HYPOTHESIZE** A student conducts an experiment to determine the effectiveness of washing hands on bacteria. He rubs an unwashed finger across an agar plate, then washes his hands and rubs the same finger across a second plate. What hypothesis might the student make for this experiment? Explain.

27. **COMPARE AND CONTRAST** Describe three ways that viruses differ from bacteria.

28. **ANALYZE** A scientist has grown cultures of bacteria on agar plates for study. Now the scientist wants to grow a culture of viruses in a laboratory for study. How might this be possible? Give an example.

29. **PROVIDE EXAMPLES** How are protists both helpful and harmful to humans? Give examples in your answer.

the BIG idea

30. **INFER** Look again at the picture on pages 6–7. Now that you have finished the chapter, how would you change or add details to your answer to the question on the photograph?

UNIT PROJECTS

If you are doing a unit project, make a folder for your project. Include in your folder a list of resources you will need, the date on which the project is due, and a schedule to track your progress. Begin gathering data.

Analyzing Data

The graph below shows growth rates of bacteria at different temperatures.

Rate of Bacterial Growth

Choose the letter of the best answer.

1. At which temperature did growth of bacteria occur at the greatest rate?

  a. 0°C   **c.** 20°C

  b. 10°C   **d.** 30°C

2. Which statement is true about the growth rate of bacteria at 10°C?

  a. Bacteria grew rapidly at first, then declined after 6 hours.

  b. Bacteria growth increased at a steady rate.

  c. Bacteria grew slowly, then declined rapidly after 10 hours.

  d. Bacteria showed neither an increase nor decrease in growth rate.

3. What is the concentration of bacteria at a temperature of 20°C after 4 hours?

  a. about 5000 per mL   **c.** about 7000 per mL

  b. about 6000 per mL   **d.** about 8000 per mL

4. During which hour was the concentration of bacteria at 20°C the greatest?

  a. hour 2   **c.** hour 8

  b. hour 4   **d.** hour 10

5. Which conclusion can be drawn from the data in the graph?

  a. The rate of bacterial growth is the greatest at the highest temperature.

  b. The rate of bacterial growth is the least at the highest temperature.

  c. The rate of bacterial growth is the greatest at the lowest temperature.

  d. The rate of bacterial growth does not change depending on temperature.

6. How much did the rate of bacterial growth increase between 2 hours and 8 hours at 30°C?

  a. 2000 per mL

  b. 4000 per mL

  c. 6000 per mL

  d. 8000 per mL

Extended Response

7. A scientist wants to test the effect of temperature on the same bacteria shown in the graph at higher temperatures. The scientist tests the growth rate of bacteria at 50°C, 75°C, and 100°C. Based on the information in the graph and your knowledge of bacteria, what results might the scientist get? Explain your reasoning.

8. Antibiotics are drugs that are used to inhibit the growth of bacterial infections. A scientist wants to test the ability of three different antibiotics to control the growth of a certain type of bacteria. The scientist has isolated the bacteria in test tubes. Each antibiotic is prepared in a tablet form. Design an experiment that will test the effectiveness of the antibiotic tablets on the bacteria. Your experiment should include a hypothesis, a list of materials, a procedure, and a method of recording data.

Introduction to Multicellular Organisms

the **BIG** idea

Multicellular organisms live in and get energy from a variety of environments.

How does an organism get energy and materials from its environment?

Key Concepts

SECTION

2.1 Multicellular organisms meet their needs in different ways.
Learn about specialized cells, tissues, and organs.

SECTION

2.2 Plants are producers.
Learn how plants get energy and respond to the environment.

SECTION

2.3 Animals are consumers.
Learn how animals get energy and how they interact with the environment.

SECTION

2.4 Most fungi are decomposers.
Learn about fungi and how they get energy.

Internet Preview

CLASSZONE.COM

Chapter 2 online resources: Content Review, Visualization, four Resource Centers, Math Tutorial, Test Practice

EXPLORE (the BIG idea)

Where Does It Come From?

Think about the things you use every day. Just like any other organism, you depend on the environment to meet your needs. The food you eat comes from plants and animals. Also, much of what you use is made of materials processed from living matter.

Observe and Think Identify three nonfood items you come into contact with every day. Where does the material for these products come from?

How Can a Multicellular Organism Reproduce on Its Own?

Take an old potato and cut it in half, making sure that there are eyes on both halves. Plant each half in a pot of soil. Water the pots once a day. After two weeks, remove the potato halves from the pots and examine.

Observe and Think What happened to the potato halves?

Internet Activity: Bee Dance

Go to **ClassZone.com** to explore how bees communicate.

Observe and Think What type of information can a bee communicate to other bees in a hive?

NSTA *SCi*LINKS
scilinks.org
Animal Behavior **Code: MDL040**

Getting Ready to Learn

◀ CONCEPT REVIEW

- Living things are organized, grow, respond, and reproduce.
- Protists get energy in three different ways.
- Single-celled organisms reproduce when the cell divides.

◀ VOCABULARY REVIEW

kingdom p. 11
producer p. 19
decomposer p. 19

See Glossary for definitions.

adaptation, DNA, genetic material

 CONTENT REVIEW
CLASSZONE.COM

Review concepts and vocabulary.

▶ TAKING NOTES

MAIN IDEA AND DETAILS

Make a two-column chart. Write the main ideas, such as those in the blue headings, in the column on the left. Write details about each of those main ideas in the column on the right.

VOCABULARY STRATEGY

Write each new vocabulary term in the center of a **four square** diagram. Write notes in the squares around each term. Include a definition, some characteristics, and some examples of the term. If possible, write some things that are not examples of the term.

See the Note-Taking Handbook on pages R45–R51.

SCIENCE NOTEBOOK

MAIN IDEAS	DETAILS
Plants respond to their environment.	1. Plants respond to different stimuli. 2. A stimulus is something that produces a response.

Definition	Characteristics
Group of same type of cells performing similar functions	Cells are similar. Different tissues do different jobs.

TISSUE

Examples	Nonexamples
skin tissue nerve tissue muscle tissue	a simple cell

2.1 Multicellular organisms meet their needs in different ways.

◀ BEFORE, you learned

- Organisms get energy and materials from the environment
- All organisms are organized, grow, respond, and reproduce
- Differences in genetic material lead to diversity

▶ NOW, you will learn

- About the functions of cells in multicellular organisms
- How multicellular organisms are adapted to different environments
- About sexual reproduction

VOCABULARY

tissue p. 44
organ p. 44
sexual reproduction p. 48
meiosis p. 48
fertilization p. 48

THINK ABOUT

Why is teamwork important?

For any team to be successful, it is important for people to work well together. Within a team, each person has a different role. For example, the team in this restaurant includes people to greet diners and seat them, people to buy and cook the food, and people to take food orders and serve the food. By dividing different jobs among different people, a restaurant can serve more customers at the same time. What would happen in a large restaurant if the diners were seated, cooked for, and served by the same person?

Multicellular organisms have cells that are specialized.

MAIN IDEA AND DETAILS
Make a chart and add notes about the main idea: *Multicellular organisms have cells that are specialized.*

In single-celled organisms, all the functions of life are performed by one cell. These functions include getting energy and materials, removing wastes, and responding to changes in the environment. In multicellular organisms, however, different jobs are done by different cells—the cells are specialized. A blood cell carries oxygen. A nerve cell sends and receives signals. Just as the different jobs of running a restaurant are divided among different people, in multicellular organisms different functions are divided among different cells.

In this chapter, you will read about plants, animals, and fungi. These three kingdoms are made up almost entirely of multicellular organisms. The cells in multicellular organisms are organized in ways that enable them to survive and reproduce.

INVESTIGATE Specialization

What are some advantages of specialization?

PROCEDURE

1. Form into two teams, each representing an organism. The single-celled team will be made up of just one person; the multicellular team will be made up of three. Each team obtains a box of materials from the teacher.

2. Each team must do the following tasks as quickly as possible: make a paper-clip chain, write the alphabet on both sides of one piece of paper, and make a paper airplane from the second piece of paper. The members of the three-person team must specialize, each person doing one task only.

MATERIALS
- two boxes, each containing 20 paper clips, 2 pieces of paper, and 1 pencil

TIME
10 minutes

WHAT DO YOU THINK?

- What are some advantages to having each person on the three-person team specialize in doing a different job?
- Why might efficiency be a factor in the activities done by cells in a multicellular organism?

CHALLENGE Suppose the "life" of the multicellular team depended on the ability of one person to make a paper airplane. How would specialization be a disadvantage if that person were not at school?

Levels of Organization

For any multicellular organism to survive, different cells must work together. The right type of cell must be in the right place to do the work that needs to be done.

Organization starts with the cell. Cells in multicellular organisms are specialized for a specific function. In animals, skin cells provide protection, nerve cells carry signals, and muscle cells produce movement. Cells of the same type are organized into **tissue,** a group of cells that work together. For example, what you think of as muscle is muscle tissue, made up of many muscle cells.

A structure that is made up of different tissues is called an **organ.** Organs have particular functions. The heart is an organ that functions as a pump. It has muscle tissue, which pumps the blood, and nerve tissue, which signals when to pump. Different organs that work together and have a common function are called an organ system. A heart and blood vessels are different organs that are both part of a circulatory system. These organs work together to deliver blood to all parts of a body. Together, cells, tissues, organs, and organ systems form an organism.

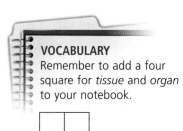

VOCABULARY
Remember to add a four square for *tissue* and *organ* to your notebook.

Organ Systems and the Organism

In almost all multicellular organisms, different organ systems take care of specific needs. Here are a few examples of organ systems found in many animals:

- nervous system enables a response to changing conditions
- muscular system produces movement and supplies heat
- respiratory system takes in oxygen and releases carbon dioxide
- circulatory system delivers oxygen and removes carbon dioxide
- digestive system breaks down food into a usable form

Organ systems allow multicellular organisms to obtain large amounts of energy, process large amounts of materials, respond to changes in the environment, and reproduce.

REMINDER

A system is a group of objects that interact, sharing energy and matter.

CHECK YOUR READING How are the functions of organ systems related to the needs of an organism? Give an example.

Different organ systems work together. For example, the respiratory system works with the circulatory system to deliver oxygen and remove carbon dioxide. When an animal such as a turtle breathes in, oxygen is brought into the lungs. Blood from the circulatory system picks up the oxygen, and the heart pumps the oxygen-rich blood out to the cells of the body. As oxygen is delivered, waste carbon dioxide is picked up. The blood is pumped back to the lungs. The carbon dioxide is released when the turtle breathes out. More oxygen is picked up when the turtle breathes in.

Organ Systems

Organ systems work together to meet the needs of an organism.

Blood vessels called **veins** return oxygen-poor blood to the lungs.

Each **lung** fills with air containing oxygen.

Blood vessels called **arteries** carry oxygen-rich blood to the body.

The **heart** pumps blood to the lungs.

Multicellular organisms are adapted to live in different environments.

READING TiP

Offspring is a word used to describe the new organisms produced by reproduction in any organism. Think of it as meaning "to spring off."

All organisms have characteristics that allow them to survive in their environment. An adaptation is any inherited characteristic that increases the chance of an organism's surviving and producing offspring that also reproduce. An adaptation may have to do with the way an organism gets its energy or processes materials. An adaptation may relate to the shape or structure of an organism's body. An adaptation can even be a form of behavior.

 CHECK YOUR READING The text above mentions different types of adaptations. Name three.

When most multicellular organisms reproduce, the offspring are not exact copies of the parents. There are differences. If a particular difference gives an organism an advantage over other members in its group, then that difference is referred to as an adaptation. Over time, the organism and its offspring do better and reproduce more.

You are probably familiar with the furry animal called a fox. Different species of fox have different adaptations that enable them to survive in different environments. Here are three examples:

- **Fennec** The fennec is a desert fox. Its large ears are an adaptation that helps the fox keep cool in the hot desert. As blood flows through the vessels in each ear, heat is released. Another adaptation is the color of its fur, which blends in with the desert sand.

- **Arctic fox** The Arctic fox lives in the cold north. Its small ears, legs, and nose are adaptations that reduce the loss of heat from its body. Its bluish-gray summer fur is replaced by a thick coat of white fur as winter approaches. Its winter coat keeps the fox warm and enables it to blend in with the snow.

- **Red fox** The red fox is found in grasslands and woodlands. Its ears aren't as large as those of the fennec or as small as those of the Arctic fox. Its body fur is reddish brown tipped in white and black, coloring that helps it blend into its environment.

The diversity of life on Earth is due to the wide range of adaptations that have occurred in different species. An elephant has a trunk for grasping and sensing. A female kangaroo carries its young in a pouch. The largest flower in the world, the rafflesia flower, is almost a meter wide, blooms for just a few days, and smells like rotting meat.

Adaptations are the result of differences that can occur in genetic material. The way multicellular organisms reproduce allows for a mixing of genetic material. You will read about that next.

INFER The strong odor of the rafflesia flower attracts flies into the plant. How might this adaptation benefit the plant?

Adaptations in Different Environments

Fennec

Habitat: warm; Sahara Desert and Saudi Arabia

Size: about 40 cm (15 in.), 1.25 kg (2.7 lb)

large ears

light brown fur

Arctic Fox

Habitat: cold; Northern Eurasia and North America

Size: about 50 cm (20 in.), 4 kg (9 lb)

small ears

winter: thick white fur

summer: thin bluish-gray fur

Red Fox

Habitat: moderate; North and Central America, Eurasia

Size: about 65 cm (25 in.), 6 kg (13 lb)

ears of moderate size

reddish-brown fur

READING VISUALS Foxes are hunters that feed on small animals. How might the coat color of each fox contribute to its survival?

Sexual reproduction leads to diversity.

Most multicellular organisms reproduce sexually. In **sexual reproduction,** the genetic material of two parents comes together, and the resulting offspring have genetic material from both. Sexual reproduction leads to diversity because the DNA in the offspring is different from the DNA in the parents.

Two different cellular processes are involved in sexual reproduction. The first is **meiosis** (my-OH-sihs), a special form of cell division that produces sperm cells in a male and egg cells in a female. Each sperm or egg cell contains only one copy of DNA, the genetic material. Most cells contain two copies of DNA.

The second process in sexual reproduction is **fertilization.** Fertilization occurs when the sperm cell from the male parent combines with the egg cell from the female parent. A fertilized egg is a single cell with DNA from both parents. Once the egg is fertilized, it divides. One cell becomes two, two cells become four, and so on. As the cells divide, they start to specialize, and different tissues and organs form.

One copy of DNA
in cell after meiosis

sperm cell   egg cell   two copies of DNA in
cell after fertilization

Differences in genetic material and in the environment produce differences in offspring. Whether a tulip flower is red or yellow depends on the genetic material in its cells. How well the tulip grows depends on conditions in the environment as well as genetic materials.

Sexual Reproduction The fertilized eggs of a sala-mander contain genetic material from two parents.

Asexual Reproduction The buds of a sea coral have the same genetic material as the parent.

Most reproduction that occurs in multicellular organisms is sexual reproduction. However, many multicellular organisms can reproduce by asexual reproduction. With asexual reproduction, a single parent produces offspring.

Budding is a form of asexual reproduction. In budding, a second organism grows off, or buds, from another. Organisms that reproduce asexually can reproduce more often. Asexual reproduction limits genetic diversity within a group because offspring have the same genetic material as the parent.

 CHECK YOUR READING How do offspring produced by sexual reproduction compare with offspring produced by asexual reproduction?

With sexual reproduction, there is an opportunity for new combinations of characteristics to occur in the offspring. Perhaps these organisms process food more efficiently or reproduce more quickly. Or perhaps they have adaptations that allow them to survive a change in their environment. In the next three sections, you will read how plants, animals, and fungi have adapted to similar environments in very different ways.

2.1 Review

KEY CONCEPTS

1. How do specialized cells relate to the different levels of organization in a multicellular organism?

2. What is an adaptation? Give an example.

3. What two cellular processes are involved in sexual reproduction?

CRITICAL THINKING

4. **Compare and Contrast** How does the genetic diversity of the offspring differ in sexual reproduction versus asexual reproduction?

5. **Predict** If fertilization occurred without meiosis, how many copies of DNA would be in the cells of the offspring?

⬥ CHALLENGE

6. **Synthesize** Do you consider the different levels of organization in a multicellular organism an adaptation? Explain your reasoning.

MATH TUTORIAL
CLASSZONE.COM
Click on Math Tutorial for
more help interpreting
circle graphs.

Making Data Visual

A circle graph is a good way to see part-to-whole relationships. To use data presented in a circle graph, do the following:

Example

Suppose, at a waterhole in a game preserve, researchers observed ten animals throughout the day. What fraction of the sightings were giraffes?

(1) The circle graph shows the data for the sightings. The whole circle represents the total sightings, 10.

(2) 3 of the 10 equal parts are shaded for giraffes.

(3) Write "3 out of 10" as a fraction $\frac{3}{10}$.

ANSWER Giraffes $= \frac{3}{10}$ of the sightings.

Answer the following questions.

1. What fraction of the sightings were lions?

2. What fraction of the sightings were gazelles?

3. Which animal did the researchers observe in greatest number?

4. Which animal did they observe in the least number? How many sightings occurred for that animal?

5. What fraction of the total does that animal represent?

6. If the researchers had seen one hundred animals, and the graph looked the same as it does, how many giraffe sightings would their graph represent?

CHALLENGE You also record the nighttime visitors: first, 2 young elephants; then a lioness with 2 thirsty cubs; then a giraffe, followed by a hyena and 3 gazelles. Calculate the fraction of the night's population that is represented by each type of animal. Use the fractions to draw a circle graph of the data on "Night Sightings at the Waterhole." Shade and label the graph with the types of animals.

2.2 Plants are producers.

 BEFORE, you learned

- Multicellular organisms have tissues, organs, and systems
- Organisms have adaptations that can make them suited to their environment
- Sexual reproduction leads to genetic diversity

 NOW, you will learn

- How plants obtain energy
- How plants store energy
- How plants respond to their environment

VOCABULARY

photosynthesis p. 52
autotroph p. 52
cellular respiration p. 53
stimulus p. 55

EXPLORE Stored Energy

In what form does a plant store energy?

PROCEDURE

1. Obtain pieces of potato, celery, and pear that have been placed in small plastic cups.

2. Place a few drops of the iodine solution onto the plant material in each cup. The iodine solution will turn dark blue in the presence of starch. It does not change color in the presence of sugar.

MATERIALS

- pieces of potato, celery, and pear
- 3 plastic cups
- iodine solution
- eye dropper

WHAT DO YOU THINK?

- Observing each sample, describe what happened to the color of the iodine solution after a few minutes.
- Starch and sugars are a source of energy for a plant. What do your observations suggest about how different plants store energy?

Plants capture energy from the Sun.

MAIN IDEA AND DETAILS
Add the main idea *plants capture energy from the Sun* to your notebook and fill in details on photosynthesis and stored energy.

If you stand outside on a warm, sunny day, you may see and feel energy from the Sun. Without the Sun's energy, Earth would be a cold, dark planet. The Sun's heat and light provide the energy almost all organisms need to live.

However, energy from the Sun cannot drive cell processes directly. Light energy must be changed into chemical energy. Chemical energy is the form of energy all organisms use to carry out the functions of life. Plants are an important part of the energy story because plants capture energy from the Sun and convert it to chemical energy.

Producing Sugars

READING TiP

The roots for *photosynthesis* are *photo-*, which means "light," and *synthesis*, which means "to put together." Together they mean "put together by light."

Plants capture energy from sunlight and convert it to chemical energy through the process of **photosynthesis.** The plant takes in water and carbon dioxide from the environment and uses these simple materials to produce sugar, an energy-rich compound that contains carbon. Oxygen is also produced. Plants are referred to as producers because they produce energy-rich carbon compounds using the Sun's energy.

The cells, tissues, and organ systems in a plant work together to supply the materials needed for photosynthesis. Most photosynthesis takes place in the leaves. The leaves take in carbon dioxide from the air, and the stems support the leaves and hold them up toward the Sun. The roots of the plant anchor it in the soil and supply water. The sugars produced are used by the plant for energy and as materials for growth.

 CHECK YOUR READING What is the product of photosynthesis?

Another name for a plant is **autotroph** (AW-tuh-TRAHF). Autotroph means self-feeder. Plants do not require food from other organisms. Plants will grow if they have energy from the Sun, carbon dioxide from the air, and water and nutrients from the soil.

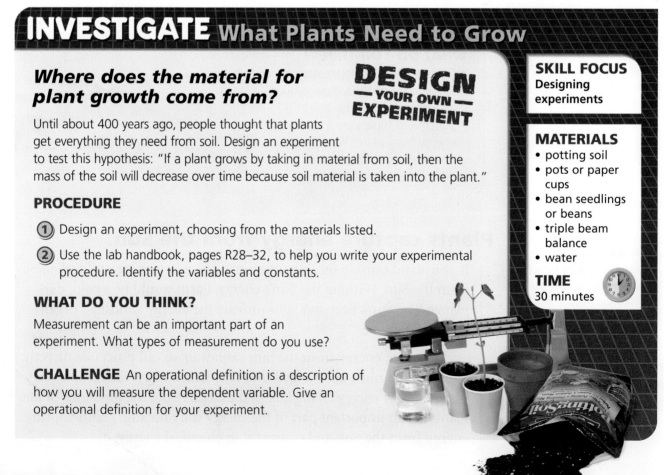

INVESTIGATE What Plants Need to Grow

Where does the material for plant growth come from?

DESIGN — YOUR OWN — EXPERIMENT

Until about 400 years ago, people thought that plants get everything they need from soil. Design an experiment to test this hypothesis: "If a plant grows by taking in material from soil, then the mass of the soil will decrease over time because soil material is taken into the plant."

PROCEDURE

1. Design an experiment, choosing from the materials listed.

2. Use the lab handbook, pages R28–32, to help you write your experimental procedure. Identify the variables and constants.

WHAT DO YOU THINK?

Measurement can be an important part of an experiment. What types of measurement do you use?

CHALLENGE An operational definition is a description of how you will measure the dependent variable. Give an operational definition for your experiment.

SKILL FOCUS
Designing experiments

MATERIALS
- potting soil
- pots or paper cups
- bean seedlings or beans
- triple beam balance
- water

TIME
30 minutes

Storing and Releasing Energy

Plants are not the only organisms that capture energy through photosynthesis. Algae and certain bacteria and protists also use photosynthesis. Plants are different from single-celled producers, however. Plants are multicellular organisms with parts of their bodies specialized for storing energy-rich material. Single-celled producers can store very little energy.

Only part of the energy captured by a plant is used as fuel for cellular processes. Some of the sugar produced is used as building material, enabling the plant to grow. The remaining sugar is stored. Often the sugars are stored as starches. Starch is an energy-rich compound made of many sugars. Starches can store a lot of chemical energy. When a plant needs energy, the starches are broken back down into sugars and energy is released. **Cellular respiration** is the process by which a cell uses oxygen to break down sugars to release the energy they hold.

Some plants, such as carrots and beets, store starch in their roots. Other plants, including rhubarb, have stems adapted for storing starch. A potato is a swollen, underground stem called a tuber. Tubers have buds—the eyes of the potato—that can sprout into new plants. The starch stored in the tuber helps the new sprouts survive.

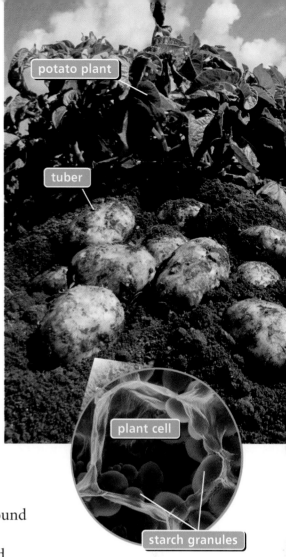

potato plant

tuber

plant cell

starch granules

 CHECK YOUR READING What is the original source of a plant's stored energy?

Plants are adapted to different environments.

Almost everywhere you look on land, you'll see plants. Leaves, stems, and roots are adaptations that enable plants, as producers, to live on land. Not all plants, however, look the same. Just as there are many different types of land environments, there are many different types of plants that have adapted to these environments.

Grasses are an example of plants that grow in several environments. Many grasses have deep roots, produce seeds quickly, and can grow in areas with a wide range of temperatures and different amounts of precipitation. Grasses can survive drought, fires, freezing temperatures, and grazing. As long as the roots of the plant survive, the grasses will grow again. Grasses are found in the Arctic tundra, as well as in temperate and tropical climates.

RESOURCE CENTER
CLASSZONE.COM

Learn more about plant adaptations.

Now compare trees to grasses. If the leaves and stems of a tree die away because of fire or drought, often the plant will not survive. Because of their size, trees require a large amount of water for photosynthesis. A coniferous (koh-NIHF-uhr-uhs) tree, like the pine, does well in colder climates. It has needle-shaped leaves that stay green throughout the year, feeding the plant continually. A deciduous (dih-SIHJ-oo-uhs) tree, like the maple, loses its leaves when temperatures turn cold. The maple needs a long growing season and plenty of water for new leaves to grow.

Plants have reproductive adaptations. It may surprise you to learn that flowering plants living on cold, snowy mountaintops have something in common with desert plants. When rain falls in the desert, wildflower seeds sprout very quickly. Within a few weeks, the plants grow, flower, and produce new seeds that will be ready to sprout with the next rainy season. The same thing happens in the mountains, where the snow may thaw for only a few weeks every summer. Seeds sprout, flowers grow, and new seeds are produced—all before the snow returns. You will read more about plant reproduction in Chapter 3.

Some plants have adaptations that protect them. Plants in the mustard family give off odors that keep many plant-eating insects away. Other plants, such as poison ivy and poison oak, produce harmful chemicals. The nicotine in a tobacco plant is a poison that helps to keep the plant from being eaten.

CHECK YOUR READING Name two different types of adaptations plants have.

ANALYZE An insect provides nutrients that this Venus flytrap cannot get from the soil. Is this plant still a producer? Ask yourself where the plant gets its energy.

Some adaptations plants have relate to very specific needs. For example, the Venus flytrap is a plant that grows in areas where the soil lacks certain materials. The leaves of the Venus flytrap fold in the middle and have long teeth all around the edges. When an insect lands on an open leaf, the two sides of the leaf fold together. The teeth form a trap that prevents the captured insect from escaping. Fluids given off by the leaf digest the insect's body, providing materials the plant can't get from the soil.

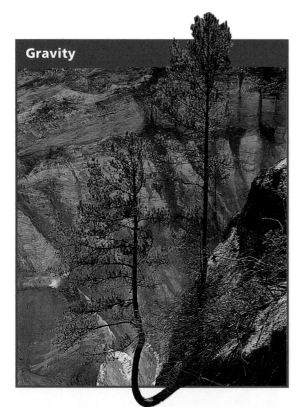

Gravity

Plant roots always grow downward and stems always grow upward. All plants respond to gravity as a stimulus.

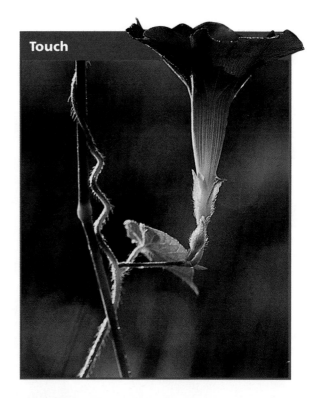

Touch

The tendril of a climbing plant grows around a nearby object. The plant responds to touch as a stimulus.

Plants respond to their environment.

During a hot afternoon, parts of the flower known as the Mexican bird of paradise close. As the Sun goes down, the flower reopens. The plant is responding to a stimulus, in this case, sunlight. A **stimulus** is something that produces a response from an organism. Plants, like all organisms, respond to stimuli in their environment. This ability helps them to survive and grow.

VOCABULARY Make a four square for the term *stimulus* in your science notebook.

Gravity

Gravity is the force that keeps you bound to Earth and gives you a sense of up and down. All plants respond to gravity. They also have a sense of up and down—roots grow down and stems grow up. Suppose you place a young seedling on its side, so that its roots and stems stretch out to the side. In a very short time, the tip of the root will begin to turn down, and the tip of the stem will turn up.

Touch

Many plants also respond to touch as a stimulus. Peas, morning glories, tropical vines, and other climbing plants have special stems called tendrils. Tendrils respond to the touch of a nearby object. As the tendrils grow, they wrap around the object. The twining of tendrils around a fence or another plant helps raise a plant into the sunlight.

How Plants Respond to Light

Auxin, a hormone, is a chemical substance that stimulates cell growth and makes plant stems bend toward light.

1 The presence of sunlight stimulates the production of auxin at the tip of the stem.

2 Auxin moves to cells on the dark side of the plant.

3 Cells with high levels of auxin grow longer than other cells, causing the plant to bend.

Light

VISUALIZATION
CLASSZONE.COM

Examine how plants respond to different stimuli.

Light is a powerful stimulus for plants. You can see that stems and leaves grow toward light by placing an indoor plant near a window. After several days, the tips of the stems start to bend toward the window. What happens if you turn the plant around so that those stems reach into the room? The stems will bend as they continue to grow, turning back toward the light.

Plants respond to light with the help of a hormone. A hormone is a chemical substance that is produced in one part of an organism and travels to a different part where it produces a reaction. Hormones act as chemical messengers. They allow an organism to respond to changes in its body or to changes in the environment around it.

Auxin (AWK-sihn), a plant hormone that stimulates cell growth, is produced at the tip of a plant stem. Auxin moves away from light. As a result, the cells on the darker side of a plant stem contain more auxin than those on the lighter side. Higher levels of auxin in plant cells on the darker side cause those cells to grow longer. The longer cells cause the plant stem to bend, moving the tip of the stem toward the light.

Plants respond to seasonal changes.

Most regions of the world go through seasonal changes every year. For example, during the summer in North America, temperatures rise and the days get longer. As winter approaches, temperatures go down and the days become shorter. These types of seasonal changes have an effect on plants.

For plants, a shorter period of daylight will affect the amount of sunlight available for photosynthesis. Shorter days cause many plants to go into a state of dormancy. When plants are dormant, they temporarily stop growing and so require less energy.

In temperate climates, the approach of winter causes the leaves of deciduous trees to die and drop to the ground. The trees enter a state of dormancy during which their growth is slowed. Other plants, such as wild cornflowers, do not survive the change. New cornflowers will grow the following season, from seeds left behind.

CHECK YOUR READING What stimulus causes a deciduous plant to respond by dropping its leaves?

For many plants, reproduction is also affected by seasonal changes. For some plants, the amount of daylight is a factor. A few plants, such as rice and ragweed, produce flowers only in autumn or winter, when days are short. They are short-day plants. Long-day plants flower in late spring and summer, when days are long. Lettuce, spinach, and irises are long day-plants. You will read more about plants in Chapter 3.

2.2 Review

KEY CONCEPTS

1. What process makes a plant a producer, and what does a plant produce?

2. Name three stimuli that plants respond to, and give examples of how a plant responds.

3. How do seasonal changes affect plants? Give an example.

CRITICAL THINKING

4. **Give Examples** Give three examples of ways that plants are adapted to their environments. How do these adaptations benefit the plant?

CHALLENGE

5. **Apply** Some experiments suggest that the hormone auxin is involved in the twining of tendrils. Use what you know about auxin to explain how it might cause tendrils to twine around anything they touch. Draw a diagram.

2.3 Animals are consumers.

BEFORE, you learned

- Plants are producers
- Plants have adaptations for capturing and storing energy
- Plants respond to different stimuli

NOW, you will learn

- How animals obtain energy
- How animals process food
- About different ways animals respond to their environment

VOCABULARY

consumer p. 58
heterotroph p. 58
behavior p. 62
predator p. 63
prey p. 63
migration p. 64
hibernation p. 64

THINK ABOUT

What can you tell from teeth?

Many animals have teeth. Teeth bite, grind, crush, and chew. A fox's sharp biting teeth capture small animals that it hunts on the run. A horse's teeth are flat and strong—for breaking down the grasses it eats. Run your tongue over your own teeth. How many different shapes do you notice? What can the shape of teeth suggest about the food an animal eats?

Animals obtain energy and materials from food.

You probably see nonhuman animals every day, whether you live in a rural area or a large city. If the animals are wild animals, not somebody's pet, then chances are that what you see these animals doing is moving about in search of food.

Animals are consumers. A **consumer** is an organism that needs to get energy from another organism. Unlike plants, animals must consume food to get the energy and materials they need to survive. Animals are heterotrophs. A **heterotroph** (HEHT-uhr-uh-TRAHF) is an organism that feeds on, or consumes, other organisms. By definition, animals are, quite simply, multicellular organisms that have adaptations that allow them to take in and process food.

READING TIP

The meaning of *heterotroph* is opposite to that of *autotroph*. The root *hetero-* means "other." *Heterotroph* means "other-feeder," or "feeds on others."

Obtaining Food

Food is a source of energy and materials for animals.

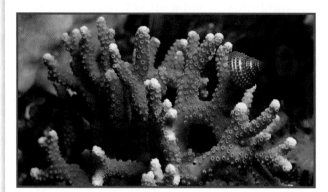

Simple feeding Some animals, such as corals, can filter food from their environment.

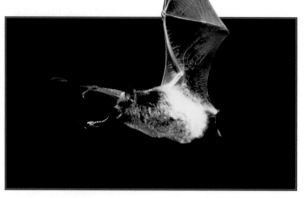

Complex feeding Many animals, such as bats, actively search for and capture food.

Animals need food and have many different ways of getting it. For some animals, feeding is a relatively simple process. An adult coral simply filters food from the water as it moves through the coral's body. Most animals, however, must search for food. Grazing animals, such as horses, move along from one patch of grass to another. Other animals must capture food. Most bats use sound and hearing to detect the motion of insects flying at night. Its wings make the bat able to move through the air quickly and silently.

What Animals Eat

Just about any type of living or once-living material is a source of food for some animal. Animals can be grouped by the type of food they eat.

- Herbivores (HUR-buh-VAWRS) feed on plants or algae.
- Carnivores (KAHR-nuh-VAWRS) feed on other animals.
- Omnivores (AWM-nuh-VAWRS) feed on both plants and animals.

Another group are those animals that feed on the remains of once-living animals. Many insects do, as do some larger animals, such as vultures. Other animals, such as worms, act as decomposers.

 CHECK YOUR READING Describe how herbivores, carnivores, and omnivores get their energy.

MAIN IDEA AND DETAILS
Make a chart about the main idea: *Animals obtain energy and materials from food.* Include *herbivore, carnivore,* and *omnivore* in the details.

Different species of animals have adapted in different ways to take advantage of all the energy-rich material in the environment. To get energy and materials from food, all animals must first break the food down—that is, they must digest it.

RESOURCE CENTER
CLASSZONE.COM

Find out more about
animal adaptations.

Processing Food

Energy is stored in complex carbon compounds in food. For the cells in an animal to make use of the energy and materials stored in this food, the large complex compounds must be broken back down into simpler compounds.

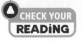 **CHECK YOUR READING** How must food be changed so an animal gets energy?

Digestion is the process that breaks food down into pieces that are small enough to be absorbed by cells. A few animals, such as sponges, are able to take food particles directly into their cells. Most animals, however, take the food into an area of their body where the materials are broken down. Cells absorb the materials they need. Animals such as jellyfish have a single opening in their bodies where food is brought into a central cavity, or gut. The unused materials are released through the same opening.

A digestive system uses both physical and chemical activity to break down food. Many animals have a tubelike digestive system. Food is brought in at one end of the animal, the mouth, and waste is released at the other end. As food moves through the system, it is continually broken down, releasing necessary materials called nutrients to the cells.

INVESTIGATE Owl Pellets

What does an owl eat, and how well does it digest its food?

PROCEDURE

1. Get an owl pellet from your teacher. Open the foil and place the pellet in a tray.

2. Use a needle tool and tweezers to sort through the materials in the pellet and separate them.

3. When you have finished, dispose of the materials according to your teacher's instructions, and wash your hands.

WHAT DO YOU THINK?

- What can you tell about what an owl eats from looking at the remains in the pellet?

- What materials are not digested?

CHALLENGE Use the bone identification key to identify what the owl ate.

SKILL FOCUS
Inferring

MATERIALS
- owl pellet
- needle tool
- tweezers
- tray
- *for Challenge:* bone identification key

TIME
30 minutes

Obtaining Oxygen

Animals need oxygen to release the energy in food.

Grasshopper

spiracles

Most insects take in oxygen through body openings called spiracles.

Bass

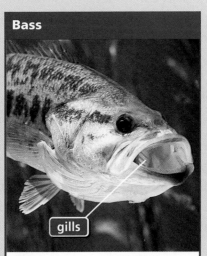

gills

Fish have gills, which pick up dissolved oxygen as water flows over them.

Tiger

lungs

This yawning tiger, like many animals, gets oxygen by inhaling air into its lungs.

Releasing and Storing Energy

Animals obtain energy from sugars and other carbon compounds the same way plants do, through the process of cellular respiration. As you read in Section 2.2, cellular respiration is a process in which energy is released when sugars are broken down inside a cell. The process requires both oxygen and water.

 CHECK YOUR READING What is the function of cellular respiration?

Many animals take in water in the same way they take in food, through the digestive system. Oxygen, however, is often taken in through a respiratory system. In many animals, the respiratory system delivers oxygen to the blood, and the blood carries oxygen to the cells.

Animals have different structures for obtaining oxygen. Many insects take in oxygen through spiracles, tiny openings in their bodies. Fish have gills, structures that allow them to pick up oxygen dissolved in the water. Other air-breathing animals take in oxygen through organs called lungs.

Most animals do not feed continuously, so they need to be able to store materials from food in their tissues or organs. Many animals, including humans, take in large amounts of food at one time. This gives an animal time to do other activities, such as caring for young or looking for more food.

Animals interact with the environment and with other organisms.

Animals, as consumers, must obtain food, as well as water, from their environment. An animal's body has many adaptations that allow it to process food. These can include digestive, respiratory, and circulatory systems. Also important are the systems that allow animals to interact with their environment to obtain food. In many animals, muscle and skeletal systems provide movement and support. A nervous system allows the animal to sense and respond to stimuli.

Animals respond to many different types of stimuli. They respond to sights, sounds, odors, light, or a change in temperature. They respond to hunger and thirst. They also respond to other animals. Any observable response to a stimulus is described as a **behavior.** A bird's drinking water from a puddle is a behavior. A lion's chasing an antelope is a behavior, just as the antelope's running to escape the lion is a behavior.

 CHECK YOUR READING What is a behavior and how does it relate to a stimulus?

Some behaviors are inherited, which means they are present at birth. For example, a spider can weave a web without being shown. Other behaviors are learned. For example, the young lion in the photograph learns that a porcupine is not a good source of food.

All behaviors fall into one of three general categories:

- individual behaviors
- interactions between animals of the same species
- interactions between animals of different species

ANALYZE Do you consider the defensive behavior of a porcupine an adaptation?

Individual behaviors often involve meeting basic needs. Animals must find food, water, and shelter. They sleep. They groom themselves. Animals also respond to changes in their environment. A lizard may warm itself in the morning sunlight and then move into the shade when the Sun is high in the sky.

Interactions that occur between animals of the same species are often described as social behaviors. Basic social behaviors include those between parents and offspring and behaviors for attracting a mate. Within a group, animals of the same species may cooperate by working together. Wolves hunt in packs and bees maintain a hive. Behaviors among animals of the same species can also be competitive. Animals often compete for a mate or territory.

 CHECK YOUR READING What are some ways that animals of the same species cooperate and compete?

For macaques, grooming is both an individual and a social behavior. Here a mother grooms her young.

Interactions that occur between animals of different species often involve the search for food. A **predator** is an animal that hunts other animals for food. Predators have behaviors that allow them to search for and capture other organisms. A cheetah first stalks an antelope, then chases it down, moving as fast as 110 kilometers per hour.

An animal that is hunted by another animal as a source of food is the **prey.** Behaviors of prey animals often allow them to escape a predator. An antelope may not be able to outrun a cheetah, but antelopes move in herds. This provides protection for the group since a cheetah will kill only one animal. Other animals, such as the pufferfish and porcupine, have defensive behaviors and structures.

VOCABULARY
Create a pair of four squares for the terms *predator* and *prey.*

unthreatened pufferfish

threatened pufferfish

Animals of different species can also interact in cooperative ways. Tickbirds remove ticks from the skin of an impala. This behavior provides food for the bird and provides relief for the impala. Sometimes animals take advantage of the behavior of other animals. Many animals eat the remains of prey left over after a predator has finished feeding.

Animals respond to seasonal changes.

Animals, like plants, are affected by seasonal changes in their environment. Certain types of food may not be available all year round. A region might go through periods of drought. Some animals do not do well in extreme heat or cold. Unlike plants, animals can respond to seasonal changes by changing their location. **Migration** is the movement of animals to a different region in response to changes in the environment.

monarch butterfly

Each spring, millions of monarch butterflies begin to fly north from Mexico and parts of southern California. As they migrate, the females lay eggs among milkweed plants. This new generation, when it matures, will continue to travel north, moving into the northern United States and parts of Canada. This second generation of monarchs also lays eggs. Monarchs cannot survive the winter temperatures of the north, so the butterflies make the long journey back to Mexico and California in the fall. These butterflies are a different generation from the butterflies that migrated from the south. This suggests their behavior is inherited, not learned. The fall migration route is shown on the map.

Not all animals migrate in response to seasonal changes. Many nonmigratory animals do change their behaviors, however. For example, when winter cold reduces the food supply, some animals hibernate. **Hibernation** is a sleeplike state that lasts for an extended time period. The body systems of a hibernating animal slow down, so the animal needs less energy to survive. Many animals, including frogs, turtles, fish, and some types of insects, hibernate. You will learn more about different types of animals in Chapters 4 and 5.

Monarch butterflies migrate each winter to California and Mexico.

2.3 Review

KEY CONCEPTS

1. In what way are animals consumers?
2. Name three body systems that relate to how an animal gets its energy.
3. What is a behavior?

CRITICAL THINKING

4. **Give Examples** Identify three categories of animal behavior and give an example of each.
5. **Analyze** How is migration similar to hibernation? How is it different?

● CHALLENGE

6. **Analyze** Scientists often look at feeding patterns as a flow of energy through the living parts of the environment. Describe the flow of energy as it relates to plants, herbivores, and carnivores.

An Animal's World

Have you ever watched a TV documentary, or flipped through the pages of a magazine and wondered, "How did the photographer ever get that picture?" For a wildlife photographer, understanding animal behavior is essential.

Cover and Protection

Photographers use camera traps and blinds. A blind, made of branches, is built upwind of an animal gathering place. Steve Winter has built camera traps, where a hidden camera emits a beam of light when an animal steps into it.

Specialized Gear

Certain environments—such as snow and cold, swamp and mud, or sea water—present challenges to a person with a camera. Underwater photographers need to use scuba gear to swim with animals like the Caribbean reef shark.

Behavior

To photograph an endangered species like the jaguar, a photographer must learn animal behavior. Steve Winter and a team of scientists used dogs with keen scent-tracking to find jaguars who are active mostly at night. They learned that jaguars have a favorite scratching tree—perfect photo opportunity!

EXPLORE

1. **OBSERVE** With or without a camera, find a spot where you are likely to find wildlife. Sit as still as possible and wait. What animals do you observe? What do they do?

2. **CHALLENGE** Interview a photographer about digital photography, and ask how technology is changing photography.

2.4 Most fungi are decomposers.

BEFORE, you learned	NOW, you will learn
• All organisms interact with the environment • Plants transform sunlight into chemical energy • Animals get energy by eating other organisms	• How fungi get energy and materials • About different types of fungi • How fungi interact with other organisms

VOCABULARY

hyphae p. 67
spore p. 67
lichen p. 70

EXPLORE Mushrooms

What does a mushroom cap contain?

PROCEDURE

1. Carefully cut the stem away from the mushroom cap, as near the cap as possible.

2. Place the mushroom cap on white paper and cover it with a plastic cup. Leave overnight.

3. Carefully remove the cup and lift the mushroom cap straight up.

4. Use a hand lens to examine the mushroom cap and the print it leaves behind.

WHAT DO YOU THINK?

• How does the pattern in the mushroom cap compare with the mushroom print?
• What made the print?

MATERIALS

• fresh store-bought mushrooms
• sharp knife
• clear plastic cup
• paper
• hand lens

Fungi absorb materials from the environment.

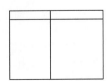

MAIN IDEA AND DETAILS
Don't forget to make a main idea chart with detail notes on the main idea: *Fungi absorb materials from the environment.*

Plants are producers; they capture energy from the Sun and build complex carbon compounds. Animals are consumers; they take in complex carbon compounds and use them for energy and materials. Fungi (FUHN-jy), at least most fungi, are decomposers. Fungi break down, or decompose, the complex carbon compounds that are part of living matter. They absorb nutrients and leave behind simpler compounds.

Fungi are heterotrophs. They get their energy from living or once-living matter. They, along with bacteria, decompose the bodies of dead plants and animals. They also decompose materials left behind by organisms, such as fallen leaves, shed skin, and animal droppings.

Characteristics of Fungi

Except for yeasts, most fungi are multicellular. The cells of a fungus have a nucleus and a thick cell wall, which provides support. Fungi are different from plants and animals in their organization. Plants and animals have specialized cells, which are usually organized into tissues and organs. Multicellular fungi don't have tissues or organs. Instead, a typical fungus is made up of a reproductive body and network of cells that form threadlike structures called **hyphae** (HY-fee).

A mass of hyphae, like the one shown in the diagram below, is called a mycelium (my-SEE-lee-uhm). The hyphae are just one cell thick. This means the cells in the mycelium are close to the soil or whatever substance the fungus is living in. The cells release chemicals that digest the materials around them, and then absorb the nutrients they need. As hyphae grow, openings can form between the older cells and the new ones. This allows nutrients to flow back to the older cells, resulting in what seems like one huge cell with many nuclei.

READING TiP

The root of the word *hyphae* means "web." Look at the diagram below to see their weblike appearance.

Reproduction

Fungi reproduce with spores, which can be produced either asexually or sexually. A **spore** is a single reproductive cell that is capable of growing into a new organism. The mushrooms that you buy at the store are the spore-producing structures of certain types of fungi. These spore-producing structures are reproductive bodies of mushrooms. A single mushroom can produce a billion spores.

Parts of a Fungus

The mycelium makes up a large part of a multicellular fungus.

reproductive body

spores

hyphae

mycelium

RESOURCE CENTER
CLASSZONE.COM

Learn more about different types of fungi.

Spores are released into the air and spread by the wind. Because they're so small and light, the wind can carry spores long distances. Scientists have found spores 160 kilometers above Earth's surface. Some spores have a tough outer covering that keeps the reproductive cell from drying out. Such spores can survive for many years. If the parent fungus dies, the spores may remain and grow when conditions are right.

Fungi reproduce in other ways. For example, a multicellular fungi can reproduce asexually when hyphae break off and form a new mycelium. Yeasts, which are single-celled fungi, reproduce asexually by simple cell division or by budding. Yeasts can also produce spores.

Fungi include mushrooms, molds, and yeasts.

A convenient and simple way to study fungi is to look at their forms. They are mushrooms, molds, and yeasts. You are probably familiar with all of them. The mushrooms on your pizza are a fungus. So is the mold that grows if you leave a piece of pizza too long in the refrigerator. The crust of the pizza itself rises because of the activity of yeast.

Mushrooms

What we call a mushroom is only a small part of a fungus. A single mushroom you buy in the store could have grown from a mycelium that fills an area 30 meters across. When you see a patch of mushrooms, they are probably all part of a single fungus.

For humans, some mushrooms are edible and some are poisonous. A toadstool is a poisonous mushroom. The cap of a mushroom is where the spores are produced. Both the cap and the stalk it grows on are filled with hyphae.

 CHECK YOUR READING What is produced in a mushroom cap?

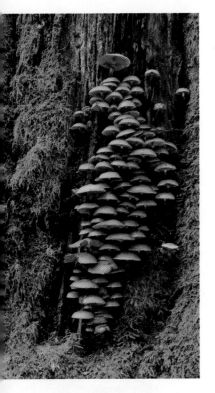

INFER Where is the mycelium of these mushrooms?

Molds

What we call mold, that fuzzy growth we sometimes see on food, is the spore-producing part of another form of fungus. The hyphae of the mold grow into the food, digesting it as they grow. Not all food molds are bad. Different species of the fungus *Penicillium* are used in the production of Brie, Camembert, and blue cheeses. Some species of the *Aspergillus* fungus are used to make soy sauce.

One interesting application of a mold is the use of the fungus *Trichoderma.* This mold grows in soil. The digestive chemicals it produces are used to give blue jeans a stonewashed look.

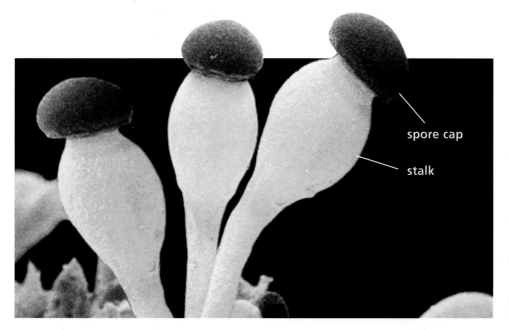

Pilobolus reacts to sunlight as a stimulus. The bend in the stalk will cause the spore cap to fly off.

Many molds cause disease. Fungal molds cause athlete's foot. Molds also affect plants. They are the cause of Dutch elm disease and the powdery white mildews that grow on plants. Compounds made from molds are also used to treat disease. Penicillin is an antibiotic that comes from the *Penicillium* fungus. It is used to fight bacterial diseases, such as pneumonia.

Molds reproduce with spores, which are typically carried by moving air. The "hat thrower" fungus *Pilobolus*, however, has an interesting adaptation for spreading spores. *Pilobolus* grows in animal droppings. It has a spore-containing cap—its hat—that grows on top of a stalk. The stalk responds to light as a stimulus and bends toward the Sun. As the stalk bends, water pressure builds up, causing the spore cap to shoot off, like a tiny cannonball. A spore cap can be thrown up to two meters away. If the spore caps land in grass, then cows and other grazing animals will eat the caps as they graze. A new cycle begins, with more *Pilobolus* being dispersed in the animal's droppings.

Yeasts

Yeasts are single-celled fungi. Some species of fungi exist in both yeast form and as multicellular hyphae. Yeasts grow in many moist environments, including the sap of plants and animal tissues. They also grow on moist surfaces, including shower curtains. Certain yeasts grow naturally on human skin. If the yeast begins to reproduce too rapidly, it can cause disease.

Yeasts are used in many food products. The activity of yeast cells breaking down sugars is what makes bread rise. The genetic material of the yeast *Saccharomyces cerevisiae* has been carefully studied by scientists. The study of this organism has helped scientists understand how genetic material controls the activities of a cell.

Yeasts are single-celled fungi.

Fungi can be helpful or harmful to other organisms.

Fungi have a close relationship to the environment and all living things in the environment. Fungi, along with bacteria, function as the main decomposers on Earth. The digestive chemicals that fungi release break down the complex compounds that come from living matter, dead matter, or the waste an organism leaves behind. A fungus absorbs what it needs to live and leaves behind simpler compounds and nutrients. These are then picked up again by plants, as producers, to start the cycle over again. Fungi also live in the sea, recycling materials for ocean-living organisms.

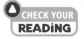 CHECK YOUR READING — What beneficial role do fungi play in the environment?

The threadlike hyphae of a fungus can grow into and decompose the material produced by another organism. This means that fungi can be helpful, for example, by releasing the nutrients in a dead tree back into the soil. Or fungi can be harmful, for example, attacking the tissues of a plant, such as the Dutch elm.

Most plants interact with fungi in a way that is helpful. The hyphae surround the plant roots, providing nutrients for the plant. The plant provides food for the fungus. Some fungi live together with single-celled algae, a network referred to as a **lichen** (LY-kuhn). The hyphae form almost a sandwich around the algae, which produce sugars and other nutrients the fungus needs.

VOCABULARY
Remember to add a four square for *lichen* to your notebook.

Lichen

A lichen is formed by a close association between algae and fungi.

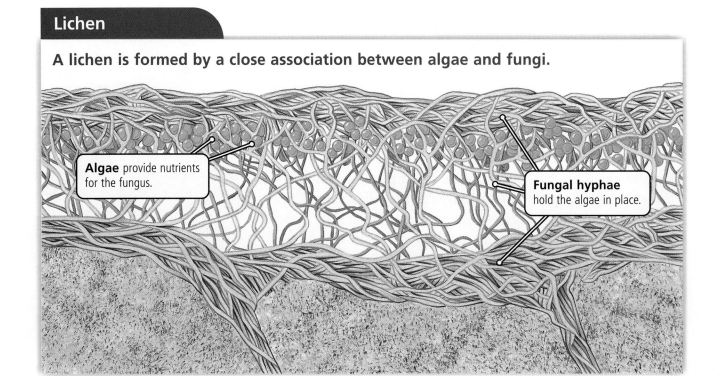

Algae provide nutrients for the fungus.

Fungal hyphae hold the algae in place.

Lichens can live just about anywhere. Lichens are found in the Arctic and in the desert. They can even grow on bare rock. The hyphae can break the rock down, slowly, and capture the particles of newly formed soil. This eventually prepares the ground for new plant growth.

On the harmful side, many fungi produce toxins, harmful chemicals. In 1845, a fungus infected Ireland's potato crop, causing the population of Ireland to drop from 8 million to about 4 million. Many people died from disease. Others died from starvation because of the loss of the important food crop. And hundreds of thousands of Irish left Ireland, many emigrating to the United States. Today, several fungal diseases are spreading through the world's banana crops.

CHECK YOUR READING Name some ways fungi can be harmful to organisms.

The toxic quality of a fungus can be put to good use, as in the case of the antibiotic penicillin. The photographs show what happens when a bacterium comes in contact with penicillin. The antibiotic prevents the bacterial cells from making new cell walls when they divide. This causes the cells to break open and the bacteria to die.

Bacterium before penicillin

Bacterium after penicillin

Penicillin is an antibiotic drug made from compounds taken from a species of the *Penicillium* fungus.

2.4 Review

KEY CONCEPTS

1. Describe the structure of a fungus.

2. How do fungi reproduce?

3. Describe two relationships between fungi and other organisms.

CRITICAL THINKING

4. **Analyze** Scientists used to classify fungi as plants. Today, scientists say that fungi are more like animals than plants. How are fungi like plants? How are they like animals?

5. **Predict** What might change in an environment where there were no fungi?

⬤ CHALLENGE

6. **Connect** Think of at least one way your life is affected by fungi in each of their three main forms: mushrooms, molds, and yeast. Are these effects beneficial or harmful to you?

CHAPTER INVESTIGATION

What Do Yeast Cells Use for Energy?

OVERVIEW AND PURPOSE Yeasts are tiny one-celled fungi that require food, water, and a warm place to grow. When they have a food source, they release carbon dioxide gas as a waste product. Yeast is used to make foods such as bread. In this activity, you will

- observe the activity of yeast
- draw conclusions about the effect of three materials on the activity of yeast

▶ Problem

How do sugar, salt, and sweetener affect the growth of yeast?

▶ Hypothesize

Write a hypothesis to explain how sugar, sweetener, and salt affect the activity of yeast in bread dough. Your hypothesis should take the form of an "If . . ., then . . ., because . . ." statement.

▶ Procedure

MATERIALS
- baking sheet
- flour
- measuring cups
- measuring spoons
- sugar
- artificial sweetener
- salt
- quick-rise yeast
- warm water
- metric ruler
- marker
- clothespins
- clear plastic straws

1. Make a data table like the one shown on page 73. Label four sheets of notebook paper *A*, *B*, *C*, and *D*.

2. Spread a very thin layer of flour over the baking sheet. Measure $\frac{1}{4}$ cup of flour and place it on the baking sheet as a mound. Repeat three times, forming separate mounds. Label the mounds *A*, *B*, *C*, and *D*.

3. Add 3 teaspoons of sugar to mound A. Add 3 tsp of sweetener to mound B. Add 3 tsp of salt to mound C. Add nothing to mound D.

4. Add $\frac{1}{4}$ tsp of the quick-rise yeast to each of the mounds. Slowly add 1 tsp of warm water to each mound to moisten the mixture. Spread a pinch of flour over your hands and knead the mounds by hand. Add water, 1 tsp at a time until the mixture has the consistency of dough. If the mixture gets too sticky, add more flour. Knead well and form each mound into a ball. Wash your hands thoroughly when you are finished. Do not taste or eat the dough.

5. Push 2 straws into each ball of dough, making sure the dough reaches at least 3 cm into the straws.

step 5

6. Squeeze the end of each straw to push the dough from the ends. Place a clothespin on the end of each straw closest to the dough. Fold and tape the other end. Mark both edges of the dough on the straw. Stand each straw upright on the appropriate piece of paper labeled A, B, C, or D.

step 6

7. Predict which mounds of dough will rise after 30 minutes. Write down your predictions in the data table.

8. After 30 minutes, measure the amount the dough has risen in each straw. Write down the results in the data table.

Observe and Analyze
Write It Up

1. **OBSERVE** In which mounds did the dough rise?

2. **OBSERVE** Did any of the remaining mounds of dough change? Explain.

3. **INFER** What was the purpose of using two straws for each of the mounds?

Conclude
Write It Up

1. **INTERPRET** Which is the most likely source of energy for yeast: salt, sugar, or sweetener? How do you know?

2. **INTERPRET** Compare your results with your hypothesis. How does your data support or disprove your hypothesis?

3. **LIMITATIONS** What limitations or sources of error could have affected your results?

4. **CONNECT** How would you account for the air spaces that are found in some breads?

5. **APPLY** Would you predict that breads made without yeast contain air spaces?

INVESTIGATE Further

CHALLENGE Design an experiment in which you can observe the production of carbon dioxide by yeast.

What Do Yeast Cells Use for Energy?

Table 1. Observations of Dough Rising

Mound	Prediction	Results
A. sugar and yeast		
B. sweetener and yeast		
C. salt and yeast		
D. yeast		

the **BIG** idea

Multicellular organisms live in and get energy from a variety of environments.

CONTENT REVIEW
CLASSZONE.COM

◀ **KEY CONCEPTS SUMMARY**

2.1 Multicellular organisms have many ways of meeting their needs.

- The bodies of multicellular organisms have different levels of organization.
- Multicellular organisms have a wide range of adaptations.
- Multicellular organisms reproduce by sexual reproduction. Some also reproduce asexually.

VOCABULARY
tissue p. 44
organ p. 44
sexual reproduction p. 48
meiosis p. 48
fertilization p. 48

2.2 Plants are producers.

Plants capture energy from the Sun and store it as sugar and starch. Plants are adapted to many environments. They respond to stimuli in the environment.

VOCABULARY
autotroph p. 52
photosynthesis p. 52
cellular respiration p. 53
stimulus p. 55

2.3 Animals are consumers.

Animals consume food to get energy and materials. Animals are adapted to many enviroments. They interact with the environment and with other organisms.

VOCABULARY
consumer p. 58
heterotroph p. 58
behavior p. 62
predator p. 63
prey p. 64
migration p. 64
hibernation p. 64

2.4 Most fungi are decomposers.

Fungi absorb energy from their surroundings. Fungi include mushrooms, molds, and yeasts. They affect people and other organisms in both helpful and harmful ways.

VOCABULARY
hyphae p. 67
spore p. 67
lichen p. 70

Reviewing Vocabulary

Draw a Venn diagram for each pair of terms. Put at least one shared characteristic in the overlap area, and put at least one difference in the outer circles.

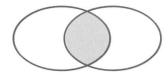

1. tissue, organ

2. autotroph, heterotroph

3. photosynthesis, cellular respiration

4. predator, prey

5. producer, consumer

6. migration, hibernation

Reviewing Key Concepts

Multiple Choice *Choose the letter of the best answer.*

7. Which body system transports materials such as nutrients and oxygen throughout an animal's body?

 a. respiratory system

 b. circulatory system

 c. digestive system

 d. nervous system

8. An example of an adaptation is

 a. a change in climate that increases plant growth

 b. the movement of a group of animals to an area that has more food and water

 c. a change in location of a squirrel's nest

 d. the ability of a plant to resist fungal disease better than other plants

9. Plants capture the Sun's energy through which process?

 a. reproduction   **c.** photosynthesis

 b. cellular respiration   **d.** digestion

10. Plants produce auxin in response to which stimulus?

 a. light

 b. gravity

 c. temperature

 d. touch

11. A plant is best described as

 a. a herbivore

 b. an omnivore

 c. a carnivore

 d. a producer

12. A carnivore is best described as an animal that

 a. eats plants

 b. eats plants and other animals

 c. eats other animals

 d. makes its own food

13. Mushrooms produce

 a. spores

 b. buds

 c. mold

 d. yeast

14. Fungi and algae together form

 a. hyphae

 b. mushrooms

 c. lichen

 d. mold

Short Answer *Write a short answer to each question.*

15. Write a short paragraph comparing sexual reproduction with asexual reproduction. How are they the same? How are they different?

16. Write a short paragraph to explain how the sugars and starches stored in plant tissue are important to the survival of animals.

17. Write a short paragraph to explain how fungi are dependent on plants and animals for their energy.

Thinking Critically

The diagram below shows a woodland food web. Each arrow starts with a food source and points to a consumer. Use the diagram to answer the next six questions.

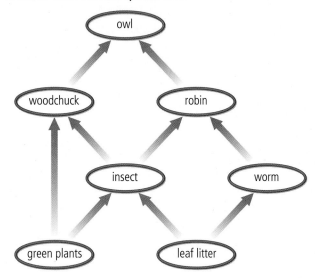

18. ANALYZE What is the original source of energy for all the animals in the food web? Explain your reasoning.

19. CLASSIFY Identify the consumers in this food web.

20. CLASSIFY Identify the animals in the food web as either herbivores, carnivores, omnivores, or decomposers.

21. EVALUATE Does an omnivore have an advantage over carnivores and herbivores in finding food?

22. ANALYZE What role does the worm play in the food web, and why it is important?

23. PREDICT How might this food web change over the course of a year, and how would that affect the feeding activity of animals in the food web?

24. CONNECT A woodchuck is sometimes referred to as a groundhog. Many people celebrate February 2 as groundhog day. The legend is that if a groundhog emerges from its burrow on this day and sees its shadow, then there will be six more weeks of winter. The groundhog is emerging from a long sleeplike state. What is this behavior, and how does it benefit the animal?

25. ANALYZE Do you think the defensive behavior of a porcupine or pufferfish is an adaptation? Explain your reasoning.

26. SYNTHESIZE A plant responds to gravity, touch, and light as stimuli. How does this relate to a plant being a producer?

27. SYNTHESIZE How are the cells of multicellular organisms like those of single-celled organisms? How are they different?

28. ANALYZE What quality of asexual reproduction makes a fungal disease spread so quickly.

the BIG idea

29. SYNTHESIZE Look again at the photograph on pages 40–41. Plants, animals, and fungi are pictured there. How do these organisms get energy and materials from the environment?

30. SUMMARIZE Write a short paragraph to describe how matter and energy move between members of the kingdoms of plants, animals, and fungi. Use the words in the box below. Underline the terms in your answer.

photosysnthesis	consumer
producer	decomposer

UNIT PROJECTS

By now you should have completed the following items for your unit project.

- questions that you have asked about the topic
- schedule showing when you will complete each step of your project
- list of resources including Web sites, print resources, and materials

Interpreting Diagrams

The diagram shows the feeding relationships between certain animals and plants in a forest environment. The size of the bars represent the relative numbers of each organism. The arrow shows the flow of energy between these groups of organisms.

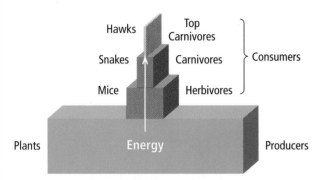

Feeding Relationships Among Plants and Animals

Use the diagram to answer the questions below.

1. Which is the largest group of organisms in the forest?
   a. plants
   b. mice
   c. snakes
   d. hawks

2. Most energy in the forest comes from
   a. top carnivores
   b. carnivores
   c. herbivores
   d. plants

3. Which description best fits the snake?
   a. a producer that feeds upon mice
   b. a consumer that is eaten by mice
   c. a consumer that feeds upon mice
   d. a consumer that feeds upon plants

4. A hawk is a top carnivore that feeds upon both snakes and mice. Which of the following best describes a top carnivore?
   a. a carnivore that feeds upon other carnivores
   b. a carnivore that feeds upon both carnivores and herbivores
   c. a consumer that gets its energy from producers
   d. a producer that supplies energy to consumers

5. Which statement best summarizes the diagram?
   a. The energy in a forest environment flows one way, from producers to consumers.
   b. Consumers don't need as much energy as producers.
   c. Energy in a forest environment goes from plants to animals and then back to plants.
   d. The number of producers depends on the number of consumers.

Extended Response

6 The diagram above shows the relative number of organisms at each level of a forest environment and the flow of energy from the producers to the consumers. Describe what happens to the amount of energy going from the producer level into the different levels of consumers. Not all the energy produced at a given level is available to organisms in the next level. What has happened to that energy? Use the words in the word box in your answer. Underline the words.

producer	energy
consumer	food

7. How would the number of plants, snakes, and hawks be affected if some disease were to reduce the numbers of mice in the forest?

TIMELINES in Science

DISCOVERIES IN Biodiversity

Scientists have discovered new species in the treetops of tropical forests and in the crannies of coral reefs. The quest to catalog the types and numbers of living things, the biodiversity of Earth, began in the late 1600s. A wave of naturalists set sail from Europe to the Americas and to Africa to find specimens of living things.

In the late 19th century, biologists reached agreement on a system for naming and classifying each new species. The mid-20th century brought an understanding of DNA and how it could be used to compare one species with another. Now new organisms could be pinpointed with precision. To this day, millions of undiscovered species lie deep in the unexplored ocean, in tropical forests, and even in heavily trafficked U.S. cities. A large concentration of Earth's known species now live in named and protected biodiversity "hotspots."

1670

Merian Illustrates from Life

In her day, it was typical to work from preserved specimens, but Maria Merian draws from life. Shown below is her illustration of the Legu Lizard she observes in South America. In 1670, she publishes a richly illustrated book of insects, the first to describe the process of metamorphosis.

EVENTS

1670

APPLICATIONS AND TECHNOLOGY

TECHNOLOGY

Improvements in Navigation

Since the Age of Exploration in the 1500s and 1600s, European ship-building and sailing had boomed. Vast improvements had been made, especially in charting and mapping. Travel from Europe to Africa, Asia, and the Americas became an important part of business and science. Still, ships often lost their way or wrecked in raging storms. The invention by John Harrison in 1765 of the marine chronometer, a clock that could work at sea, changed navigation forever. Nobody expected a land-locked clockmaker to solve the puzzle, but the sea clock provided an accurate way to record sightings of stars and planets, and thus plot longitude at sea. The ocean remained a dangerous passage, but now, if tossed off course, a captain could still steer clear.

1775
A Catalog of Living Things

In 1775 Carl Linnaeus completed a book called *Systema Naturae*. His book outlines a system to organize and name plants and animals. The naming system gave scientists a precise and consistent method for sharing discoveries.

1859
Naturalists in the Amazon

Henry Walter Bates travels from England to the Amazon rainforest in South America with Alfred Russell Wallace. Bates sails home in 1859, bringing over 14,000 specimens, mostly insects. About 8000 of Bates's finds are new discoveries. Wallace loses his collection in a shipwreck.

1889
Naming Discoveries

At the height of discovering new species, conflicts arise over who gets to name living things. In 1889, a conference settles the matter. The first person to publish a description of an organism has the right to claim the discovery and to name it.

| 1770 | 1780 | | 1860 | 1870 | | 1880 |

TECHNOLOGY
Living Things Too Small to See

Before the 1600s, scientists were unable to see microorganisms. Anton van Leeuwenhoek, a drapery maker who made microscopes in his spare time, was one of the first to observe these tiny organisms. He made the first observation of bacteria, and viewed lake water through a microscope like the one shown to the far right. Others used microscopes to draw detailed close-ups, such as an insect's compound eye shown here.

1970
The Bacteria Kingdom Divides

Dr. Carl Woese discovers that bacterialike organisms living in places with extremely high temperatures have genetic material very different from bacteria. Woese suggests a new kingdom or domain called archaebacteria, which is later shortened to Archaea.

1990
Diver, SCUBA Pioneer, Heads Research

Dr. Sylvia Earle is the first woman to serve as chief scientist at the National Oceanic and Atmospheric Administration (NOAA). Earle uses SCUBA diving and discovers many new fish and marine species—especially new seaweeds in the Gulf of Mexico. Here she shows a sample to a student in a submersible vehicle.

1974
Fogging the Rainforest

Terry Erwin spouts plumes of insecticide into trees and discovers thousands of new insects species in the rainforest canopy. Erwin uses an organic insecticide that does not harm other parts of the ecosystem. Erwin spreads ground sheets or big funnels around a tree, sprays, and, after an hour or so catches the fallen insects, which look like jewels.

| 1970 | 1980 | 1990 |

TECHNOLOGY

Submersibles

To explore great depths, scientists use manned submersibles or robots. Scientists used the submersible, Alvin, to discover giant worms around thermal vents. This was at a depth where people thought that life could not exist. Underwater submersibles were also used to discover life in cold springs and to collect bacteria to be used for biomedical research. In addition, unmanned submersibles, such as robots, search for giant squids and other life deep in the ocean.

2002 to Present
New Plant Genera

Scientists who study plants and insects in tropical rain forests discover so many new species that they are sometimes backlogged in naming them. In the plant kingdom, it has been estimated that for every 1000 species discovered, one new genus will be found. Occasionally a new plant genus is found in the wild. In 2002 scientists found a new genus of ginger in the wild in Singapore. More and more, genera are identified in the laboratory using DNA.

RESOURCE CENTER
CLASSZONE.COM

Read about current biodiversity discoveries and research.

2000

APPLICATION

Biodiversity Hotspots

In 1988, environmentalist Mike Meyers creates a list of 18 areas that he calls biodiversity "hotspots." In 2000, Myers increases the number of hotspots to 34. How does an area get to be called a hotspot? It has to have a large number of species that exist only in that location and it has to be a region in great danger of habitat loss. Hotspots cover only 2.3 percent of the Earth's surface yet they contain 50 percent of all species of higher plants and 42 percent of all land vertebrates. Scientists place most of their effort in discovering new species in these hotspots.

cold hot

SPOTLIGHT on
MARJORIE COURTENAY-LATIMER

Biologists thought coelacanth fish had been extinct for 70 million years. At least they did until 1938. This was when Marjorie Courtenay-Latimer (1907–2004) identified the body of one that was recently caught off the southern coast of Africa. The fish got the scientific name *Latimeria chalumnae* in her honor.

Ms. Courtenay-Latimer was the first curator of the East London Museum in South Africa. She built the museum's collection. This collection included seashells, wild flowers, butterflies, and insects as well as fossils. She remained an active speaker about museums until her death in 2004.

ACTIVITIES

Writing About Science: Documentary

Research one hotspot and report on the diverse species living there. Note any legal steps or other efforts to conserve biodiversity in that area.

Reliving History

Devise an animal classification system based on a criterion such as habitat, diet, or behavior. What are the strengths and weaknesses of your system?

CHAPTER

3 Plants

the **BIG** idea

Plants are a diverse group of organisms that live in many land environments.

Key Concepts

SECTION
3.1 Plants are adapted to living on land.
Learn about plant characteristics and structures.

SECTION
3.2 Most mosses and ferns live in moist environments.
Learn about how mosses and ferns live and reproduce.

SECTION
3.3 Seeds and pollen are reproductive adaptations.
Learn about seeds, pollen, and gymnosperms.

SECTION
3.4 Many plants reproduce with flowers and fruit.
Learn about flowers, fruit, and angiosperms.

Internet Preview

CLASSZONE.COM

Chapter 3 online resources: Content Review, Simulation, Visualization, four Resource Centers, Math Tutorial, Test Practice

How does such a large tree get what it needs to survive?

EXPLORE (the BIG idea)

How Are Plants Alike, How Are They Different?

Find samples of plants in your area. Draw or take pictures of them for your science notebook. Note each plant's shape, size, and the environment where you found it.

Observe and Think Do all plants have leaves? Do all plants have flowers?

How Are Seeds Dispersed?

Make a model of a seed with wings, such as a seed from a maple tree. Fold a strip of paper in half the long way and then unfold it. Cut a little less than halfway along the fold. Refold the uncut part of the paper and bend out the two cut strips so they look like wings. Put a paper clip on the bottom of the folded part. Drop your seed.

Observe and Think How does having seeds with wings benefit a plant?

Internet Activity: Sprouting Seeds

Go to **ClassZone.com** to watch a time-lapse video of a seed sprouting.

Observe and Think If plants come from seeds, where do seeds come from?

NSTA
scilinks.org
SCi LINKS

Plant Kingdom Code: MDL041

Getting Ready to Learn

◀ CONCEPT REVIEW

- All organisms get water and other materials from the environment.
- Plants have specialized tissues with specific functions.
- Plants are producers.

◀ VOCABULARY REVIEW

meiosis p. 48

fertilization p. 48

photosynthesis p. 52

spore p. 67

cycle *See Glossary.*

 CONTENT REVIEW
CLASSZONE.COM
Review concepts and vocabulary.

▶ TAKING NOTES

MIND MAP

Write each main idea, or blue heading, in an oval; then write details that relate to each other and to the main idea. Organize the details so that each spoke of the web has notes about one part of the main idea.

VOCABULARY STRATEGY

Draw a **word triangle** diagram for each new vocabulary term. On the bottom line, write and define the term. Above that, write a sentence that uses the term correctly.
At the top, draw a small picture to remind you of the definition.

See the Note-Taking Handbook on pages R45–R51.

SCIENCE NOTEBOOK

cells have a nucleus   two-part life cycle

cells have cell walls   producers

PLANTS SHARE COMMON CHARACTERISTICS

multicellular

live on land

Sunlight and wind can cause transpiration.

Transpiration: the movement of water vapor out of a plant and into the air

Plants are adapted to living on land.

◀ BEFORE, you learned

- All organisms have certain basic needs and characteristics
- The bodies of multicellular organisms are organized
- Plants are producers

▶ NOW, you will learn

- About plant diversity
- About common characteristics of plants
- How the bodies of plants are organized

VOCABULARY

vascular system p. 87
transpiration p. 88

EXPLORE Leaf Characteristics

What is a leaf?

PROCEDURE

① Examine the leaf your teacher gives you carefully. Try to notice as many details as you can.

② Make a drawing of both sides of your leaf in your notebook. Label as many parts as you can and write down your ideas describing each part's function.

③ Compare your diagram and notes with those of your classmates.

MATERIALS
- assorted leaves
- hand lens

WHAT DO YOU THINK?
- What characteristics did most or all of your leaves have?
- How would you describe your leaf to someone who could not see it?

MIND MAP
Make a mind map for the first main idea:
Plants are a diverse group of organisms.

Plants are a diverse group of organisms.

Plants are nearly everywhere. Walk through a forest, and you're surrounded by trees, ferns, and moss. Drive along a country road, and you pass fields planted with crops like cotton or wheat. Even a busy city has tree-lined sidewalks, grass-covered lawns, and weeds growing in vacant lots or poking through cracks in the pavement.

Earth is home to an amazing variety of plant life. Plants come in all shapes and sizes, from tiny flowers no bigger than the head of a pin to giant trees taller than a 12-story building. Plants are found in all types of environments, from the icy Arctic to the steamy tropics.

Plant species live in a variety of environments and have a wide range of features.

Orchids

Seed pods of the vanilla orchid are used to flavor food.

Horsetails

Horsetails have a distinctive shape and texture.

Bristlecone Pine

Bristlecone pines are some of the oldest trees on Earth.

Plants share common characteristics.

Scientists estimate that at least 260,000 different species of plants live on Earth today. The photographs on this page show three examples of plants that are very different from one another.

Orchids are flowering plants that mostly grow in tropical rain forests. To get the sunlight they need, many orchids grow not in the soil but on the trunks of trees. Horsetails are plants that produce tiny grains of a very hard substance called silica. Sometimes called scouring rushes, these plants were once used to scrub clean, or scour, dishes and pots. Bristlecone pine trees live on high mountain slopes in North America, where there is little soil and often high winds. These trees grow very slowly and can live for several thousand years.

You can see from these three examples that plant species show great diversity. Despite how different an orchid is from a horsetail and a bristlecone pine, all three plants share certain characteristics. These are the characteristics that define a plant as a plant:

- Plants are multicellular organisms.
- A plant cell has a nucleus and is surrounded by a cell wall.
- Plants are producers. They capture energy from the Sun.
- Plant life cycles are divided into two stages, or generations.

READING TiP

The word *species* comes from a root word meaning "kind" or "type." In science, *species* is a classification for a group of organisms that are so similar that members of the group can breed and produce offspring that can also reproduce.

 CHECK YOUR READING   What characteristics are shared by all plants?

Plant parts have special functions.

You could say that a plant lives in two worlds. The roots anchor a plant in the ground. Aboveground, reaching toward the Sun, are stems and leaves. Together, stems and leaves make up a shoot system. These two systems work together to get a plant what it needs to survive.

A plant's root system can be as extensive as the stems and leaves that you see aboveground. Roots absorb water and nutrients from the soil. These materials are transported to the leaves through the stems. The leaves use the materials, along with carbon dioxide from the air, to make sugars and carbohydrates. The stems then deliver these energy-rich compounds back to the rest of the plant.

CHECK YOUR READING What are two plant systems, and what are their functions?

Transporting Water and Other Materials

Stems serve as the pathway for transporting water, nutrients, and energy-rich compounds from one part of a plant to another. In most plants, the materials move through a **vascular system** (VAS-kyuh-lur) that is made up of long, tubelike cells. These tissues are bundled together and run from the roots to the leaves. A vascular bundle from the stem of a buttercup plant is shown.

Transport is carried out by two types of tissue. Xylem (ZY-luhm) is a tissue that carries water and dissolved nutrients up from the roots. Phloem (FLOH-em) is a tissue that transports energy-rich materials down from the leaves. Xylem cells and phloem cells are long and hollow, like pipes. The xylem cells are a little larger than the phloem cells. Both tissues include long fibers that help support the plant body, as well as cells that can store extra carbohydrates for energy.

REMINDER

Plants, like animals, have several levels of oranization. The root system and shoot system are organ systems.

phloem

xylem

This vascular bundle has been magnified 113×.

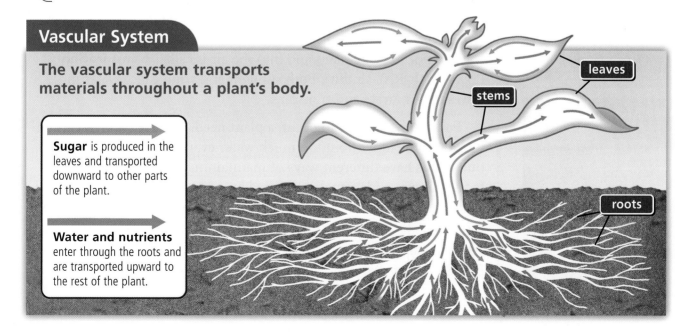

Vascular System

The vascular system transports materials throughout a plant's body.

Sugar is produced in the leaves and transported downward to other parts of the plant.

Water and nutrients enter through the roots and are transported upward to the rest of the plant.

leaves

stems

roots

Making Sugars

Plants produce sugars through the process of photosynthesis. Photosynthesis is a series of chemical reactions that capture light energy from the Sun and convert it into chemical energy stored in sugar molecules. The starting materials needed are carbon dioxide, water, and light. The end products are sugars and oxygen. The chemical reactions for photosynthesis can be summarized like this:

carbon dioxide + water + sunlight → sugars + oxygen

Photosynthesis takes place in chloroplasts, structures that contain chlorophyll. Chlorophyll absorbs the sunlight that the chloroplasts need to produce the reaction. Most chloroplasts in a plant are located in leaf cells. As you can see from the illustration on page 89, the structure of the leaf is specialized for capturing light energy and producing sugar.

 CHECK YOUR READING What is photosynthesis, and why is it important?

The upper surface of the leaf, which is turned toward the Sun, has layers of cells filled with chloroplasts. Vascular tissue located toward the center of the leaf brings in water and nutrients and carries away sugars and other carbohydrates. Tiny openings at the bottom of the leaf, called stomata (STOH-muh-tuh), lead to a network of tiny spaces where gases are stored. The carbon dioxide gas needed for photosynthesis comes in through the stomata, and oxygen gas moves out. This process is called gas exchange.

Open Stomata

214×

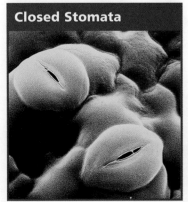

Closed Stomata

Controlling Gas Exchange and Water Loss

For photosynthesis to occur, a plant must maintain the balance of carbon dioxide and water in its body. Carbon dioxide gas from the air surrounding a plant enters through the stomata in its leaves. Open stomata allow carbon dioxide and oxygen to move into and out of the leaf. These openings also allow water to evaporate. The movement of water vapor out of a plant and into the air is called **transpiration** (TRAN-spuh-RAY-shuhn). Both sunlight and wind cause water in leaves to evaporate and transpire.

For photosynthesis to occur, a plant needs to have enough carbon dioxide come in without too much water evaporating and moving out. Plants have different ways of maintaining this balance. The surfaces of leaves and stems are covered by a waxy protective layer, called a cuticle. The cuticle keeps water from evaporating. Also, when the air is dry, the stomata can close. This can help to prevent water loss.

 CHECK YOUR READING What are two ways plants have to keep from losing too much water?

Inside a Leaf

The leaf is an organ that produces sugars. It is made up of different types of cells and tissues.

Cells at the surface produce a waxy cuticle that keeps the leaf from losing water.

Most chloroplasts are located in cells of the upper layer of the leaf.

Xylem transports water and nutrients up from the roots.

Phloem transports energy-rich compounds made in the leaf down to other parts of the plant.

Carbon dioxide, oxygen, and water vapor move into and out of the leaf through stomata.

READING VISUALS How is the top of a leaf different from the bottom of a leaf?

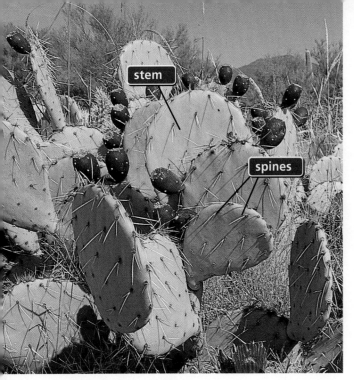

stem

spines

The stomata are an adaptation that allows a plant to adjust to daily changes in its environment. Plants can respond to hot, dry weather by keeping their stomata closed. Stomata can be open during the night, when evaporation is less likely to occur. Most plants have stomata.

Some species of plants have special adaptations for survival in a particular environment. For example, a cactus plant has adaptations that allow it to survive in a desert. The spines of a cactus are actually modified leaves. A plant with regular leaves would lose too much water through transpiration. In cacti, most photosynthesis occurs in the thick fleshy stem, where the cactus also stores water and carbon dioxide gas.

APPLY Plant stems branch as they grow. Do cactus plants have branches?

Plants grow throughout their lifetimes.

Plants grow as long as they live. This is true for plants that live for only one season, such as sunflowers, and for plants that can live for many years, such as trees. Plants grow bigger when cells at the tips of their roots and stems divide and multiply more rapidly than other plant cells do. A plant's roots and stems can grow longer and thicker and can branch, or divide. However, only stems grow leaves. Leaves grow from buds produced by growth tissue in a plant's stems. The bud of an oak tree is shown on page 91.

Plant stems are structures with more than one function. You have read that a plant's stem includes its vascular system, which allows the plant to transport materials between its leaves and roots. Long stiff fibers in the tissues of the vascular system provide support and give the plant shape. Plant stems can also store the sugars produced by photosynthesis. Many plants, including broccoli, celery, and carrots, convert sugars into starch and then store this energy-rich material in their stems or roots.

CHECK YOUR READING What are three functions of plant stems?

Plants with Soft Stems

RESOURCE CENTER
CLASSZONE.COM

Learn more about plant systems.

The soft stems and leaves of many wildflowers, garden flowers, and vegetables die when the environment they live in becomes too cold or too dry. This type of plant survives by using the carbohydrates stored in its roots. Then, when the environment provides it with enough warmth, water, and sunlight, the plant will grow new, soft, green stems and leaves.

Plant Growth

Plants, such as these oak trees, grow most when there is enough warmth, water, and sunlight.

Oak Bud

The tips of the shoots produce buds, which become new leaves and stems.

Plants with Woody Stems

Some plants, such as trees and shrubs, have tough, thick stems that do not die each year. These stems keep growing longer and thicker. As the stems grow, they develop a type of tough xylem tissue that is not found in soft stems. This tough xylem tissue is called wood. The growing tissues in woody stems are located near the outer surface of the stem, right under the bark. This means that, for a tree like one of the oaks in the photograph above, the center of the trunk is the oldest part of the plant.

 Review

KEY CONCEPTS

1. What characteristics do all plants have in common?

2. How does the structure of a leaf relate to its function?

3. What tissues move materials throughout a plant?

CRITICAL THINKING

4. **Summarize** Describe how the structure of a leaf allows a plant to control the materials involved in photosynthesis.

5. **Analyze** Do you think the stems of soft-stemmed plants have chloroplasts? How about woody-stemmed plants? Explain your reasoning. Hint: Think about the color of each.

⚫ CHALLENGE

6. **Evaluate** Scientists who study the natural world say that there is unity in diversity. How does this idea apply to plants?

3.2

KEY CONCEPT

Most mosses and ferns live in moist environments.

 BEFORE, you learned

- All plants share common characteristics
- The body of a plant has specialized parts
- Plants grow throughout their lifetimes

NOW, you will learn

- About the first plants
- About reproduction in nonvascular plants, such as mosses
- About reproduction in vascular plants, such as ferns

EXPLORE Moss Plants

What do moss plants look like?

PROCEDURE

1. Use a hand lens to examine a moss plant. Look for different structures and parts you can identify.

2. Draw a diagram of the moss plant in your notebook. Label parts you identified and parts you would like to identify.

3. Write a brief description of each part's function.

MATERIALS
- live moss plant
- hand lens

WHAT DO YOU THINK?
- How would you describe a moss plant to someone who had never seen one?
- How does a moss plant compare with the other plants you are familiar with?

Plant species adapted to life on land.

Evidence indicates that life first appeared on Earth about 3.8 billion years ago. Tiny single-celled and multicellular organisms lived in watery environments such as warm shallow seas, deep ocean vents, and ponds. Fossil evidence suggests that plant life did not appear on land until about 475 million years ago. The ancestors of the first plants were among the first organisms to move onto land.

What did these plantlike organisms look like? Scientists think they looked much like the green algae you can find growing in watery ditches or shallow ponds today. Both green algae and plants are autotrophs, or producers. Their cells contain chloroplasts that enable them to convert the Sun's light energy into the chemical energy stored in sugars.

RESOURCE CENTER
CLASSZONE.COM

Explore plant evolution.

The First Plants

Suppose that hundreds of millions of years ago, the area now occupied by your school was a shallow pond full of tiny, floating organisms that could photosynthesize. The Sun overhead provided energy. The pond water was full of dissolved nutrients. The organisms thrived and reproduced, and over time the pond became crowded. Some were pushed to the very edges of the water. Then, after a period of dry weather, the pond shrank. Some organisms at the edge were no longer in the water. The ones that were able to survive were now living on land.

Scientists think that something like this took place in millions of watery environments over millions of years. Those few organisms that were stranded and were able to survive became ancestors to the first plants. Life on land is very different from life in water. The first plants needed to be able to get both nutrients and water from the land. There is no surrounding water to provide support for the body or to keep body tissues from drying out. However, for organisms that survived, life on land had many advantages. There is plenty of carbon dioxide in the air and plenty of direct sunlight.

Scientists think the first plants shared a common ancestor with green algae, shown here magnified about 80×.

 CHECK YOUR READING Why is having plenty of sunlight and water an advantage for a plant? Your answer should mention photosynthesis.

Mosses and Ferns

Among the first plants to live on Earth were the ancestors of the mosses and ferns you see today. Both probably evolved from species of algae that lived in the sea and in freshwater. Mosses are simpler in structure than ferns. Mosses, and two closely related groups of plants known as liverworts and hornworts, are descended from the first plants to spread onto the bare rock and soil of Earth. Ferns and their relatives appeared later.

This diorama shows what a forest on Earth might have looked like about 350 million years ago.

INVESTIGATE Capturing the Sun's Energy

How much sunlight reaches an organism living in water?

PROCEDURE

1. Thread the string through the holes in the button so that the button hangs flat. Fill the empty bottle with clean water.

2. Look down through the top of the bottle. Lower the button into the water until it either disappears from view or reaches the bottom. Have a classmate measure how far the button is from the surface of the water.

3. Add two spoonfuls of kelp granules to the water. Repeat step 2.

WHAT DO YOU THINK?

- How did the distance measured the second time compare with your first measurement?

- Why might a photosynthetic organism living on land get more sunlight than one living in water?

CHALLENGE What do the kelp granules in this experiment represent? What does that suggest about the advantages of living on land?

SKILL FOCUS
Measuring

MATERIALS
- white button
- string
- empty clear plastic bottle
- water
- ruler
- kelp granules
- tablespoon

TIME
20 minutes

Mosses are nonvascular plants.

Moss plants have adaptations for life on land. For example, each moss cell, like all plant cells, is surrounded by a thick wall that provides it with support. Moss cells also have special storage areas for water and nutrients. Mosses do not grow very large, but they have simple structures that function like roots, stems, and leaves. These adaptations help moss plants survive on land, while algae survive only in water.

If you look closely at a clump of moss, you will see that it is actually made up of many tiny, dark green plants. Mosses belong to a group called nonvascular plants. Nonvascular plants do not have vascular tissue. Water and nutrients simply move through nonvascular plants' bodies cell by cell. A plant can get enough water this way as long as its body is no more than a few cells thick.

 CHECK YOUR READING What limits the size of moss plants?

Water also plays a part in the reproductive cycle of a moss plant. In the first part of the cycle, the moss grows and maintains itself, producing the male and female structures needed for sexual reproduction. If conditions are right and there is enough water, the plant enters a spore-producing stage, the second part of the cycle.

Mosses reproduce with spores.

Mosses, ferns, and fungi all reproduce with spores. Spores are an important adaptation that allowed the ancestors of these organisms to reproduce on land. A spore is a single reproductive cell that is protected by a hard, watertight covering. The covering prevents the cell from drying out. Spores are small and can be transported through the air. This means offspring from spores can grow in places that are distant from the parent organisms.

The green moss plants you are familiar with have grown from spores. They represent the first generation. Within a clump of moss are both male and female reproductive structures. When conditions are right, these structures produce sperm and eggs. Fertilization can occur only if water is present because the tiny moss sperm move by swimming. A layer of water left by rain is one way sperm can move to the eggs on another part of the plant.

The fertilized egg grows into a stalk with a capsule on the end—the second generation of the plant. The stalk and capsule grow from the female moss plant. Inside the capsule, the process of meiosis produces thousands of tiny spores. When the spores are released, as shown in the photograph, the cycle can begin again.

REMINDER

Sexual reproduction involves two processes: fertilization and meiosis.

Moss Releasing Spores

capsule

stalk

spores

moss plant

IDENTIFY Point out the two generations of the moss plant shown here.

Mosses, like other plants, can also reproduce asexually. A small piece of a moss plant can separate and can grow into a new plant, or new plants can branch off from old ones. Asexual reproduction allows plants to spread more easily than sexual reproduction. However, the genetic material of the new plants is the same as that of the parent. Sexual reproduction increases genetic diversity and the possibility of new adaptations.

 CHECK YOUR READING Compare and contrast sexual and asexual reproduction. Your answer should mention *genetic material.*

Ferns are vascular plants.

Ferns, and two closely related groups of plants known as horsetails and club mosses, were the first plants on Earth with vascular systems. The tubelike tissue of a vascular system moves water through a plant's body quickly and effectively. Because of this transport system, vascular plants can grow much larger than nonvascular plants. Vascular tissue also provides support for the weight of a larger plant.

The presence of vascular tissue has an effect on the development of roots, stems, and leaves. The root system can branch out more, anchoring a larger plant as well as providing water and nutrients. Vascular tissue moves materials more efficiently and gives extra support. The stems can branch out and more leaves can grow. This results in more sugars and other materials needed for energy and growth.

Nonvascular

Liverworts are tiny nonvascular plants. The liverworts shown here are life-size.

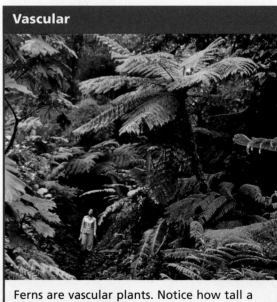

Vascular

Ferns are vascular plants. Notice how tall a tree fern can grow.

READING VISUALS COMPARE AND CONTRAST How do the penny and the person help to show that the tree ferns are much larger than the liverworts?

Ferns reproduce with spores.

You may have seen ferns growing in the woods or in a garden. The leaves of ferns, called fronds, are often included in a flower bouquet. The next time you have a chance to look at a fern frond, take a look at the back. You will probably see many small clusters similar to those shown to the right. The clusters are full of spores.

spores

spore cluster

Ferns, like mosses, have a two-part life cycle. In ferns, spores grow into tiny structures that lie very close to the ground. You would have to look closely to find these structures on the ground, for they are usually smaller than the size of your thumbnail. Within these structures are the sperm- and egg-producing parts of the fern plant. This is the first generation of the plant. Like mosses, the sperm of a fern plant need water to swim to the egg. So fertilization occurs only when plenty of moisture is present.

The second part of a fern life cycle is the plant with fronds that grows from the fertilized egg. As the fronds grow, the small egg-bearing part of the plant dies away. The fronds produce clusters, and cells within those clusters undergo meiosis and produce spores. The more the fern grows, the more clusters and spores it produces. The spores, when they are released, spread through the air. If conditions are right where the spores land, they grow into new fern plants and a new cycle begins. This is sexual reproduction. Ferns, like mosses, also reproduce asexually. New ferns branch off old ones, or pieces separate from the plant and grow.

As fern fronds grow, they produce clusters of spores on the back of the fronds.

CHECK YOUR READING Explain one way that sexual reproduction in ferns is similar to reproduction in mosses. Explain one way it is different.

3.2 Review

KEY CONCEPTS

1. For the ancestors of the first plants, what were some advantages to living on land?

2. What are three adaptations that make mosses able to live on land?

3. What are two characteristics you can observe that distinguish vascular plants from nonvascular plants?

CRITICAL THINKING

4. **Synthesize** Vascular plants such as ferns can grow bigger and taller than nonvascular plants such as mosses. Does this mean they can also capture more sunlight? Explain your answer.

5. **Compare** Make a chart that shows how the life cycles of mosses and ferns are different, and how they are similar.

CHALLENGE

6. **Evaluate** Consider the conditions that are needed for mosses and ferns to reproduce sexually. Sexual reproduction increases genetic diversity within a group of plants, while asexual reproduction does not. Explain why asexual reproduction is still important for both moss and fern plants.

3.3 Seeds and pollen are reproductive adaptations.

◀ **BEFORE, you learned**

- Plant species evolved from algaelike ancestors
- Mosses are nonvascular plants that reproduce with spores
- Ferns are vascular plants that reproduce with spores

▶ **NOW, you will learn**

- How some plants reproduce with pollen and seeds
- About the advantages of pollen and seeds

VOCABULARY

seed p. 98
embryo p. 98
germination p. 99
pollen p. 100
gymnosperm p. 102

THINK ABOUT

Is a seed alive?

A lotus is a type of pond lily that is commonly found in water gardens. The plants take root in the bottom of a pond. A plant scientist in California experimented with lotus seeds from China that were over 1000 years old. The scientist made a small opening in the hard covering of each seed and planted the seeds in wet soil. Some of the seeds sprouted and grew. What made it possible for these seeds to survive for such a long time? Is a seed alive?

Seeds are an important adaptation.

Spores are one adaptation that made it possible for plants to reproduce on land. Seeds are another. A **seed** is a young plant that is enclosed in a protective coating. Within the coating are enough nutrients to enable the plant to grow. Seeds and spores can both withstand harsh conditions. Seed plants, however, have several survival advantages over seedless plants. These advantages make it possible for seed plants to spread into environments where seedless plants are less likely to survive.

In all plants, fertilization brings about the growth of the next generation of the plant, beginning with an embryo. An **embryo** (EHM-bree-OH) is the immature form of an organism that has the potential to grow and develop. In seed plants, the embryo is protected. The seed coat protects the immature plant until conditions are right for it to grow.

VOCABULARY
Remember to make word triangles for *seed* and *embryo* in your notebook.

An embryo can remain inside a seed for a long time without growing. When moisture, temperature, and other conditions are right, a seed will start to grow. **Germination** (JUR-muh-NAY-shuhn) is the beginning of growth of a new plant from a spore or a seed. If you've ever planted a seed that sprouted, you've observed germination.

 What is germination?

When a seed germinates, it takes in water from its surroundings. As the embryo begins to grow, it uses the stored nutrients in the seed for energy and materials. The nutrients need to last until the new plant's roots and shoots can start to function.

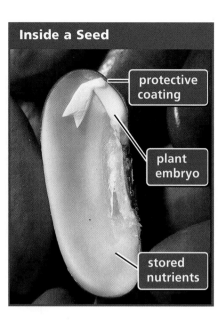

Inside a Seed

protective coating

plant embryo

stored nutrients

Some plants reproduce with seeds.

In most places, plants that reproduce with seeds are common and easy to see. Trees, bushes, flowers, and grasses are all seed plants. It's a bit harder to find plants that reproduce with spores, such as mosses or ferns. Why are there so many more seed plants in the world? The diagram below shows some of the differences and similarities between seeds and spores.

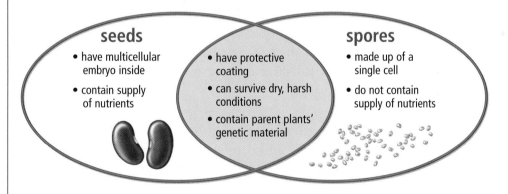

seeds
- have multicellular embryo inside
- contain supply of nutrients

- have protective coating
- can survive dry, harsh conditions
- contain parent plants' genetic material

spores
- made up of a single cell
- do not contain supply of nutrients

One important difference between a seed and a spore is that the seed contains a multicellular organism. If you look closely at the photograph above you can see the tiny leaves at the top of the embryo, with the root below. Spores are just a single cell. Seeds can be spread by wind, animals, or water. Spores are mostly carried by the wind. The sperm of seed plants, unlike the sperm of mosses and ferns, do not need water to reach the egg. One important similarity between a seed and a spore is that both can grow into a new plant.

 Name three ways seeds are different from spores.

RESOURCE CENTER
CLASSZONE.COM

Learn more about seeds.

Pine trees reproduce with pollen and seeds.

Seed plants, such as pine trees, do not have swimming sperm. Instead, they have pollen. A **pollen** grain is a small multicellular structure that holds a sperm cell. It has a hard outer covering to keep the sperm from drying out. Pollen grains can be carried from one plant to another by wind, water, or by animals such as insects, bats, or birds. The process of pollination is completed when a pollen grain attaches to the part of a plant that contains the egg and releases the sperm.

The life cycle of a pine tree provides an example of how seed plants reproduce.

READING TiP

As you read the numbered paragraphs on this page, follow the numbers on the labels of the diagram on page 101.

1 The reproductive structures of a pine tree are the pinecones. Meiosis occurs in the pine cones, producing sperm and egg cells. Each tree has separate male and female cones.

Pinecones release lots of pollen into the air.

2 In male cones, the sperm cells are contained in pollen grains, which are released into the air. In female cones, the egg cells are enclosed in protective compartments within the cone scales.

3 The female cone produces a sticky substance. When a pollen grain lands, it sticks. A pollen tube begins to grow from the pollen grain through the scale to the egg. Fertilization occurs when the pollen tube reaches the protective compartment and sperm travel through it to one of the eggs.

4 The fertilized egg grows into an embryo. The compartment, with its protective covering and supply of nutrients, becomes the seed. The pinecone eventually releases its seeds. The winged seeds can float through the air and may be carried long distances by the wind. If the seed lands on the ground and germinates, it can become a new pine tree.

In the life cycle of a pine tree, meiosis and fertilization occur completely within the tissue of the mature plant. Fertilization doesn't require an outside source of water. The sperm cells in a pollen grain and the egg cells in a cone scale represent the first generation of the plant. The seed and the tree that grows from the seed represent the second generation.

 CHECK YOUR READING What do pollen grains and cone scales contain?

Life Cycle of a Pine Tree

open
female
cone

④ Seeds

Each fertilized egg becomes an embryo in a seed. A female cone can contain many seeds. The cone opens and the seeds are released.

seed

① Meiosis

A mature pine tree has both male and female cones. Meiosis occurs inside the cones, producing sperm and egg cells.

Male Cones

Female Cone

③ Fertilization

Sperm move through the pollen tube to fertilize one of the egg cells at the base of the female cone scale.

pollen tube

sperm   egg

pollen grain

② Pollination

Male cones release pollen into the air. A pollen grain sticks to the scales of a female cone, and a pollen tube begins to grow.

scales

READING VISUALS Use the definition of a cycle to predict what happens after seeds are released from pinecones.

INVESTIGATE Pinecones

What conditions make a pinecone open?

PROCEDURE

1. Place your pinecone in the beaker of water. Observe any changes that take place. Leave the cone in the water until the changes stop.

2. Remove the cone from the water and place it on a paper towel to dry. Observe any changes that take place as the cone dries.

WHAT DO YOU THINK?

- What did you observe when the cone was in the water?
- What happened when the cone dried out?

CHALLENGE Try this procedure on cones from different plant species.

Gymnosperms are seed plants.

Pollen and seeds are reproductive adaptations. They did not appear in plants until millions of years after seedless plants such as mosses and ferns had already begun to live on land. Today, however, most of the plant species on Earth reproduce with seeds, and many species of seedless plants have become extinct. Some scientists think this is because over time Earth's climate has become drier and cooler. Seed plants are generally better at reproducing in dry, cool environments than seedless plants are.

Fossil evidence shows that species of seed plants in the **gymnosperm** (JIHM-nuh-SPURM) group have existed on Earth for more than 250 million years. Plants classified as gymnosperms produce seeds, but the seeds are not enclosed in fruit. The word *gymnosperm* comes from the Greek words for "naked seed." There are four types of gymnosperms living on Earth today.

 What is distinctive about gymnosperm seeds?

Conifers

The conifers, or cone-bearing trees, are the type of gymnosperm you are probably most familiar with. The conifers include pine, fir, spruce, hemlock, cypress, and redwood trees. Many conifers are adapted for living in cold climates, where there is relatively little water available. Their leaves are needle-shaped and have a thick cuticle. This prevents the plant from losing much water to transpiration. Conifers can also keep their needles for several years, which means the plants can produce sugars all year.

MIND MAP
Make a mind map for the main idea that *gymnosperms are seed plants.* Don't forget to include the definition of a gymnosperm in your mind map.

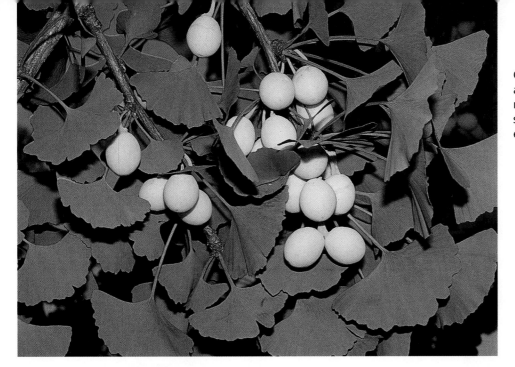

Ginkgo trees like this one are gymnosperms that do not produce cones. Their seeds are exposed to the environment.

Other Gymnosperms

The other types of living gymnosperms are cycads, gnetophytes (NEE-toh-fyts), and ginkgoes. These three types of gymnosperms appear to be quite different from one another. Cycads are palmlike plants that are found in tropical areas. They produce cones for seeds. Many cycads produce poisonous compounds. Gnetophytes are another type of tropical gymnosperm that produces cones. Chemicals taken from certain gnetophyte plants have been used to treat cold symptoms for thousands of years.

Ginkgoes are gymnosperms with fleshy seeds that hang from their branches. Ginkgoes are often grown in parks and along streets, but you will not often see them with seeds. People avoid putting male and female ginkgo trees together because the seed coat of a ginkgo produces a particularly foul smell.

 Review

KEY CONCEPTS

1. How are seeds different from spores?

2. How does fertilization in seed plants differ from fertilization in seedless plants?

3. Seed plants are found in environments where seedless plants are not. List at least two reasons why.

CRITICAL THINKING

4. **Compare and Contrast** What is the difference between a spore and a pollen grain? In what ways are spores and pollen grains similar?

5. **Hypothesize** Gymnosperms produce a lot of pollen, and most of it blows away, never fertilizing an egg. Why might this characteristic help a plant species survive?

○ CHALLENGE

6. **Analyze** Like all plants, a pine tree has a two-part life cycle. Look again at the diagram on page 101, and then make a new version of it in your notebook. Your version should show where in the life cycle each generation begins and ends. Hint: reread the text on page 100.

CHAPTER INVESTIGATION

Which Seeds Will Grow?

OVERVIEW AND PURPOSE Many of the foods you eat come from seed plants. What seeds or parts of seed plants have you eaten lately? What seeds can you find outside in your neighborhood? What conditions do the seeds from these plants need to grow? In this investigation, you will
- plant a variety of seeds
- observe differences in germination and growth among seeds planted in similar conditions

▶ Problem

How successfully will a variety of seeds germinate in conditions that can be provided in your classroom?

▶ Hypothesize

Read through all of the steps of the procedure and then write a hypothesis. Your hypothesis should explain what you think will happen when your class plants its collection of seeds and observes their growth for at least ten days. Your hypothesis should take the form of an "If . . . , then . . . , because . . ." statement.

▶ Procedure

MATERIALS
- assorted seeds
- potting soil
- paper cups
- water
- paper towels
- labels

1. Make a data table in your **Science Notebook** like the one shown on page 105.

2. Examine the seeds you will use in this investigation. Try to identify them. Record your observations in the data table.

step 2

RICE
NEY BEAN
SUNFLOWER SE

3 Use the materials provided to plant the seeds. Remember that the planting conditions should be the same for each of the seeds. Label each container.

4 Decide where you will keep your seeds while they are growing and how often you will check and water them. Be sure to keep the growing conditions for all of the seeds the same. Wash your hands.

5 Observe your seeds for at least ten days. Check and water them according to the plan you made.

step 5

▶ Observe and Analyze

Write It Up

1. In your **Science Notebook**, draw and label a diagram showing how you planted the seeds, the materials you used, and the place where they are being kept.

2. Each time you check on your seeds, record your observations in your data table.

3. **IDENTIFY** Which seeds germinated? What differences in growth and development did you observe in the different types of seeds?

▶ Conclude

Write It Up

1. **INTERPRET** Compare your results with your hypothesis. Did your data support your hypothesis?

2. **INFER** What patterns or similarities did you notice in the seeds that grew most successfully?

3. **IDENTIFY LIMITS** What unexpected factors or problems might have affected your results?

4. **APPLY** Use your experience to tell a young child how to grow a plant from a seed. What type of seeds would you suggest? Write directions for planting and caring for seeds that a younger child could understand.

▶ INVESTIGATE Further

CHALLENGE Some seeds need special conditions, such as warmth or a certain amount of moisture, before they will germinate. Design an experiment in which you test just one type of seed in a variety of conditions to learn which results in the most growth. Include a hypothesis, a materials list, and a procedure when you write up your experiment.

Which Seeds Will Grow?

Table 1. Observations of Seeds

Seed	Observations
Kidney bean	sprouted March 3
Popcorn	
Sunflower	
Rice	

Forest Fires release jackpine seeds from their pinecones to sprout after the fire stops.

Seed Survivors

Not only can seeds survive harsh conditions, but sometimes harsh conditions actually make it possible for seeds to grow into new plants.

Forest Fires

Jackpine seeds are locked inside pinecones by a sticky resin. The pinecones survive hot forest fires that melt the resin and release the seeds. In fact, without the high temperatures from fires, the seeds would never get the chance to germinate and grow into jackpine trees.

Bomb Damage

In 1940, during World War II, the British Museum was firebombed. People poured water over the burning museum and its contents. In the museum were silk-tree seeds collected in China and brought to the museum in 1793. After the firebombing 147 years later, the seeds sprouted.

Dodo Digestion

Seeds of Calvaria trees, which live on the island of Mauritius have very hard outer shells. The outer shell must be softened before the seeds can sprout. Hundreds of years ago, dodo birds ate the Calvaria fruits. Stones and acids in the birds' digestive tract helped soften the seed. After the dodo birds deposited them, the softened seeds would sprout. Dodo birds went extinct in 1681, and no young Calvaria trees grew. In 1975, only about 13 Calvaria trees remained. Recently, scientists have used artificial means to grind and break down the Calvaria seed cover and foster new tree growth.

EXPLORE

1. **INFER** Why do you think the silk tree seeds sprouted? Think about how the seeds' environment changed.

2. **CHALLENGE** If you were a scientist who wanted to help the Calvaria trees make a comeback, what methods might you try for softening the seeds?

RESOURCE CENTER
CLASSZONE.COM

Find out more about extreme seeds.

3.4 Many plants reproduce with flowers and fruit.

◀ **BEFORE, you learned**

- Seed plants do not have swimming sperm
- Gymnosperms reproduce with pollen and seeds

▶ **NOW, you will learn**

- About flowers and fruit
- About the relationship between animals and flowering plants
- How humans need plants

VOCABULARY

angiosperm p. 107
flower p. 108
fruit p. 108

EXPLORE Fruit

What do you find inside fruit?

PROCEDURE

1. Place the apple on a paper towel. Carefully cut the apple in half. Find the seeds.

2. Place the pea pod on a paper towel. Carefully split open the pea pod. Find the seeds.

3. Both the apple and the pea pod are examples of fruits. In your notebook, draw a diagram of the two fruits you examined. Label the fruit and the seeds.

WHAT DO YOU THINK?

- How many seeds did you find?
- What part of an apple do you eat? What part of a pea?

MATERIALS

- apple
- paper towel
- plastic knife
- pea pod

MIND MAP
Make a mind map diagram for the main idea: *Angiosperms have flowers and fruit.*

Angiosperms have flowers and fruit.

Have you ever eaten peanuts, grapes, strawberries, or squash? Do you like the way roses smell, or how spider plants look? All of these plants are angiosperms, or flowering plants. An **angiosperm** (AN-jee-uh-SPURM) is a seed plant that produces flowers and fruit. Most of the species of plants living now are angiosperms. The grasses at your local park are angiosperms. Most trees whose leaves change color in the fall are angiosperms.

The sperm of a flowering plant are protected in a pollen grain and do not need an outside source of water to reach the eggs. The eggs develop into embryos that are enclosed within seeds. Both generations of angiosperms and gymnosperms occur within a single plant.

The reproductive cycles of angiosperms and gymnosperms are alike in many ways. Both angiosperms and gymnosperms have separate male and female reproductive structures. In some species, male and female parts grow on the same plant, but in others there are separate male and female plants.

An important difference between angiosperms and gymnosperms is that in angiosperms, the sperm and egg cells are contained in a flower. The **flower** is the reproductive structure of an angiosperm. Egg cells develop in a part of the flower called an ovary. Once the eggs are fertilized and the seed or seeds form, the ovary wall thickens and the ovary becomes a **fruit.**

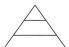 **CHECK YOUR READING**
What reproductive structures do angiosperms have that gymnosperms do not?

The diagram on page 109 shows the life cycle of one type of angiosperm, a cherry tree. As you read the numbered paragraphs below, follow the numbers on the labels in the diagram.

1 The reproductive structures of a cherry tree are its flowers. The anther is the male part. The pistil is the female part. Meiosis in the anther produces sperm cells enclosed within pollen grains. Meiosis in the ovary of the pistil produces egg cells.

2 The pollen grains are released. When a pollen grain is caught on the pistil of a flower, a pollen tube starts to grow. Within the ovary one of the egg cells matures.

3 Fertilization occurs when the pollen tube reaches the ovary and a sperm fertilizes the egg. The fertilized egg grows into an embryo and develops a seed coat. The ovary develops into a fruit.

4 The fruit may fall to the ground or it may be eaten by animals. If the seed inside lands in a place where it can germinate and survive, it will grow into a new cherry tree.

 CHECK YOUR READING
What is the flower's role in the sexual reproduction of an angiosperm?

Many flowering plants also reproduce asexually. New shoots can grow out from the parent plant. For example, strawberries and spider plants can reproduce by sending out shoots called runners. New plants grow from the runners, getting nutrients from the parent until the roots of the new plant are established. Plants can spread quickly this way. This form of asexual reproduction allows plants to reproduce even when conditions are not right for the germination of seeds.

VOCABULARY
Remember to add word triangles for *flower* and *fruit* to your notebook.

Life Cycle of a Cherry Tree

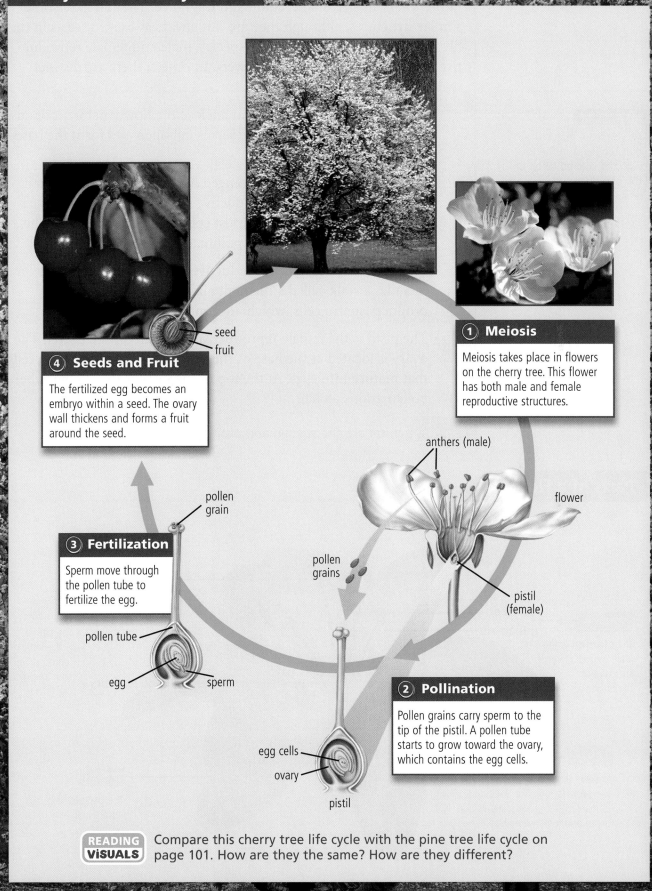

seed
fruit

④ Seeds and Fruit

The fertilized egg becomes an embryo within a seed. The ovary wall thickens and forms a fruit around the seed.

① Meiosis

Meiosis takes place in flowers on the cherry tree. This flower has both male and female reproductive structures.

anthers (male)

flower

pollen grains

pistil (female)

pollen grain

③ Fertilization

Sperm move through the pollen tube to fertilize the egg.

pollen tube

egg

sperm

② Pollination

Pollen grains carry sperm to the tip of the pistil. A pollen tube starts to grow toward the ovary, which contains the egg cells.

egg cells

ovary

pistil

READING ViSUALS Compare this cherry tree life cycle with the pine tree life cycle on page 101. How are they the same? How are they different?

Flowers

Flowers vary in size, shape, color, and fragrance. They all have some similar structures, although they are not always as easy to see as in the lily pictured below. Also, in some species, male and female reproductive structures are on different flowers. In others, there are distinct male and female plants.

READING TiP

As you read, match the bulleted items in the text with the colored labels on the photograph below.

- Sepals are leafy structures that enclose the flower before it opens. When the flower blooms, the sepals fall open and form the base of the flower.

- Petals are leafy structures arranged in a circle around the pistil. The petals open as the reproductive structures of the plant mature. Petals are often the most colorful part of a flower. The petals help to attract animal pollinators.

- The stamen is the male reproductive structure of a flower. It includes a stalk called a filament and the anther. The anther produces sperm cells, which are contained in pollen grains.

- The pistil is the female reproductive structure of the flower. The ovary is located at the base of the pistil and contains the egg cells that mature into eggs. At the top of the pistil is the stigma, where pollen grains attach.

CHECK YOUR READING What are the stamen and pistil?

Parts of a Flower

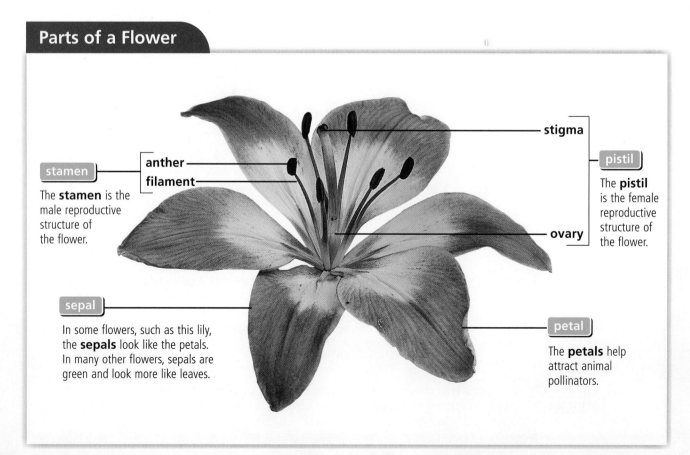

stamen
The **stamen** is the male reproductive structure of the flower.

anther
filament

stigma

pistil
The **pistil** is the female reproductive structure of the flower.

ovary

sepal
In some flowers, such as this lily, the **sepals** look like the petals. In many other flowers, sepals are green and look more like leaves.

petal
The **petals** help attract animal pollinators.

What parts of a flower can you identify?
PROCEDURE

① Examine the flower you are given. Try to notice as many details as you can. Draw a diagram of the flower in your notebook and label its parts.

② Carefully take your flower apart. Sort the parts. Draw and label one example of each part in your notebook.

WHAT DO YOU THINK?

• Which of the parts of a flower labeled in the diagram on page 110 did you find in your flower?

• Based on your experience, what would you look for if you were trying to decide whether a structure on an unfamiliar plant was a flower?

SKILL FOCUS
Observing

MATERIALS
• assorted flowers
• hand lens

TIME
15 minutes

Fruit

A fruit is a ripened plant ovary. Some ovaries contain more than one seed, such as an apple. Some contain only one seed, like a cherry. Apples and cherries are called fleshy fruits, because they have juicy flesh. The corn you eat as corn on the cob is a fleshy fruit. There are also dry fruits. Peanuts, walnuts, and sunflowers are dry fruits. The shells of dry fruits help protect the seeds. Some dry fruits, like the winged fruit of a maple tree or the feathery tip of a dandelion seed, have structures that allow the seeds to be carried by the wind.

Animals spread both pollen and seeds.

Reproduction in many types of flowering plants includes interactions between plants and animals. The plants are a source of food for the animal. The animals provide a way to transport pollen and seeds. As they eat, animals move pollen from flower to flower and seeds from place to place.

Have you ever watched a honeybee collect nectar from a flower? Nectar is a sweet sugary liquid located at the bottom of the flower. As the bee crawls around in the flower, reaching down for the nectar, it rubs against the anthers and picks up pollen grains. When the bee travels to another flower, some of that pollen rubs off onto the pistil of the second flower.

 CHECK YOUR READING How do bees benefit from the flowers they pollinate?

pollen grains

An animal that pollinates a flower is called a pollinator. Bees and other insects are among the most important pollinators. Bees depend on nectar for food, and they collect pollen to feed their young. Bees recognize the colors, odors, and shapes of flowers. Thousands of species of plants are pollinated by bees, including sunflowers and lavender.

The relationship between angiosperms and their pollinators can be highly specialized. Sometimes the nectar is located in a tube-shaped flower. Only certain animals, for example hummingbirds with long, slender beaks, can pollinate those flowers. Some flowers bloom at night. These flowers attract moths and bats as pollinators. Night-blooming flowers are usually pale, which means they are visible at night. Also, they may give off a strong scent to attract animal pollinators.

The advantage of animal pollination is that the pollen goes to where it is needed most. The pollen collected by a bee has a much better chance of being brought to another flower. By comparison, pollen grains that are spread by the wind are blown in all directions. Each grain has only a small chance of landing on another flower. Wind-pollinated plants produce a lot more pollen than plants that are pollinated by animals.

 CHECK YOUR READING What is the advantage of animal pollination over wind pollination?

The fruits produced by angiosperms help to spread the seeds they contain. Some seeds, like dandelion and maple seeds, are carried by the wind. Many seeds are scattered by fruit-eating animals. The seeds go through the animal's digestive system and are eventually deposited on the ground with the animal's waste. Wide scattering of seeds ensures that some seeds will land in an area with enough resources and room to grow.

READING TiP

The word *pollinate* means "to transfer pollen from an anther to a stigma." Note the differences in spelling between *pollen* and *pollinate, pollinator.*

SIMULATION
CLASSZONE.COM

Compare the different ways seeds are dispersed.

Animals eat fleshy fruit and distribute the seeds with their waste.

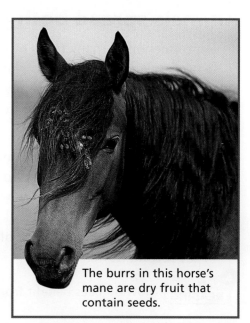
The burrs in this horse's mane are dry fruit that contain seeds.

Animals also help to scatter some types of dry fruits—not by eating them, but by catching them on their fur. Have you ever tried to pet a dog that has run through a grassy field? You might have noticed burrs stuck in the animal's fur. The seeds of many grasses and wildflowers produce dry fruits that are covered with spines or have pointed barbs. Seeds protected by these types of dry fruits stick to fur. The seeds travel along with the animal until the animal rubs them off.

Humans depend on plants for their survival.

Without plants, humans and all other animals would not be able to live on Earth. After plants adapted to life on land, it became possible for animals to live on land as well. Land animals rely on plants for food and oxygen. Many animals live in or near plants. Plants also supply materials humans use every day.

Food and Oxygen

All organisms must have energy to live. For animals, that energy comes from food. Plants, especially angiosperms, are the ultimate source of food for all land animals. Plants capture energy from the Sun to make sugars and other carbohydrates. Those same energy-rich materials are then consumed by animals as food. Even animals that eat other animals depend on plants for survival, because plants may provide food for the animals they eat.

Photosynthesis, the process that plants use to produce sugars and carbohydrates, also produces oxygen. The oxygen in the air you breathe is the product of the photosynthetic activity of plants and algae. Animals, including humans, need oxygen to release the energy stored in food.

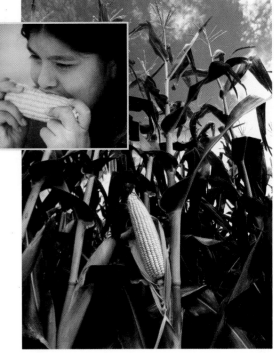

Plants capture light energy from the Sun and store it in sugars and other carbohydrates.

Energy Resources and Soil

Plants are an important source of many natural resources. Natural gas and coal are energy resources that formed deep underground from the remains of plants and other organisms. Natural gas and coal are important fuels for many purposes, including the generation of electricity.

Even the soil under your feet is a natural resource associated with plants. Plant roots can break down rock into smaller and smaller particles to form soil. When plants die, their bodies decay and add richness to the soil.

From Plants to Products

1 Cotton Plant

U.S. farmers harvest over 17 million bales of cotton each year.

2 Cotton Bale

A typical bale of cotton contains over 200 kg of cotton fibers.

3 Cotton Mill

Cotton mills clean the fiber, remove the seeds, and separate the fibers into strands.

4 Final Product

A bale of cotton has enough fiber for over 200 pairs of jeans.

Other Products

Plant materials are part of many products people use every day. Plants provide the wood used to build houses and the wood pulp used to make paper for books like the one you are reading. The cotton in blue jeans comes from plants. So do many dyes that are used to add color to fabrics. Aspirin and many other medicines made by drug companies today are based on chemicals originally found in plants.

3.4 Review

KEY CONCEPTS

1. How do flowers relate to fruit?
2. How are animals involved in the life cycles of some flowering plants?
3. List three ways that humans depend upon plants.

CRITICAL THINKING

4. **Predict** If you observed three plants in a forest—a moss, a fern, and a flowering plant—which would have the most insects nearby? Why?
5. **Connect** Draw an apple like the one shown on page 107. Label three parts of the fruit and explain from which part of an apple flower each part grew.

⚠ CHALLENGE

6. **Synthesize** There are more species of flowering plants on Earth than species of mosses, ferns, or cone-bearing plants such as pine trees. How do you think the different ways spores, pollen, and seeds are spread affect the genetic diversity of different types of plants? Explain your reasoning.

Chloroplast Math

You can't count the number of chloroplasts in a leaf very easily, but you can estimate the number. For example, if you know the number of chloroplasts in a small area, you can estimate the number of chloroplasts in a whole leaf.

MATH TUTORIAL
CLASSZONE.COM

Click on Math Tutorial for more help with perimeter and area.

Example

Suppose you are studying how lilacs make food from sunlight. You read that there are 50 million chloroplasts for every square centimeter of a leaf. You want to know the number in a whole leaf.

(1) Cover the leaf with centimeter grid paper.

(2) Count the number of whole squares covering the leaf.
7

(3) Match pairs or sets of partly covered squares, that add up to a whole square.
7 + 5 = 12

(4) Add on any remaining 0.5 (half), 0.25 (quarter), or 0.75 (three-quarters) of a square.
12 + .5 = 12.5

(5) Finally, multiply the number of squares by the number of chloroplasts in one square.

ANSWER 50,000,000 × 12.5 = 625,000,000.

Give estimates for the following amounts.

1. Trace the beech leaf shown on this page onto a sheet of centimeter grid paper. What is the leaf's approximate area in cm^2?

2. About how many chloroplasts are in this beech leaf?

3. A eucalyptus leaf is long and thin. Suppose a healthy leaf is 1.5 centimeters wide and 6 centimeters long. Estimate its area. Hint: Make a sketch.

4. What is the approximate number of chloroplasts in the eucalyptus leaf described above?

CHALLENGE Collect two leaves. Trace the leaves on centimeter grid paper. Label each tracing with its name, estimated area, and its approximate number of chloroplasts.

3 Chapter Review

the BIG idea

Plants are a diverse group of organisms that live in many land environments.

KEY CONCEPTS SUMMARY

3.1 Plants are adapted to living on land.

All plants share common characteristics. The parts of a plant are specialized to get water and nutrients from the soil, gases from the air, and energy from the Sun. Plants have tissues, organs, and organ systems.

VOCABULARY
vascular system p. 87
transpiration p. 88

3.2 Most mosses and ferns live in moist environments.

The ancestors of present-day mosses and ferns were among the first land plants. Mosses are small nonvascular plants. Ferns are larger vascular plants. Both reproduce with spores and need moisture for a sperm to reach an egg.

3.3 Seeds and pollen are reproductive adaptations.

Gymnosperms, such as the pine tree, reproduce with **pollen** and seeds.

Seeds provide protection for the young plant as well as a supply of nutrients.

VOCABULARY
seed p. 98
embryo p. 98
germination p. 99
pollen p. 100
gymnosperm p. 102

3.4 Many plants reproduce with flowers and fruit.

Angiosperms use flowers and fruit to reproduce. **Flowers** produce pollen and contain the plant's reproductive structures.

Fruit develops after pollination and contains seeds. Animals eat fruit and transport seeds to new locations.

VOCABULARY
angiosperm p. 107
flower p. 108
fruit p. 108

Reviewing Vocabulary

Write a statement describing how the terms in each pair are related to each other.

1. transpiration, cuticle

2. spores, seeds

3. seed, embryo

4. flower, fruit

The table below shows Greek (G.) and Latin (L.) words that are roots of words used in this chapter.

angeion (G.)	vessel or holder
gymnos (G.)	naked
sperma (G.)	seed
germinatus (L.)	sprout
pollen (L.)	fine flour

Describe how these word roots relate to the definitions of the following words.

5. angiosperm

6. gymnosperm

7. germination

8. pollen

Reviewing Key Concepts

Multiple Choice *Choose the letter of the best answer.*

9. Which of these is a characteristic of only some plants?
- **a.** They produce sugars.
- **b.** They are multicellular.
- **c.** They have a vascular system.
- **d.** They have a two-stage life cycle.

10. Which part of a plant anchors it in the soil?
- **a.** shoot system
- **b.** root system
- **c.** vascular system
- **d.** growth tissue

11. Which plant system transports water to different parts of the plant?
- **a.** vascular
- **b.** leaf
- **c.** stomata
- **d.** cuticle

12. Which part of a leaf does *not* allow transpiration?
- **a.** stomata
- **b.** cell wall
- **c.** stem
- **d.** cuticle

13. Which of these structures do mosses and ferns reproduce with?
- **a.** seeds
- **b.** growth tissue
- **c.** spores
- **d.** pollen

14. How are mosses different from ferns, pine trees, and flowering plants?
- **a.** Mosses reproduce through sexual reproduction.
- **b.** Mosses need moisture to reproduce.
- **c.** Mosses produce sugar through photosynthesis.
- **d.** Mosses have no vascular tissue.

15. What do seeds have that spores and pollen do not?
- **a.** a supply of nutrients
- **b.** a reproductive cell
- **c.** a protective covering
- **d.** a way to be transported

Short Answer *Write a short answer to each question.*

16. What are three ways plants are important to humans?

17. Explain how the bat in these photographs is interacting with the flower. How might the activity benefit the plant?

Thinking Critically

The next four questions refer to the labeled parts of the diagram of the leaf below.

18. **CLASSIFY** Identify the layer that covers a leaf. What function does it serve, and why is that function important?

19. **CLASSIFY** What are the two tissues shown here, how do they function, and what system do they belong to?

20. **PREDICT** Identify the structure and predict what would happen to this structure if the air around the plant was very hot and dry.

21. **ANALYZE** What are these structures? What is their function? What are the advantages of having more of them at the top of the leaf than at the bottom?

22. **COMMUNICATE** A leaf is made up of different tissues and specialized cells. What is the main function of a leaf? How does the organization of tissues and cells in a leaf help it to carry out this function? Include the following terms in your answer: *sunlight, energy, oxygen gas, carbon dioxide gas, water,* and *sugar.*

23. **CLASSIFY** What is the name of the group of plants pine trees belong to? What group of plants do cherry trees belong to? Which of the two groups is more widespread?

24. **CONNECT** You or someone you know may be allergic to pollen that is in the air during some plants' growing seasons. What is the advantage of a plant producing so much pollen?

25. **SUMMARIZE** Copy and complete the table below, indicating which reproductive structures are part of the life cycles of mosses, ferns, pine trees, and cherry trees. The first row is done.

	moss	fern	pine tree	cherry tree
sperm	✓	✓	✓	✓
egg				
pollen				
seed				
cone				
flower				
fruit				

26. **SYNTHESIZE** Plants were among the first organisms to live on land. Name at least two ways that plants made land habitable for animals. In what way did animals help plants to spread farther onto the land?

27. **INFER** Describe how a plant might reproduce asexually. Explain one advantage and one disadvantage asexual reproduction might have for the plant you described.

the BIG idea

28. **SUMMARIZE** Look again at the photograph on pages 82-83. Now that you have finished the chapter, how would you change or add details to your answer to the question on the photograph?

29. **SYNTHESIZE** Think of three different types of plants that you have seen. Use what you know about those plants as supporting evidence in a paragraph you write on one of these topics:

Plants are a diverse group of organisms.

Plants share common characteristics.

UNIT PROJECTS

Check your schedule for your unit project. How are you doing? Be sure that you have placed data or notes from your research in your project folder.

Analyzing Data

A pesticide is a material that kills pests, such as insects. A plant specialist wants to know if a new pesticide has any effect on the production of oranges. Grove A is planted using the same pesticide that was used in previous years. The new pesticide is used in grove B. Both groves have the same number of orange trees. The bar graph shows the data for one season.

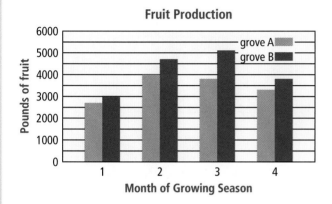

Fruit Production

Choose the letter of the best response.

1. About how many pounds of fruit were grown in grove A during month 1 of the growing season?
   a. about 2000 lb
   b. about 2700 lb
   c. about 3000 lb
   d. about 3500 lb

2. During which month in the growing season was the most fruit produced?
   a. month 1   c. month 3
   b. month 2   d. month 4

3. About how many pounds of fruit were produced altogether by both groves in month 2?
   a. about 4000 lb
   b. about 4700 lb
   c. about 5000 lb
   d. about 8700 lb

4. Comparing the production in both groves, during which month was there the least amount of difference in the number of pounds of fruit produced?
   a. month 1
   b. month 2
   c. month 3
   d. month 4

5. Based on the data in the graph, what might the plant specialist conclude about the effectiveness of the new pesticide used in grove B?
   a. The pesticide is effective only after three months of growth.
   b. The pesticide does not have any effect on orange production.
   c. The pesticide used in grove A is more effective than the pesticide used in grove B.
   d. The pesticide increases the overall production of oranges throughout the growing season.

Extended Response

6. Pesticides are intended to kill insects that harm the growth of a plant. However, not all insects are harmful. Insects often pollinate the flowers of fruit trees. Pollination leads to fertilization of the flower, and fruit grows from the fertilized flower. Describe what might happen if a pesticide kills insects that are pollinators. What effect might such a pesticide have on the flowers of the plant and on its fruit?

7. Pesticides are only one factor that affect the growth of plants and the number of flowers or fruit the plant produces. Write a paragraph that names some other factors that may affect plant growth. Include environmental factors and factors that are controlled by humans.

Invertebrate Animals

the **BIG** idea

Invertebrate animals have a variety of body plans and adaptations.

How does this jellyfish find food and eat?

Key Concepts

SECTION
4.1
Most animals are invertebrates.
Learn about sponges and other invertebrates.

SECTION
4.2
Cnidarians and worms have different body plans.
Learn how the body plans of cnidarians are different from those of worms.

SECTION
4.3
Most mollusks have shells, and echinoderms have spiny skeletons.
Learn about how mollusks and echinoderms meet their needs.

SECTION
4.4
Arthropods have exoskeletons and joints.
Learn about insects, crustaceans, and arachnids.

Internet Preview

CLASSZONE.COM

Chapter 4 online resources: Content Review, Visualization, four Resource Centers, Math Tutorial, Test Practice

EXPLORE (the BIG idea)

Worm-Watching

Find a worm and observe it for a while in its natural environment. How much can you learn about how a worm meets its needs by watching it for a short time? Record your observations in your notebook.

Observe and Think
What body parts can you identify on a worm? How would you describe a worm's activities and behavior?

Insects and You

Think about times when you have seen or noticed insects. Make a list of your experiences in your notebook. Then, start keeping a list of all the insects you see for the next week. How long do you think this list will be?

Observe and Think How many different types of insects did you see? Where did you see them? What characteristics do you think insects share?

Internet Activity: Invertebrate Diversity

Go to **ClassZone.com** to learn more about different types of invertebrates.

Observe and Think
Of every 20 animal species on Earth, 19 are invertebrates. How many types of invertebrates can you name?

NSTA
scilinks.org

SC*i*LINKS

Sponges Code: MDL042

Getting Ready to Learn

CONCEPT REVIEW

- All animals need energy, materials, and living space.
- Animals get energy and materials from food.
- Animals have different adaptations and behaviors for meeting their needs.

VOCABULARY REVIEW

predator p. 63

prey p. 63

adaptation *See Glossary.*

 CONTENT REVIEW
CLASSZONE.COM

Review concepts and vocabulary.

TAKING NOTES

COMBINATION NOTES

To take notes about a new concept, first make an informal outline of the information. Then make a sketch of the concept and label it so you can study it later. Use arrows to connect parts of the concept when appropriate.

CHOOSE YOUR OWN STRATEGY

For each new vocabulary term, take notes by choosing one of the strategies from earlier chapters—**description wheel, four square,** or **word triangle.** You can also use other vocabulary strategies that you might already know.

See the Note-Taking Handbook on pages R45–R51.

SCIENCE NOTEBOOK

Notes

Sponges are simple animals

- no organs
- attached to one place
- remove food from water

Description Wheel

Four Square

Word Triangle

Most animals are invertebrates.

BEFORE, you learned	NOW, you will learn
• Animals are consumers; they get food from the environment • Most animals have body systems, including tissues and organs • Animals interact with the environment and other animals	• About the diversity of invertebrates • About six groups of invertebrates • How sponges get energy

VOCABULARY

invertebrate p. 123
sponge p. 125
sessile p. 125
larva p. 126

THINK ABOUT

What makes an animal an animal?

A sponge is an animal. It has no head, eyes, ears, arms, or legs. A sponge doesn't have a heart or a brain or a mouth. It doesn't move. Typically, it spends its life attached to the ocean floor. Many people used to think that sponges were plants that had adapted to life in the water. Scientists, however, classify them as animals. How might you decide if the organism in the photograph is an animal?

Invertebrates are a diverse group of organisms.

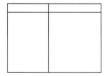

COMBINATION NOTES
Make notes and diagrams for the first main idea: *Invertebrates are a diverse group of organisms*. Include a sketch of a member of each group.

About one million invertebrate species live on Earth. **Invertebrates** are animals that do not have backbones. In fact, invertebrates do not have any bone tissue at all. Invertebrates can be found just about everywhere, from frozen tundra to tropical forests. Some invertebrates live in water, while others survive in deserts where there is almost no water. Many invertebrates live inside other organisms.

Most invertebrate animals are small. Crickets, oysters, sea stars, earthworms, ants, and spiders are some examples of invertebrates. The fact that invertebrates do not have backbones for support tends to limit their size. However, some ocean-dwelling invertebrates can be quite large. For example, the giant squid can grow to 18 meters (59 ft) in length and can weigh over 450 kilograms (992 lb).

INVESTIGATE Invertebrates

Which types of invertebrates live near you?

PROCEDURE

1. Cut the potato in half lengthwise. Scoop out a hole and carve a channel so it looks like the photograph below.

2. Put the two halves back together and wrap them with masking tape. Leave the channel uncovered. It is the entrance hole.

3. Take the potato trap outside and bury it upright in soil, with the entrance hole sticking out of the ground. Wash your hands.

4. Collect the potato the next day. Remove the masking tape and look inside.

WHAT DO YOU THINK?

• Observe the contents of the potato. Record your observations.

• Would you classify the contents of the potato as living or nonliving? Do you think they are animals or plants?

CHALLENGE Predict how your observations would be different if you buried the potato in a different place.

In this chapter, you will learn about six groups of invertebrates:

• **Sponges** are the simplest invertebrates. They live in water. They filter food from the water that surrounds them.

• **Cnidarians** also live in water. Animals in this group have a central opening surrounded by tentacles. They take in food and eliminate waste through this opening. Jellyfish, sea anemones, hydras, and corals are cnidarians.

• **Worms** are animals with soft, tube-shaped bodies and a distinct head. Some worms live inside other animals. Others live in the water or on land.

• **Mollusks** have a muscular foot that allows them to move and hunt for food. Some mollusks live on land. Others live in water. Clams, snails, and octopuses are mollusks.

• **Echinoderms** are water animals that have a central opening for taking in food. Sea stars and sand dollars are echinoderms.

• **Arthropods** are invertebrates that are found on land, in the water, and in the air. They have legs. Some have wings. Insects, spiders, crabs, and millipedes are arthropods.

Sponges are simple animals.

Sponges are the simplest multicellular animals on Earth. These invertebrates are **sessile** (SEHS-EEL) organisms, which means they live attached to one spot and do not move from place to place. Most live in the ocean, although some live in fresh water. Sponges have no tissues or organs. The body of a sponge is made up of a collection of cells. The cells are organized into a body wall, with an outside and an inside. Sponges are adapted to feed continuously. They feed on plankton and other tiny organisms that live in the water.

VOCABULARY
Make a description wheel for *sponge*. Include information on its specialized cells.

Specialized Cells

A sponge meets its needs with cells specialized for different functions. Pore cells along the body wall create tiny openings throughout the body. The pores lead into larger canals and sometimes a central opening, where cells with tiny hairs, or flagella, move water through the sponge. As water moves out, more water enters, as shown in the diagram below. Specialized cells filter out food particles and oxygen. Other specialized cells digest the food.

 CHECK YOUR READING What adaptations does a sponge have for obtaining food?

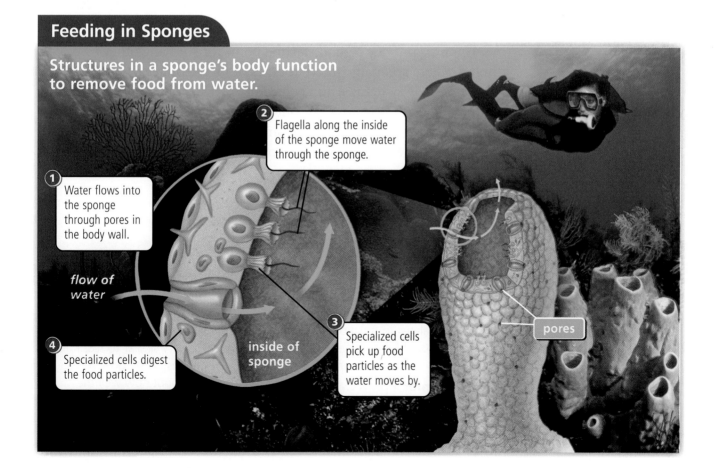

Feeding in Sponges

Structures in a sponge's body function to remove food from water.

1. Water flows into the sponge through pores in the body wall.

2. Flagella along the inside of the sponge move water through the sponge.

3. Specialized cells pick up food particles as the water moves by.

4. Specialized cells digest the food particles.

flow of water

inside of sponge

pores

Another adaptation sponges have are structures that make the body stiff. Most sponges have spicules (SPIHK-yoolz), which are needlelike spines made of hard minerals such as calcium or silicon. Spicules help give the sponge its shape and provide support. In some sponges, spicules stick out from the body. This may make the sponge less likely to become a source of food for other animals.

Reproduction

Sponges can reproduce asexually. Buds form alongside the parent sponge or the buds break off and float away. Tiny sponges can float quite a distance before they attach to the ocean floor or some underwater object and start to grow.

Sponges also reproduce sexually, as most multicellular organisms do. In sponges, sperm are released into the water. In some sponges, the eggs are released too. In this case, fertilization occurs in the water. In other sponges, the eggs are contained in specialized cells in the body wall. Sperm enter the sponge to fertilize the eggs.

A fertilized egg becomes a larva. A **larva** is an immature form—an early stage—of an organism that is different from the parent. Sponge larvae are able to swim. They move away from the parent and will grow into a sponge once they attach to some underwater surface. Then they become sessile, like their parents.

Sponges provide a good starting point for studying other invertebrates. There are many different types of invertebrates, with a wide range of body structures and behaviors. Invertebrates have adapted to many different environments. But the sponge is a simple organism that has changed very little over time. Sponges today look very similar to fossil sponges that are millions of years old.

This basket sponge is releasing microscopic larvae into the water.

4.1 Review

KEY CONCEPTS

1. Make a table with six columns. Write the name of an invertebrate group above each column. Fill in the table with a characteristic and an example for each group.

2. What does it mean that sponges are sessile?

3. How do sponges meet their need for energy?

CRITICAL THINKING

4. **Apply** Give two examples of how structure in a sponge relates to function. You should use the words *flagella* and *spicule* in your answer.

5. **Infer** How is water involved in the reproductive cycle of a sponge?

⬥ CHALLENGE

6. **Analyze** Sponges have lived on Earth for hundreds of millions of years. Sponges today look very similar to fossil sponges. What does this suggest about how well the simple structure of a sponge meets its needs? Do species always change over time?

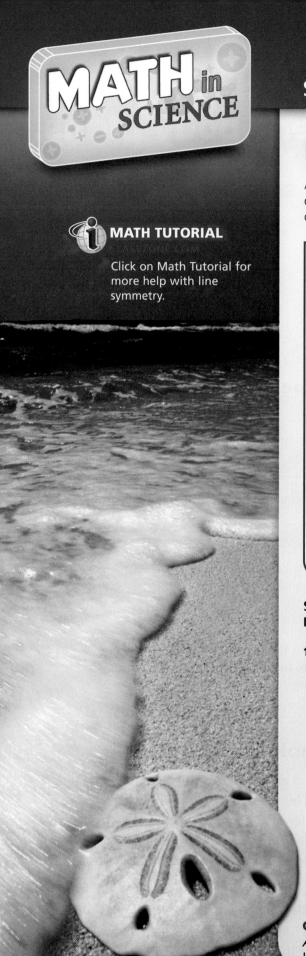

MATH in SCIENCE

MATH TUTORIAL

Click on Math Tutorial for more help with line symmetry.

Mirror, Mirror

A pattern or shape that has *line symmetry* contains a mirror image of its parts on either side of a straight line. Think about the shapes of a sea star or a butterfly.

Example

If you were to cut these shapes out of flat paper, you could fold the paper along a line of symmetry. The two halves would match.

Some shapes have more than one line of symmetry. The shapes of most anemones and sea stars can fold along two, three, or more lines of symmetry.

Sketch each shape. Then draw any lines of symmetry. If there are none, write "zero."

1)

2)

3)

4)

5)

CHALLENGE Write out the uppercase letters of the alphabet *A* to *Z*. For each letter, write whether it has zero, one, or two lines of symmetry.

4.2 Cnidarians and worms have different body plans.

◀ BEFORE, you learned	▶ NOW, you will learn
• Invertebrates are a diverse group of animals • Sponges are sessile organisms • Sponges meet their needs with simple bodies and specialized cells	• About body systems in cnidarians • About body symmetry and feeding patterns • About body systems in worms

VOCABULARY

cnidarian p. 128
tentacle p. 128
mobile p. 130

EXPLORE Worm Movement

How does body shape affect movement?

PROCEDURE

1. Put a thin layer of soil on the tray and gently place the worm on it. Use the spray bottle to keep the soil and your hands moist.

2. Draw a sketch of the worm and try to identify the parts of its body.

3. Record your observations of its movement.

4. Follow your teacher's instructions in handling the worm and materials at the end of the lab. Wash your hands.

MATERIALS
• worm
• tray
• soil
• spray bottle filled with distilled water

WHAT DO YOU THINK?
• How does the shape of a worm's body affect its movement?
• How would you describe a worm to someone who has never seen one?

Cnidarians have simple body systems.

COMBINATION NOTES
Make notes and diagrams for the main idea: *Cnidarians have simple body systems.*

Cnidarians (ny-DAIR-ee-uhnz) are invertebrates. Like sponges, cnidarians are found only in water. This group includes jellyfish, corals, sea anemones, and small freshwater organisms called hydras. Most cnidarians feed on small plankton, fish, and clams. Many cnidarians are sessile for most of their lives. Like sponges, cnidarians have adaptations that allow them to pull food in from the water that surrounds them.

All cnidarians have **tentacles,** fingerlike extensions of their body that reach into the water. Other animals have tentacles, but the tentacles of cnidarians have specialized stinging cells. The tentacles, with their stinging cells, are an adaptation that enables cnidarians to capture prey.

Stinging Cells in Cnidarians

Jellyfish have specialized cells on their tentacles.

Stinging Cell

Each stinging cell contains a nematocyst, a capsule with a coiled filament inside.

- trigger
- coiled filament
- nematocyst
- stinging cell

released filament

tentacles

Each stinging cell has a nematocyst (NEHM-uh-tuh-SIHST), a capsule that holds a barbed filament. The filament is like a tiny hollow tube coiled up inside the capsule. When prey comes into contact with the stinger cell, the filament is released. Sometimes this stinger wraps itself around the prey. In most species of cnidarians, the stinger stabs the prey and releases a poison from its tip. These stingers are what produce the sting of a jellyfish. Stinging cells have a second function. They protect cnidarians from predators.

 CHECK YOUR READING Describe how the structure of a nematocyst allows it to function in capturing food and providing protection.

READING TiP

Refer to the diagram above as you read the description of a nematocyst and its structure.

Tissues and Body Systems

A cnidarian's body is made up of flexible layers of tissue. These tissues, along with specialized cells, make up its body systems. The tissues are organized around a central opening where food is taken in and wastes are released. The tentacles bring the prey into this opening. The opening leads into a cavity, a gut, where the food is digested.

Cnidarians have a simple muscle system for movement. Even though cnidarians are sessile during most of their lives, they still move their bodies. Cnidarians bend from side to side and extend their tentacles. Adult jellyfish swim. The movement is produced by muscle cells that run around and along the sides of its body. When the muscle cells shorten, or contract, they produce movement.

When cnidarians move, they interact with the environment. They sense and respond to the prey that come in contact with their tentacles. This behavior is the result of a simple nervous system. Cnidarians have a network of nerve cells, a nerve net that extends throughout their bodies.

Reproduction

VOCABULARY
Choose a strategy from earlier chapters, such as a four square, or one of your own to take notes on the term *mobile*.

Cnidarians reproduce both sexually and asexually, and water plays a role in both processes. Buds produced by asexual reproduction are carried away from the sessile parent by water. In sexual reproduction, sperm are carried to the egg. Fertilization results in a free-swimming larva. The larva, if it survives, develops into an adult.

Jellyfish are cnidarians with a life cycle that includes several stages. A jellyfish's body, or form, is different at each stage, as you can see in the diagram below. When a jellyfish larva settles on the ocean floor, it grows into a form called a polyp. The polyp, which is sessile, develops disk-shaped buds that stack up like a pile of plates. The buds, once they are released, are called medusas. Each medusa is an adult jellyfish. In the medusa stage, jellyfish are **mobile,** which means they can move their bodies from place to place.

Jellyfish Life Cycle

Young Medusa

Column of Discs

Jellyfish have a two-part life cycle that includes both a mobile and a sessile form.

1 Adult female medusa releases fertilized eggs.

free-swimming larva

2 Larva settles on ocean floor.

polyp

3 Disks begin to form and later separate.

late polyp

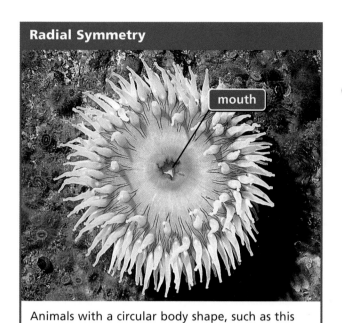

Radial Symmetry

mouth

Animals with a circular body shape, such as this sea anemone, have radial symmetry.

Bilateral Symmetry

mouth

Animals with identical right and left sides, such as this butterfly, have bilateral symmetry.

Animals have different body plans.

Scientists sometimes use the term *body plan* to describe the shape of an animal's body. Most cnidarians have a body plan with radial symmetry. This means the body is organized around a central point, a mouthlike opening that leads into a gut. You can see from the diagram of the jellyfish life cycle on page 130 that both the polyp and medusa have radial symmetry.

A radial body plan allows a sessile organism, such as the sea anemone shown in the photograph above, to capture food from any direction. A radial body plan also affects how a mobile animal moves. A jellyfish medusa moves forward by pushing down on the water. It has to stop moving to change direction.

Most animals, including worms, butterflies, birds, and humans, have a body plan with bilateral symmetry. One half looks just like the other, as you can see in the photograph of the butterfly above. You can recognize a bilaterally symmetrical shape because there is only one way to draw a line dividing it into two equal halves.

Animals with bilateral symmetry have a forward end where the mouth is located. This is the animal's head. The animal moves forward, head first, in search of food. A bilateral body shape works well in animals that are mobile. Food enters at one end, and is processed as it moves through the body. Once all the nutrients have been absorbed, the remaining wastes are released at the other end.

READING **TiP**

The root of the word *radial* means "ray," like the spoke of a wheel. The roots of the word *bilateral* are *bi-*, meaning "two," and *lateral,* meaning "side."

CHECK YOUR READING Describe how radial symmetry and bilateral symmetry affect an animal's feeding behaviors.

Most worms have complex body systems.

RESOURCE CENTER
CLASSZONE.COM

Learn more about the
many types of worms.

Some worms have simple bodies. Others have well-developed body systems. Worms have a tube-shaped body, with bilateral symmetry. In many worms, food enters at one end and is processed as it moves through a digestive tract. Worms take in oxygen, dissolved in water, through their skin. Because of this, worms must live in moist environments. Many live in water.

Segmented Worms

Segmented worms have bodies that are divided into individual compartments, or segments. These worms are referred to as annelids (AN-uh-lihdz), which means "ringed animals." One annelid you might be familiar with is the earthworm. As the diagram below shows, an earthworm's segments can be seen on the outside of its body.

An earthworm has organs that are organized into body systems. The digestive system of an earthworm includes organs for digestion and food storage. It connects to the excretory system, which removes waste. Earthworms pass soil through their digestive system. They digest decayed pieces of plant and animal matter from the soil and excrete what's left over. A worm's feeding and burrowing activity adds nutrients and oxygen to the soil.

CHECK YOUR READING Name two body systems found in earthworms.

Inside an Earthworm

An earthworm has organs and body systems.

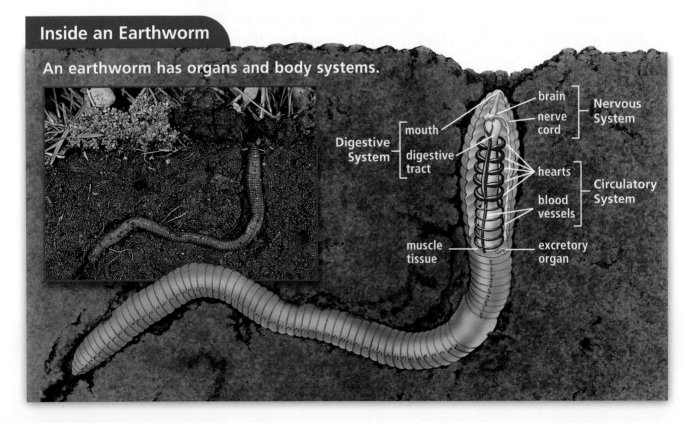

brain — Nervous System
nerve cord

mouth
Digestive System — digestive tract

hearts — Circulatory System
blood vessels

muscle tissue
excretory organ

Earthworms have several layers of muscle tissue in their body wall. Hairlike bristles on the segments help to anchor a worm in the soil as it moves. The nervous system includes a brain and a nerve cord that runs through the body. An earthworm can detect strong light and vibrations in the soil. These stimuli signal danger to a worm. An earthworm also has a circulatory system. It is made up of several hearts that pump blood through blood vessels.

Some annelids reproduce asexually, while others reproduce sexually. There are no distinct male or female worms. Earthworms, for example, carry both male and female reproductive structures. To reproduce, two worms exchange sperm. The sperm fertilize eggs the worms carry in their bodies. The eggs are laid and later hatch into larvae.

Flatworms and Roundworms

Flatworms are the worms with the simplest bodies. Some are so small and flat that they move with cilia, not muscles. These flatworms absorb nutrients directly through the skin. Many flatworms live as parasites, feeding off other organisms. For example, tapeworms are flatworms that infect humans and other animals. The tapeworm has no need for a digestive system because it gets digested nutrients from its host.

Roundworms are found just about everywhere on Earth. The bodies of roundworms are more complex than those of flatworms. They have muscles to move with, and a nervous system and digestive system. Some roundworms are important decomposers on land and in the water.

Three Types of Worms

segmented worm

flatworm

roundworm

Segmented worms, flatworms, and roundworms are the most common worms on Earth.

4.2 Review

KEY CONCEPTS

1. What adaptation do cnidarians have for capturing prey?

2. What is the difference between radial symmetry and bilateral symmetry?

3. Pick two systems found in an earthworm and describe how they work together.

CRITICAL THINKING

4. **Predict** How might having sense organs located at the front end of the body benefit an animal?

5. **Infer** Would the food of a jellyfish medusa be different from the food of a polyp? Support your answer.

⬤ CHALLENGE

6. **Compare and Contrast** Describe how the different body symmetries of cnidarians and segmented worms affect their movement and feeding behaviors.

CHAPTER INVESTIGATION

Worm Behavior

OVERVIEW AND PURPOSE Earthworms do not have eyes, so they cannot see. An earthworm needs an environment that provides it with moisture, food, and protection from predators. How do worms gather information about their surroundings? How do they respond to changes in their environment? In this investigation you will

- observe worm behavior
- predict how worms will respond to surfaces with different textures

▶ Problem

Write It Up

How is worm behavior affected by environmental conditions?

▶ Hypothesize

Write It Up

You should complete steps 1–9 in the procedure before writing your hypothesis. Write a hypothesis to explain how worms will respond to different surface textures in an environment. Your hypothesis should take the form of an "If . . . , then . . . , because . . ." statement.

▶ Procedure

1. Make a data table in your **Science Notebook** like the one shown on page 135.

2. Cover one half of the bottom of the aquarium with potting soil and the other half with sand.

3. Fill the beaker with 250 mL of distilled water and use it to fill the spray bottle. Spray all the water over the potting soil so it is evenly moistened.

MATERIALS
- aquarium
- potting soil
- coarse sand
- small beaker
- distilled water
- spray bottle
- filter paper
- 5 or more worms
- 2 containers, one for untested worms and one for tested worms
- stopwatch
- *for Challenge* flashlight

4 Repeat step 3, but this time moisten the sand. Refill the spray bottle.

5 Place a piece of filter paper in the middle of the aquarium so it is half on the soil and half on the sand, as shown.

step 5

6 Put on your gloves. Spray your hands with water. Gently remove one worm and observe it until you can tell which end is its head.

step 6

7 Start the stopwatch as you place the worm on the middle of the filter paper. Note which part of the aquarium the worm's head points toward.

8 Observe the worm's behavior for two minutes and then remove it carefully from the aquarium and place it in the container for tested worms.

9 Write your observations in your data table. State your hypothesis.

10 Fix the sand, soil, and paper in the aquarium so they are arranged as they were for the first worm. Then repeat steps 6–9 with at least four more worms.

11 Return the worms to their original living place. Wash your hands.

▶ Observe and Analyze
Write It Up

1. **OBSERVE** What behaviors suggest that worms get information about their surroundings?

2. **OBSERVE** What evidence did you see to suggest that worms respond to information they get about their surroundings?

3. **INTERPRET DATA** What patterns did you notice in the behavior of the worms you tested?

▶ Conclude
Write It Up

1. **INTERPRET** Compare your results with your hypothesis. Does your data support your hypothesis?

2. **IDENTIFY LIMITS** What sources of error could have affected your investigation?

3. **EVALUATE** Based on your observations and evidence, what conclusions can you draw about the connection between worm behavior and environmental conditions?

▶ INVESTIGATE Further

CHALLENGE Worms respond to light as a stimulus. Design an experiment to test the reaction of worms to the presence of light.

Worm Behavior

Hypothesis

Table 1. Observations of Tested Worms

	Starting Position	Ending Position	Description of Behavior
Worm 1			
Worm 2			
Worm 3			
Worm 4			
Worm 5			

KEY CONCEPT
Most mollusks have shells, and echinoderms have spiny skeletons.

 BEFORE, you learned

- Body shape affects how animals move and behave
- Cnidarians have radial symmetry and simple body systems
- Worms have bilateral symmetry and segmented body systems

▶ **NOW, you will learn**

- About different types of mollusks and their features
- About different types of echinoderms and their features

VOCABULARY

mollusk p. 136
gill p. 137
lung p. 137
echinoderm p. 139

THINK ABOUT

How does a snail move?

Snails belong to a group of mollusks called gastropods. The name means "belly foot." Snails are often put into aquariums to clean up the algae that can build up along the walls of the tank. If you get a chance, look at a snail moving along the glass walls of an aquarium, observe how it uses its foot to move. How would you describe the action of the snail's foot?

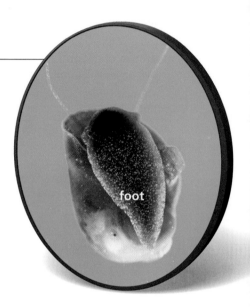

foot

Mollusks are soft-bodied animals.

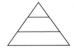

VOCABULARY
Choose a strategy from earlier chapters, such as a word triangle, or one of your own to take notes on the term *mollusk*.

One characteristic that is shared by all **mollusks** is a soft body. Many of these invertebrate animals also have an outer shell to protect their body. Oysters, clams, snails, and mussels are all mollusks. So are octopuses, squids, and slugs. Mollusks live on land and in freshwater and saltwater environments. You will read about three groups of mollusks: bivalves, gastropods, and cephalopods.

Most mollusks have well-developed organ systems. They have muscles, a digestive system, a respiratory system, a circulatory system, and a nervous system with sensory organs. Mollusks reproduce sexually, and in most species there are distinct male and female organisms. Two adaptations distinguish mollusks as a group. First, all mollusks have a muscular foot. A mollusk's head is actually attached to its foot. Second, all mollusks have a mantle, a layer of folded skin that protects its internal organs.

Bivalves

Bivalves are named for a hard shell that is made up of two matching halves. Clams, mussels, scallops, and oysters are all bivalves. The shell, when it is closed, completely encloses the body. If you've ever seen a raw oyster, you know that a bivalve's body looks like a mass of tissue. Bivalves do not have a distinct head, but they do have a mouth and sensory organs. The scallop shown in the photograph has light-sensitive organs that look like tiny eyes.

Bivalves are filter feeders, they filter food from the surrounding water. To move, a bivalve balances upright, opens its shell, and extends its foot. The animal moves by pushing the foot in and out. The foot is also used for burrowing, digging down into the sand.

The invertebrates you've studied so far—sponges, cnidarians, and worms—take in oxygen all along the surface of their bodies. A bivalve takes in oxygen through a pair of gills. A **gill** is an organ that filters dissolved oxygen from water. The gill is an adaptation that allows an organism to take in a lot of oxygen in just one area of its body. It is made up of many folds of tissue that create a large surface area. Blood picks up the oxygen and moves it to the rest of the animal's body. In most bivalves, the gills also filter food from the water.

Bivalve

Most of this blue-eyed scallop's body is inside its two-part shell.

RESOURCE CENTER
CLASSZONE.COM

Discover more about mollusks.

CHECK YOUR READING What are the two functions of gills and how do those functions relate to where bivalves live?

Gastropods

Gastropods are the most diverse group of mollusks. Some, such as snails and slugs, live on land. Many live in water, for example, conches, whelks, and periwinkles. Many gastropods are protected by a spiral-shaped shell. To protect itself, a gastropod withdraws into the shell.

The gastropod's head is located at the end of its foot. The head has eyes and specialized tentacles for sensing. Many gastropods have a cutting mouth part, called a radula, that shreds their food. Some gastropods eat animals, but most feed on plants and algae. Gastropods that live in water have gills. Some gastropods that live on land have lungs. A **lung** is an organ that absorbs oxygen from the air. Like gills, lungs have a large surface area.

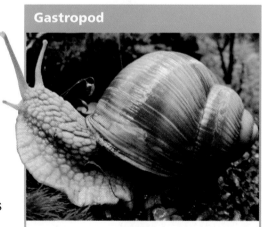

Gastropod

This brown-lipped snail extends most of its body out of its shell when it moves.

How do mollusk shells compare with echinoderm skeletons?

PROCEDURE

① Closely observe the mollusk shells and skeletons of sea stars and sand dollars you are given.

② Examine the shape and texture of each. Sort them by their characteristics.

WHAT DO YOU THINK?

How are the shells and skeletons the same? How are they different?

CHALLENGE Based on your observations, what can you infer about the bodies of living mollusks, sea stars, and sand dollars?

SKILL FOCUS
Observing

MATERIALS
Selection of mollusk shells, sea stars, and sand dollars

TIME
15 minutes

Cephalopods

Cephalopods (SEHF-uh-luh-PAHDZ) live in saltwater environments. Octopuses, squids, and chambered nautiluses are cephalopods. Among mollusks, cephalopods have the most well-developed body systems.

Cephalopods

This Maori octopus has a well-developed head attached to a foot with eight tentacles.

Cephalopods have a brain and well-developed nerves. They have a pair of eyes near their mouth. The foot, which surrounds the mouth, has tentacles for capturing prey. The mantle is adapted to push water forcefully through a tube-shaped structure called a siphon. This produces a jet of water that moves the animal. Gills take in oxygen, which is picked up by blood vessels and pumped through the body by three hearts.

Octopuses and squids do not have protective shells. They do have protective behaviors, however. Some can change body color to match their surroundings. Some release dark clouds of inklike fluid into the water, to confuse their predators. The lack of a shell lets them move freely through the water.

The nautilus is the only cephalopod that has a shell. The shell is made up of separate compartments, or chambers. The nautilus itself lives in the outermost chamber. The inner chambers are filled with gas, which makes the animal better able to float. The chambered shell also provides the soft-bodied nautilus with protection from predators.

VISUALIZATION
CLASSZONE.COM

Watch how different cephalopods move.

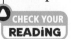
CHECK YOUR READING How is the foot of a cephalopod adapted for hunting?

Mollusks show a range of adaptations.

You might not think that a clam would belong to the same group as an octopus. These organisms look very different from one another. They also interact with the environment in different ways. The great variety of mollusks on Earth today provides a good example of how adaptations within a group can lead to great diversity. A good example of this is the range of adaptations shown in the shape and function of a mollusk's foot.

The foot of the bivalve is a simple muscular structure that moves in and out of its shell. The foot allows a bivalve to crawl along the ocean floor and to bury itself in the sand. Gastropods have a head at the end of the foot, which runs the length of the body. Muscles in the foot produce ripples that allow the gastropod to glide over a surface as it searches for food. In cephalopods, the foot has tentacles to pull food into its mouth. The tentacles also help some cephalopods move along the ocean floor.

foot

COMPARE How does the foot of this clam compare with the foot of an octopus?

Echinoderms have unusual adaptations.

Echinoderms are a group of invertebrates that live in the ocean. In their adult form, their bodies have radial symmetry. Sea stars, sea urchins, sea cucumbers, and sand dollars belong to this group. Echinoderms feed off the ocean floor as they move along. An echinoderm's mouth is located at the center of the body, on the underside. Some echinoderms, such as sea urchins and sand dollars, filter food from their surroundings. Others, such as sea stars, are active predators that feed on clams, snails, and even other echinoderms.

COMBINATION NOTES
Remember to take notes and make sketches for the main idea: *Echinoderms have unusual adaptations.*

Spines and Skeletons

Echinoderm means "spiny-skinned." Some of the more familiar echinoderms have long, sharp spines, like the sea urchin in the photograph at the bottom of this page. However, some echinoderm species, such as sea cucumbers, have spines that are very small.

One unusual adaptation that echinoderms have is a type of skeleton. Remember that echinoderms are invertebrates, they have no bone tissue. The echinoderm skeleton is made up of a network of stiff, hard plates. The plates lie just under the surface of the echinoderm's skin. Some echinoderms, such as sea stars, have skeletons with loosely connected plates and flexible arms. In other echinoderms, such as sand dollars, the plates grow close together, so the skeleton does not allow for much flexibility.

This purple sea urchin has very obvious spines.

This sea star has captured a bivalve and is using its tube feet to open the shell.

tube feet

This sea star's arms have been pulled up to show how its tube feet are attached to the bivalve's shell.

Water Vascular System and Tube Feet

Another adaptation that is unique to echinoderms is a water vascular system. This system is made up of water-filled tubes that radiate out from the center of the echinoderm's body. Tiny openings along the upper surface of the echinoderm's body feed water into these tubes. At the base of the tubes is a series of tube feet.

Muscles attached to the top of each tube can close the tube off, producing suction at the base of the tube. The tube feet stick to the ocean floor, allowing the echinoderm to pull itself along. The tube feet can also be used for hunting prey. For example, a sea star can surround a clam or oyster with its body, as shown in the photograph on the left. The tube feet pull the shell open. Then, the sea star's stomach is pushed out through its mouth and into the bivalve's shell, where it begins to digest the bivalve's body. Not all echinoderms eat other animals. Some, like sea urchins, feed off algae on the ocean floor.

4.3 Review

KEY CONCEPTS

1. What two features do all mollusks have?
2. What are two features all echinoderms have?
3. What are two functions of tube feet in echinoderms?

CRITICAL THINKING

4. **Analyze** For mollusks and echinoderms, what are the advantages and disadvantages of having a shell or spiny skeleton?
5. **Compare and Contrast** Compare the foot of mollusks with the tube feet of echinoderms.

⬥ CHALLENGE

6. **Analyze** Animals with lungs or gills can be larger than animals that take in oxygen through their skin. What feature do both lungs and gills have that affect the amount of oxygen they can absorb? What role does the circulatory system play?

Eating Well

Common sea stars have five arms. When one arm is missing, sea stars are, amazingly, able to grow another. Scientists interested in this amazing ability designed an experiment to see how having four arms instead of five affects a sea star's ability to consume prey. The sea stars use tube feet on each arm to pry open the shells of mussels and eat the animals' insides.

Scientists, working in 1999 and 2000, examined common sea stars caught in fishing gear. The study divided them into two groups: one group with five arms and one group with only four arms. Each sea star was tested to see how well it could open and eat a mussel.

◗ Observations

Scientists made these observations:

> a. Most of the sea stars with all five arms opened and ate a mussel.
> b. Fewer than half of the sea stars with four arms opened and ate a mussel.
> c. All the sea stars that opened a mussel took about 13 hours to finish eating it.

◗ Conclusions

Here are some conclusions about sea stars eating mussels:

> a. Common sea stars are most likely to feed successfully if they have all their arms.
> b. A common sea star with only four arms will starve.
> c. Common sea stars eat slowly regardless of how many arms they have.
> d. Common sea stars with only four arms choose mussels that are difficult to open.

◗ Evaluate the Conclusions

On Your Own Think about each observation that the scientists noted. Do they support the conclusions? Do some observations support one conclusion but not another? If a conclusion is not supported, what extra observations would you need to make?

With a Partner Compare your thinking with your partner's thinking. Do you both agree with the conclusions?

CHALLENGE Why do you think the sea stars with only four arms were less likely to open and eat a mussel?

The common sea star *(Asterias rubeus)* can regrow a missing arm. Its main prey is the mussel.

4.4 Arthropods have exoskeletons and joints.

 BEFORE, you learned

- Mollusks are invertebrates with soft bodies, some have shells
- Echinoderms have spiny skeletons
- Different species adapt to the same environment in different ways

 NOW, you will learn

- About different groups of arthropods
- About exoskeletons in arthropods
- About metamorphosis in arthropods

VOCABULARY

arthropod p. 142
exoskeleton p. 143
molting p. 143
insect p. 145
metamorphosis p. 146

EXPLORE Arthropods

What are some characteristics of arthropods?

PROCEDURE

1. Observe the pillbugs in their container. Draw a sketch of a pillbug.

2. Gently remove the pillbugs from their container and place them in the open end of the box. Observe and make notes on their behavior for several minutes.

3. Return the pillbugs to their container.

WHAT DO YOU THINK?

- Describe some of the characteristics you noticed about pillbugs.
- Are pillbugs radially or bilaterally symmetrical?

MATERIALS

- clear container
- shoebox with half of cover removed
- pillbugs
- hand lens

Most invertebrates are arthropods.

COMBINATION NOTES
Make notes and diagrams for the main idea: *Most invertebrates are arthropods.*

There are more species of arthropods than there are any other type of invertebrate. In fact, of all the animal species classified by scientists, over three-quarters are arthropods. An **arthropod** is an invertebrate that has a segmented body covered with a hard outer skeleton. Arthropods can have many pairs of legs and other parts that extend from their body. Insects are arthropods, as are crustaceans such as the shrimp and arachnids such as the spider.

Fossil evidence shows that arthropods first appeared on land about 420 million years ago, around the same time as plants. Arthropods are active animals that feed on all types of food. Many arthropods live in water, but most live on land.

segmented body

jointed legs

RESOURCE CENTER
CLASSZONE.COM

Find out more about the diversity of arthropods.

The exoskeleton of this crayfish completely covers its body.

Exoskeletons and Jointed Parts

One adaptation that gives arthropods the ability to live in many different environments is the exoskeleton. An **exoskeleton** is a strong outer covering, made of a material called chitin. The exoskeleton completely covers the body of an arthropod. In a sense, an exoskeleton is like a suit of armor that protects the animal's soft body. For arthropods living on land, the exoskeleton keeps cells, tissues, and organs from drying out.

 CHECK YOUR READING What are two functions of an exoskeleton?

A suit of armor is not much good unless you can move around in it. The arthropod's exoskeleton has joints, places where the exoskeleton is thin and flexible. There are joints along the different segments of the animal's body. An arthropod body typically has three sections: a head at one end, a thorax in the middle, and an abdomen at the other end. Legs are jointed, as are other parts attached to the body, such as antennae and claws. Muscles attach to the exoskeleton around the joints, enabling the arthropod to move.

The exoskeleton is like a suit of armor in one other way. It doesn't grow. An arthropod must shed its exoskeleton as it grows. This process is called **molting.** For an arthropod, the times when it molts are dangerous because its soft body is exposed to predators.

COMPARE How does the shape of this cicada's molted exoskeleton compare to the shape of its body?

Complex Body Systems

Arthropods have well-developed body systems. They have a nervous system with a brain and many different sensory organs. Their digestive system includes a stomach and intestines. Arthropods have an open circulatory system, which means the heart moves blood into the body directly. There are no blood vessels. Arthropods reproduce sexually. An arthropod has either a male or a female reproductive system.

Three Major Groups of Arthropods

Scientists have named at least ten groups of arthropods, but most arthropod species belong to one of three groups: insects, crustaceans, or arachnids.

Insects

- Includes beetles, bees, wasps, ants, butterflies, moths, and grasshoppers
- 3 pairs of legs, 3 body segments, 1 pair of antennae
- Most live on land

Crustaceans

- Includes shrimp, crabs, lobsters, barnacles, and pill bugs
- Number of body segments and pairs of legs varies, 2 pairs of antennae
- Most live in water; some live on land

Arachnids

- Includes spiders, ticks, mites, and scorpions
- 4 pairs of legs, 2 body segments, no antennae
- Most live on land

READING VISUALS What body features can you see that are shared by all of these arthropods?

Parts of an Insect's Body

Adult insects have three body segments and six jointed legs.

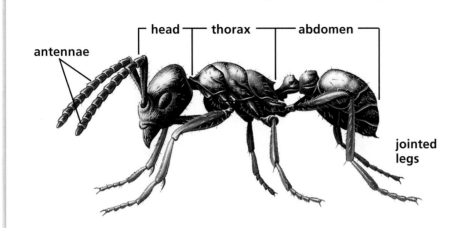

antennae — head — thorax — abdomen

jointed legs

READING TiP
The word *insect* relates to its body being **in sect**ions. Note the three sections in the diagram of the ant.

Insects are six-legged arthropods.

Scientists have so far identified over 700,000 insect species. **Insects** are arthropods that as adults have three body segments, a pair of antennae, and six legs attached to the middle segment, the thorax. Insect species have adapted to all sorts of environments and live on every continent. Most insects live on land. These insects obtain oxygen through spiracles, small openings in their exoskeleton.

 CHECK YOUR READING What are two characteristics all adult insects share?

VOCABULARY
Don't forget to take notes on the term *insect,* using a strategy from an earlier chapter or one that you already know.

Insects show great diversity in appearance. Many species have adaptations in color and shape that allow them to blend into their environments. For example, a stick insect is the same color and shape as a twig. Insect bodies also have different adaptations. Many insects have compound eyes and antennae, which are sensory organs. Many insects fly, having one or two pairs of wings.

Many insects are herbivores. And many insect species have mouth parts adapted for feeding on specific plants. A butterfly, for example, has a tubelike mouth that can reach into a flower to get nectar. Insects that feed on flowers often help the plants reproduce because the insects carry pollen from flower to flower. Other insects harm the plants they feed on. A grasshopper has jawlike mouth parts that crush parts of a plant. Many plants have defensive adaptations, such as poisons in leaves and stems, to keep insects from eating them.

Some insects, for example, ants, termites, and some bees, are social insects. They must live in groups in order to survive. Members of the group work together to gather food, maintain the nest, and care for the offspring. Often with social insects, just one female, called a queen, produces and lays eggs.

INVESTIGATE Insect Metamorphosis

How often do mealworms molt?

PROCEDURE

1. Prepare the jar for the mealworms. Fill it halfway with oat bran for food. Place a slice of potato and a piece of carrot on top for moisture.

2. In your notebook, note how many mealworms you have. Carefully place the mealworms inside the jar and close the lid. Wash your hands.

3. Without opening the jar, look for signs of activity every day. Once a week, open the container and pour some of the contents into a tray. Examine this sample for molted exoskeletons. Then return it to the jar. Replace the vegetables and add new oats as needed. Wash your hands.

WHAT DO YOU THINK?

• What changes did you observe in the mealworms?

• Did you see any sign of other stages of development?

CHALLENGE Use tweezers and a petri dish to collect the molted exoskeletons. How do the number of molts compare to the number of worms? Estimate how often the worms molt.

SKILL FOCUS
Observing

MATERIALS
• glass jar
• lid with air holes
• oat bran
• potato
• carrot
• mealworms
• *for Challenge:* petri dish tweezers

TIME
20 minutes

All insects can reproduce sexually. Females lay eggs, often a large number of eggs. The queen honey bee can lay over a million eggs in her lifetime. Many insect eggs have a hard outer covering. This adaptation protects the egg from drying out and can allow hatching to be delayed until conditions are right.

During their life cycle, insects undergo a process in which their appearance and body systems may change dramatically. This process is called **metamorphosis.** There are three stages to a complete metamorphosis. The first stage is the larva, which spends its time eating. The second stage is the pupa. During this stage, the insect body develops within a protective casing. The final stage is the adult, which is capable of going on to produce a new generation.

> **READING TiP**
> The word *metamorphosis* means "many changes."

CHECK YOUR READING What happens to an insect during metamorphosis?

Not all insects go through complete metamorphosis. Some insects, such as grasshoppers, have a simple metamorphosis. When a young grasshopper hatches from an egg, its form is similar to an adult's, just smaller. A grasshopper grows and molts several times before reaching adult size.

1 A female mosquito lays a mass of eggs on the surface of the water.

2 Each egg develops into a larva that swims head down, feeding on algae.

3 The larva develops into a pupa. Inside, the body of the insect matures.

4 At the adult stage, the mosquito leaves the water and flies away.

You have probably seen many insects in their larval form. A caterpillar is a larva; so is an inchworm. Often the larval form of an insect lives very differently from its adult form. A mosquito, for example, begins its life in the water. The larva swims about, feeding on algae. The pupa forms at the water's surface. The developing mosquito is encased in a protective covering. The adult form of the mosquito, the flying insect, leaves the water. The female is a parasite that feeds off the blood of other animals.

Crustaceans live in water and on land.

Most crustacean species live in the water. Several of these, including the Atlantic lobster and the Dungeness crab, are used by people as a source of food. Crustaceans are important to the ocean food web. Tiny crustaceans such as krill and copepods are a food source for many other animals, including other invertebrates, fish, and whales. Some species of crustaceans live in freshwater and a few, such as pill bugs, live on land.

 CHECK YOUR READING Where do most crustaceans live?

IDENTIFY How many pairs of legs does this crab have?

Crustaceans have three or more pairs of legs and two pairs of sensory antennae. Many of the larger, water-living crustaceans, such as crabs, have gills. Most crustaceans, like other arthropods, have a circulatory system that includes a heart but no blood vessels. Crustaceans reproduce sexually. Their young hatch from eggs.

The eating habits of crustaceans vary. Lobsters and shrimp eat plants and small animals. Many crustaceans are scavengers, feeding off the remains of other organisms. Some, such as barnacles, are filter feeders. The larval form of a barnacle is free swimming. However, as an adult this arthropod attaches itself to a rock or another hard surface, such as a mollusk's shell or the hull of a ship. It uses its tentacles to capture food from the surrounding water.

Arachnids are eight-legged arthropods.

This mite is an arachnid that lives in dust. This micrograph shows it magnified 150×.

Spiders, mites, ticks, and scorpions belong to a group called the arachnids. Like all arthropods, arachnids have an exoskeleton, jointed limbs, and segmented bodies. But the bodies of arachnids have some characteristics that distinguish them from other arthropods. Arachnids always have four pairs of legs and only two body segments. Arachnids do not have antennae.

Some arachnids, including ticks and chigger mites, are parasites. Other arachnids, such as spiders and scorpions, are predators. Recall that predators get their food by capturing and consuming other animals. Predatory arachnids kill their prey by stinging them, biting them, or injecting them with venom.

The spiders are the largest group of arachnids. Many spiders have a unique adaptation for capturing their prey. They produce an extremely strong material, called silk, inside their bodies and use the silk to make webs for capturing food. The spider spins strands of silk out from tubes called spinnerets at the rear of its abdomen. It weaves the strands into a nearly invisible web. The web serves as a net for catching insects and other small organisms that the spider eats. This adaptation allows web-building spiders to wait for their prey to come to them. Other invertebrates, such as silkworms, produce silk, but they do not weave webs.

CHECK YOUR READING How is the way some spiders capture prey unusual?

Some arachnids obtain oxygen through spiracles, as insects do. However, certain species of spiders have a unique type of respiratory organ referred to as book lungs. Book lungs are like moist pockets with folds. They are located inside the animal's abdomen.

This spider has wrapped its prey in silk.

prey

silk

spinneret

Millipede

Centipede

READING VISUALS COMPARE AND CONTRAST With their long segmented bodies, a millipede and a centipede look very similar. How are they different?

Millipedes and centipedes are arthropods.

At first glance, the members of two other arthropod groups look similar. Both centipedes and millipedes have long, segmented bodies and many legs. However, animals from these groups differ in their body features and their behavior.

Millipedes are arthropods with two pairs of walking legs on each body segment. Millipedes move rather slowly and eat decaying leaves and plant matter. When disturbed, many millipedes emit a foul odor that can be harmful to predators.

Centipedes can move more quickly. They have one pair of walking legs per body segment. They have antennae and jawlike mouthparts. Many centipedes also have pincers on their rearmost segment. Centipedes are predators. They can use their jaws and pincers to paralyze prey and protect themselves from predators.

 Review

KEY CONCEPTS

1. Describe the characteristics of insects, crustaceans, and arachnids.

2. What is molting and how does it relate to an exoskeleton?

3. Name three arthropods and the adaptations they have for feeding.

CRITICAL THINKING

4. **Analyze** How does the form of an exoskeleton relate to its function?

5. **Connect** Mosquitoes can spread disease, such as the West Nile virus. People are advised not to leave open containers of water in the yard. How does standing water contribute to an increase in the number of mosquitoes?

⬥ CHALLENGE

6. **Evaluate** Many plant-eating insects live less than a year. An adult will lay eggs in the fall and then die as winter comes. The eggs hatch the next spring. How does the life cycle of the insect fit in with the life cycle of plants? What role does the egg play in the survival of the insect species in this case?

the BIG idea

Invertebrate animals have a variety of body plans and adaptations.

KEY CONCEPTS SUMMARY

4.1 Most animals are invertebrates.

Invertebrates are a diverse group of animals. Species of invertebrates live in almost every environment.

Sponges are simple invertebrates that have several types of specialized cells.

VOCABULARY
invertebrate p. 123
sponge p. 125
sessile p. 125
larva p. 126

4.2 Cnidarians and worms have different body plans.

Cnidarians have simple bodies with specialized cells and tissues.

Most **worms** have organs and complex body systems.

VOCABULARY
cnidarian p.128
tentacle p. 128
mobile p. 130

4.3 Most mollusks have shells, and echinoderms have spiny skeletons.

Mollusks include bivalves, gastropods, and cephalopods.

Echinoderms have a water vascular system and tube feet.

VOCABULARY
mollusk p. 136
gill p. 137
lung p. 137
echinoderm p. 139

4.4 Arthropods have exoskeletons and joints.

Arthropods, which include insects, crustaceans, and arachnids, are the most abundant and diverse group of animals.

VOCABULARY
arthropod p. 142
exoskeleton p. 143
molting p. 143
insect p. 145
metamorphosis p. 146

Reviewing Vocabulary

Copy and complete the chart below.

Word	Definition	Example
1. mollusk		clam, snail, squid
2. arthropod	invertebrate with jointed legs, segmented body, and an exoskeleton	
3.	ocean-dwelling animal with spiny skeleton	sea star
4. sessile		sponge
5. larva		caterpillar
6. metamorphosis		caterpillar changing into a butterfly
7. molting	process by which an arthropod sheds its exoskeleton	
8.	arthropod with three body segments, one pair of antennae, and six legs	grasshopper, mosquito, beetle

Reviewing Key Concepts

Multiple Choice *Choose the letter of the best answer.*

9. Which of the following groups of animals is the most abundant?
   a. worms   **c.** echinoderms
   b. mollusks   **d.** arthropods

10. In what way are all invertebrates alike?
    a. They do not have backbones.
    b. They live in the ocean.
    c. They are predators.
    d. They have a closed circulatory system.

11. Sponges bring food into their bodies through a
    a. system of pores
    b. water vascular system
    c. mouth
    d. digestive tract

12. Which group of invertebrates has a mantle?
    a. echinoderms
    b. crustaceans
    c. cnidarians
    d. mollusks

13. Bivalves, cephalopods, and gastropods are all types of
    a. echinoderms
    b. mollusks
    c. crustaceans
    d. cnidarians

14. As they grow, arthropods shed their exoskeleton in a process called
    a. metamorphosis
    b. symmetry
    c. molting
    d. siphoning

15. Which invertebrate animals always have three body segments: a head, a thorax, and an abdomen?
    a. segmented worms
    b. adult insects
    c. arachnids
    d. echinoderms

16. Which group of invertebrates have a water vascular system and tube feet?
    a. echinoderms   **c.** cnidarians
    b. crustaceans   **d.** mollusks

Short Answer *Write a short answer to each question.*

17. Describe the stages in the life cycle of an insect that has complete metamorphosis.

18. Explain one advantage and one disadvantage an exoskeleton has for an organism.

19. Is a spider an insect? Explain.

Thinking Critically

20. CLASSIFY What characteristics does a sponge have that make it seem like a plant? What characteristic makes a sponge an animal?

21. PROVIDE EXAMPLES Arthropods are the most diverse and abundant group of animals on Earth. Give three examples of arthropod features that enable them to be active in their environment.

22. INFER Worms have a tube-shaped body with openings at either end. How does this body plan relate to the way a worm obtains its food and processes it?

23. COMPARE Jellyfish go through a life cycle that involves different stages of development. Insects also go through different stages of development in a process called metamorphosis. What are some similarities between metamorphosis in a mosquito, for example, and a jellyfish life cycle? Use the terms in the table below in your answer.

larva	polyp	medusa
pupa	adult	mobile
sessile		

Refer to the chart below as you answer the next three questions.

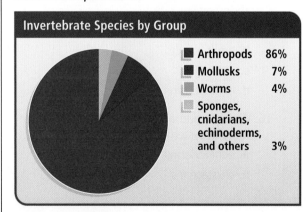

Invertebrate Species by Group

■ Arthropods	86%
■ Mollusks	7%
■ Worms	4%
▨ Sponges, cnidarians, echinoderms, and others	3%

24. APPLY What percentage of invertebrate species are arthropods?

25. CALCULATE What is the combined percentage of all other invertebrate species, not including arthropods?

26. APPLY How could you modify this pie chart to show that insects, crustaceans, and arachnids are types of arthropods?

27. APPLY A sea star has a radial body plan. A spider has a bilateral body plan. How does the shape of these animal's bodies affect how they capture their food?

28. COMPARE AND CONTRAST How are the three main groups of arthropods similar? How are they different?

29. SYNTHESIZE Animal bodies need support as well as protection. What structures do the bodies of a sponge, a bivalve, and an insect have for protection and support? Use the terms in the table below in your answer.

spicule	shell	exoskeleton

30. PREDICT Many people think of insects as pests, but some species of insects are important pollinators for many flowering plants. Also, many animals eat insects. What problems would humans face if Earth's insect species became extinct?

the BIG idea

31. INFER How does a cnidarian such as the jellyfish in the photograph on pages 120–121 respond to its environment? Is the diver in the photograph in danger? Explain your answer.

32. COMPARE AND CONTRAST Make a chart showing the key features of the body plans of three different invertebrate animal groups. For each group, identify one characteristic that is an adaptation.

UNIT PROJECTS

If you need to create graphs or other visuals for your project, be sure you have grid paper, poster board, markers, or other supplies.

Analyzing Data

Reef-building corals are invertebrates that live in clear, warm ocean water. As a coral grows, it produces a hard external skeleton. If many generations of corals grow near each other over a long period of time, their accumulated skeletons form a structure called a reef. Many ocean life-forms live in and around coral reefs. This table shows the maximum growth rates of five species of reef-building corals.

Species	Rate of Growth (mm per year)	Number of Years to Grow a 1400-m Reef
A	143	9,790
B	99	14,100
C	120	11,700
D	100	14,000
E	226	6,190

Choose the letter of the best response

1. Which has the fastest rate of growth?
   a. Species C
   b. Species B
   c. Species D
   d. Species E

2. What is the growth rate for Species B ?
   a. 99 mm per year
   b. 120 mm per year
   c. 143 mm per year
   d. 14,100 mm per year

3. Which takes the shortest amount of time to grow to 1400 meters?
   a. Species B
   b. Species C
   c. Species D
   d. Species E

4. Which have about the same rate of growth?
   a. Species A and C
   b. Species B and D
   c. Species C and E
   d. Species D and E

5. How many years does it take Species A to grow into a 1400-m reef?
   a. 143
   b. 226
   c. 9790
   d. 14,000

6. Based on the information in the table, which statement is true?
   a. Coral species with the fastest growth rates take the greatest amount of time to grow.
   b. Coral species with the slowest growth rates take the least amount of time to grow.
   c. Coral species have different rates of growth that affect how long it takes them to grow.
   d. Coral species that grow more than 100 mm per year take the longest to grow.

Extended Response

7. Corals are cnidarians. They are sessile animals that live attached to one place. Other ocean-dwelling animals are mobile and can move about their environment. Crustaceans like the lobster are mobile, so are mollusks like the octopus. How does being sessile or mobile affect the feeding behaviors of an animal? Do you think the bodies and systems of sessile animals are going to be different from those of mobile animals? Use some of the terms in the word box in your answer.

digestive system	sessile	mobile
nervous system	filter	mouth
muscle tissue	food	sensory organs

Vertebrate Animals

Vertebrate animals live in most of Earth's environments.

What do these penguins have in common with this seal?

Key Concepts

SECTION

5.1 **Vertebrates are animals with endoskeletons.**
Learn how most of the vertebrates on Earth are fish.

SECTION

5.2 **Amphibians and reptiles are adapted for life on land.**
Learn how most amphibians hatch in water and most reptiles hatch on land.

SECTION

5.3 **Birds meet their needs on land, in water, and in the air.**
Learn how adaptations for flight affect how birds meet their needs.

SECTION

5.4 **Mammals live in many environments.**
Learn about mammals' many adaptations.

Internet Preview

CLASSZONE.COM

Chapter 5 online resources: Content Review, Visualization, five Resource Centers, Math Tutorial, Test Practice.

EXPLORE (the **BIG** idea)

What Animals Live Near You?

Make a list of animals you think live in your neighborhood. Remember that some animals are small! Organize the animals on your list into groups.

Observe and Think Where do you think you would see the most animals? What about the widest variety?

How Is a Bird Like a Frog?

Fish, frogs, snakes, birds, dogs, and humans are all vertebrate animals. Choose two vertebrates and quickly sketch their body plans, including their skeletons.

Observe and Think Where do you think each animal's brain, heart, and stomach are located?

Internet Activity: Where in the World?

Go to **ClassZone.com** to learn more about the distribution of reptiles and amphibians across the world.

Observe and Think In what area of the world do the greatest number of species live? the least? What features of these animals might help explain the pattern of distribution?

NSTA
scilinks.org
SCiLINKS

Bird Characteristics **Code: MDL043**

Getting Ready to Learn

◀ CONCEPTS REVIEW

- All living things have common needs.
- Plants and some invertebrates have adaptations for life on land.
- Most multicellular organisms can reproduce sexually.

◀ VOCABULARY REVIEW

migration p. 64

embryo p. 98

gill p. 137

lung p. 137

exoskeleton p. 143

ⓘ CONTENT REVIEW
CLASSZONE.COM

Review concepts and vocabulary.

▶ TAKING NOTES

CHOOSE YOUR OWN STRATEGY

Take notes using one or more of the strategies from earlier chapters – **main idea webs, main idea and details, mind maps**, or **combination notes**. You can also use other note-taking strategies that you may already know.

VOCABULARY STRATEGY

Think about a vocabulary term as a **magnet word** diagram. Write other terms and ideas related to that term around it.

See the Note-Taking Handbook on pages R45–R51.

SCIENCE NOTEBOOK

Main Idea Web

Main Idea and Details

Mind Map

bird

mammal

transforms food into heat

ENDOTHERM

hair, feathers, blubber

shivers, sweats, pants

active in cold environments

5.1 Vertebrates are animals with endoskeletons.

 BEFORE, you learned

- Most animals are invertebrates
- Animals have adaptations that suit their environment
- Animals get energy by consuming food

 NOW, you will learn

- About the skeletons of vertebrate animals
- About the characteristics of fish
- About three groups of fish

VOCABULARY

vertebrate p. 157
endoskeleton p. 157
scale p. 161

EXPLORE Streamlined Shapes

How does a fish's shape help it move?

PROCEDURE

MATERIALS
tub of water

1. Place your hand straight up and down in a tub of water. Keep your fingers together and your palm flat.

2. Move your hand from one side of the tub to the other, using your palm to push the water.

3. Move your hand across the tub again, this time using the edge of your hand as if you were cutting the water.

WHAT DO YOU THINK?

- In which position was the shape of your hand most like the shape of a fish's body?
- How might the shape of a fish's body affect its ability to move through water?

Vertebrate animals have backbones.

VOCABULARY
Add magnet word diagrams for *vertebrate* and *endoskeleton* to your notebook.

If you asked someone to name an animal, he or she would probably name a vertebrate. Fish, frogs, snakes, birds, dogs, and humans are all **vertebrates,** or animals with backbones. Even though only about 5 percent of animal species are vertebrates, they are among the most familiar and thoroughly studied organisms on Earth.

Vertebrate animals have muscles, a digestive system, a respiratory system, a circulatory system, and a nervous system with sensory organs. The characteristic that distinguishes vertebrates from other animals is the **endoskeleton,** an internal support system that grows along with the animal. Endoskeletons allow more flexibility and ways of moving than exoskeletons do.

Vertebrate Skeleton and Muscles

Like all vertebrates, the cheetah has an internal skeleton, which supports and protects its body.

vertebrae (backbone)

skull

ribs

leg bones

muscle

Muscles attached to bones aid in movement.

READING VISUALS How does this cheetah's endoskeleton relate to the cheetah's shape?

Vertebrates are named for specialized bones called vertebrae. These bones are located in the middle of each vertebrate animal's central body segment. Together, the vertebrae are sometimes called a backbone. The vertebrae support muscles and surround the spinal cord, which connects the animal's brain to its nerves. Other bones, such as the ribs and skull, protect organs like the heart, lungs, and brain.

CHECK YOUR READING What is one function of the endoskeleton for vertebrate animals?

Most vertebrates are fish.

NOTETAKING STRATEGY
Choose a strategy from an earlier chapter to take notes on the idea that most vertebrates are fish. Be sure to include information on adaptations to water.

Fish are the most diverse group of vertebrate animals. There are more than 29,000 species of fish, ranging in size from tiny minnows to huge whale sharks. Fish live in nearly every aquatic environment, from freshwater lakes to the bottom of the sea. Some fish even are able to survive below the ice in the Antarctic!

Fish are adapted for life in water. Like all living things, fish need to get materials from their environment. For example, fish must be able to get oxygen from water. Fish must also be able to move through water in order to find food. Fish that live in water where sunlight does not penetrate need special organs to help them find food.

Most fish move by using muscles and fins to push their stream-lined bodies through water. These muscles allow fish to move more quickly than most other vertebrates. Most fish also have an organ called a swim bladder, which allows them to control the depth at which they float.

Fish have sensory organs for taste, odor, and sound. Most fish species have eyes that allow them to see well underwater. Most fish also have a sensory system unlike that of other vertebrates. This system includes an organ called a lateral line, which allows fish to sense vibrations from objects nearby without touching or seeing them.

Fish, like some invertebrates, remove oxygen from water with specialized respiratory organs called gills. You can locate most fishes' gills by looking for the openings, called gill slits, on the sides of their head. You can see what gills look like in the diagram of a fish below.

VISUALIZATION
CLASSZONE.COM
Explore how fish breathe.

 How are gills similar to lungs?

Fish gills are made up of many folds of tissue and are filled with blood. When a fish swims, it takes water in through its mouth and then pushes the water back over its gills. In the gills, oxygen dissolved in the water moves into the fish's blood. Carbon dioxide, a waste product of respiration, moves from the blood into the water. Then the water is forced out of the fish's body through its gill slits. The oxygen is transported to the fish's cells. It is a necessary material for releasing energy.

Inside a Fish

Fish are vertebrates that live in water.

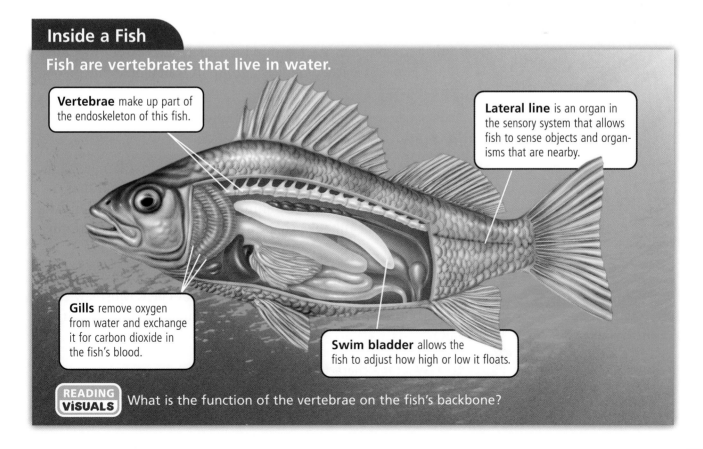

Vertebrae make up part of the endoskeleton of this fish.

Lateral line is an organ in the sensory system that allows fish to sense objects and organisms that are nearby.

Gills remove oxygen from water and exchange it for carbon dioxide in the fish's blood.

Swim bladder allows the fish to adjust how high or low it floats.

READING VISUALS What is the function of the vertebrae on the fish's backbone?

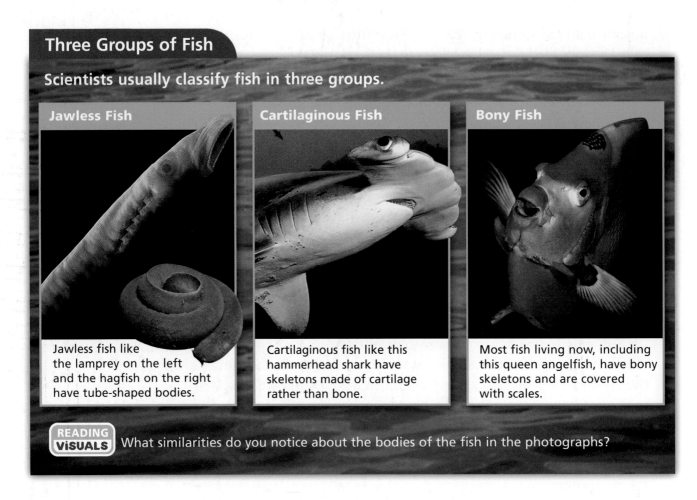

Three Groups of Fish

Scientists usually classify fish in three groups.

Jawless Fish

Jawless fish like the lamprey on the left and the hagfish on the right have tube-shaped bodies.

Cartilaginous Fish

Cartilaginous fish like this hammerhead shark have skeletons made of cartilage rather than bone.

Bony Fish

Most fish living now, including this queen angelfish, have bony skeletons and are covered with scales.

READING VISUALS What similarities do you notice about the bodies of the fish in the photographs?

Fish can be classified in three groups.

Scientists classify fish into three major groups: jawless fish, cartilaginous fish, and bony fish. Each group is characterized by body features. As you read on and learn about each group of fish, look at the photographs above.

Jawless Fish

Scientists think that fish in this group, which includes lampreys and hagfish, are the living animals most similar to the first fish that lived on Earth. Jawless fish have simpler bodies than the other fish. They have a slender tubelike shape and a digestive system without a stomach.

As the name of the group implies, these fish do not have jaw bones. Although they do have teeth, they cannot chew. Most jawless fish eat by biting into another animal's body and then sucking out flesh and fluids.

RESOURCE CENTER
CLASSZONE.COM

Learn more about fish.

 CHECK YOUR READING What is a characteristic of jawless fish?

Cartilaginous Fish

This group includes sharks, rays, and skates. Their skeletons are not made of hard bone, but of a flexible tissue called cartilage (KAHR-tuhl-ihj). Some species of sharks are dangerous to humans, but most cartilaginous fish feed primarily on small animals such as mollusks and crustaceans. Whale sharks and basking sharks, which are the largest fish on Earth, feed by filtering small organisms from the water as they swim.

Rays are flat-bodied cartilaginous fish that live most of their lives on the ocean floor. Their mouths are on the underside of their bodies. Most rays eat by pulling small animals out of the sand. A ray's flat body has fins that extend on either side of its vertebrae like wings. When rays swim, these fins wave so it looks as if the fish is flying through the water.

 CHECK YOUR READING Describe three ways cartilaginous fish species obtain food.

Bony Fish

Most fish species, including tuna, flounder, goldfish, and eels, are classified in this large, diverse group. Of the nearly 29,000 fish species, about 96 percent are bony fish. Bony fish have skeletons made of hard bone, much like the skeleton in your body. Most bony fish are covered with overlapping bony structures called **scales.** They have jaws and teeth and several pairs of fins.

The range of body shapes and behavior in bony fish shows how living things are adapted to their environments. Think of the bright colors and patterns of tropical fish in an aquarium. These eye-catching features are probably adaptations for survival in the fishes' natural environment. In a coral reef, for example, bright stripes and spots might provide camouflage or might advertise the fish's presence to other animals, including potential mates.

Most young fish develop inside an egg.

Most fish species reproduce sexually. The female produces eggs, and the male produces sperm. In many fish species, individual animals select a mate. For example, a female fish might release eggs into the water only when a certain male can fertilize them. After the eggs are fertilized, the parent fish usually leave the eggs to develop and hatch on their own. Most fish reproduce this way, but there are many exceptions.

 REMINDER

In sexual reproduction the genetic material from two parents is combined in their offspring.

This young shark is developing from an egg that is covered by an egg case. In this photograph, light shining through the egg case allows you to see the shark and the yolk inside.

yolk

developing shark

egg case

REMINDER

An embryo is the immature form of an organism that has the potential to grow to maturity.

All animals and plants that can reproduce sexually produce egg cells and sperm cells. However, the structure and size of eggs vary among species. In Chapter 3, you learned that the eggs of flowering plants are found inside the seeds in fruit. In Chapter 4, you read about the eggs of different types of invertebrates. You learned that some eggs have a food supply and a protective covering. For some animals, the food supply is called yolk, and the covering is called an egg case.

Most fish eggs are surrounded by a soft egg case that water can pass through. Since fish lay eggs in the water, this means that a fish embryo inside an egg gets the water and oxygen it needs directly from its surroundings. The egg's yolk provides the developing fish with food. Such eggs can develop on their own, without needing care from adults. However, many animals eat fish eggs. Fish often lay and fertilize many eggs, but few of them survive to maturity.

CHECK YOUR READING How are fish eggs different from invertebrate eggs?

 Review

KEY CONCEPTS

1. Why are fish classified as vertebrate animals?
2. What are three adaptations that suit fish for life in water?
3. Name a feature for fish from each of these groups: jawless, cartilaginous, and bony.

CRITICAL THINKING

4. **Apply** If you wanted to choose tropical fish that could live comfortably in the same tank, what body features or behaviors might you look for?
5. **Infer** Some fish do not lay eggs. Their eggs develop inside the female fish. How might the offspring of one of these fish differ from those of an egg-laying fish?

CHALLENGE

6. **Synthesize** Fossils indicate that species of fish with bodies very similar to today's sharks have lived in aquatic environments for hundreds of millions of years. What can you infer about the adaptations of sharks from this?

MATH in SCIENCE

MATH TUTORIAL
CLASSZONE.COM

Click on Math Tutorial for more help dividing by decimals.

Great Growth

The leatherback sea turtle is one of the largest reptiles alive. Full-grown, adult leatherbacks can weigh 880 kilograms. This huge turtle starts out life weighing just 44 grams.

Example

How many times heavier is the 880 kg adult than the 44 g baby?

(1) Convert the units so they are all in kilograms.
$44 \text{ g} \times 0.001 \text{ kg/g} = 0.044 \text{ kg}$

(2) Divide 880 by 0.044 to get the answer.

(3) To divide by a decimal, multiply the divisor and the dividend by a multiple of 10. Since the decimal number is in thousandths, multiply by 1000.

$$0.044{\overline{\smash{)}880000}} \qquad 44{\overline{\smash{)}880000}}^{\,20,000}$$

ANSWER The adult leatherback is 20,000 times heavier than the baby leatherback hatchling.

Answer the following questions.

1. An adult leatherback has been measured as 1.5 m from nose to tail. The same animal measured just 6 cm as a baby hatchling. How many times longer is the adult?

2. A typical box turtle grows to 12.5 cm long. How many times longer is the adult leatherback than the adult box turtle?

3. Suppose the box turtle hatched with a length of 2.5 cm. By how many times has its length grown at adulthood?

4. How many times longer is the leatherback hatchling than the box turtle hatchling?

CHALLENGE What fraction of its adult weight is the leatherback hatchling in the example?

KEY CONCEPT

5.2 Amphibians and reptiles are adapted for life on land.

 BEFORE, you learned

- Fish are vertebrates that live in water
- Fish gills remove oxygen from water
- Most young fish develop inside eggs laid in the water

NOW, you will learn

- About amphibians, vertebrates that can live on land for part of their lives
- About reptiles, vertebrates that can live on land for their whole lives
- About the body temperature of amphibians and reptiles

VOCABULARY

amphibian p. 167
reptile p. 168
ectotherm p. 170

 EXPLORE Moving on Land

What good are legs?

PROCEDURE

MATERIALS
meter stick

1. Measure and record your height in meters.

2. Jump as far as you can, and have your partner record the distance.

3. Divide the distance you jumped by your height.

4. Some frogs can jump a distance that's equal to 10 times their body length. Calculate the distance you would be able to jump if you were a frog.

WHAT DO YOU THINK?
How might the ability to jump help a frog survive on land?

Vertebrates adapted to live on land.

Most of the groups of invertebrates and all of the vertebrates you have read about so far live in water. Organisms such as plants and insects became very diverse after adapting to live on land. Some vertebrate animals adapted to live on land as well. In this section you will learn about the first vertebrates to live on land, a group called the amphibians, and the group that came next, the reptiles.

Amphibians living today include frogs, toads, and salamanders. Reptiles include turtles, snakes, lizards, and crocodiles. Some people find it hard to tell animals from these two groups apart, but there are some important characteristics that distinguish them.

More than 350 million years ago, Earth was already inhabited by many species of vertebrate animals. All of them were fish. They

Amphibian

Reptile

READING VISUALS **COMPARE AND CONTRAST** Just by looking at these two animals, what physical differences can you see? What similarities do you see?

lived in salt water and fresh water, consumed other organisms as food, and obtained oxygen using specialized organs called gills.

Recall the pond you imagined in Chapter 3, when you learned that plants adapted to land. Now imagine the same pond a hundred million years later. The pond is crowded with invertebrates and fish, all competing for oxygen and food.

Suppose a period of dry weather makes the pond start to dry up. Many animals die, and food and oxygen become scarce. On the banks of the pond it might be less crowded. Invertebrates living there are sources of food. Air on land contains more oxygen than water does. Fish that could survive on land would be better off than the fish in the pond in this situation.

However, the gills of fish work only when they are wet. Fins can function to make a fish move through water, but they are not good for moving on land. Water provides more support for the body than air. Plus, fish sensory organs are specialized for detecting sounds and smells in water, not in air.

It took millions of years and many generations before different adaptations occurred and amphibians became a distinct group. These early amphibians were able to survive on land. Today there are fish that can breathe air and fish that can walk for short distances on land. There are also some modern amphibian species that have adapted to life only in water.

NOTETAKING STRATEGY
Choose a strategy from an earlier chapter or use one of your own to take notes on how vertebrates adapted to life on land.

CHECK YOUR READING How are amphibians different from fish?

Wood Frog Life Cycle

Wood frogs live in moist forest environments and breed once a year, in early spring.

A female adult wood frog deposits a mass of eggs in a pool of fresh water.

The young wood frog climbs out of the water. From now on, it will live on land and breathe with lungs.

Some of the eggs hatch and become tadpoles. Tadpoles swim and breathe like fish.

The wood frog will grow until fall and slow its activity in winter. In spring females lay eggs and the cycle repeats.

The tadpole's legs develop, and its tail shrinks. Many changes occur inside the tadpole's body as well.

READING VISUALS What visible changes occur in a wood frog tadpole's body as it transforms into an adult wood frog?

Amphibians have moist skin and lay eggs without shells.

As adults, most **amphibians** have these characteristics:

- They have two pairs of legs, or a total of four limbs.
- They lay their eggs in water.
- They obtain oxygen through their smooth, moist skin. Many also have respiratory organs called lungs.
- Their sensory organs are adapted for sensing on land.

Most amphibians live in moist environments. Their skin is a respiratory organ that functions only when it is wet. Most species of amphibians live close to water or in damp places. Some are most active at night, when the ground is wet with dew. Others live mostly underground, beneath wet leaves, or under decaying trees.

Amphibians reproduce sexually. In most amphibian species, a female lays eggs in water, a male fertilizes them with sperm, and then the offspring develop and hatch on their own. Yolk inside the eggs provides developing embryos with nutrients. Like fish eggs, amphibian eggs do not have hard shells. This means developing amphibians can get water and oxygen directly from their surroundings.

 CHECK YOUR READING How is the way most amphibians reproduce similar to the way most fish reproduce?

RESOURCE CENTER
CLASSZONE.COM
Learn more about amphibians.

Amphibian Life Cycle

The diagram shows the life cycle of one amphibian, the wood frog. When a young amphibian hatches, it is a larva. In Chapter 4 you learned that a larva is an early stage that is very different from the animal's adult form. For example, the larvae of frogs and toads are called tadpoles. Tadpoles look and behave like small fish. They breathe with gills, eat mostly algae, and move by pushing against the water with their tails.

After a few weeks, a tadpole's body begins to change. Inside, the lungs develop and parts of the digestive system transform. The tadpole begins to have some of the external features of a frog. It develops legs, its tail shrinks, and its head changes shape.

As a young wood frog's body changes, its gills stop functioning, and it begins breathing air with its lungs. The frog starts using its tongue to capture and eat small animals. It leaves the water and begins using its legs to move around on land. Some amphibians, such as sirens and bullfrogs, remain in or near water for all of their lives. Others, like wood frogs, most toads, and some salamanders, live in moist land environments as adults.

READING TiP

As you read about the amphibian life cycle in these paragraphs, look at the diagram on page 166 to see what a wood frog looks like at each stage.

Reptiles have dry, scaly skin and lay eggs with shells.

VOCABULARY
Add a magnet word diagram for *reptile* to your notebook.

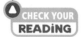

Reptiles evolved soon after amphibians and are closely related to them. However, animals in the reptile group have adaptations that allow them to survive in hotter, drier places than amphibians. For many millions of years they were the largest and most diverse verte-brate animal group living on land. Most of the animals classified as reptiles have these characteristics:

- They have two pairs of legs, for a total of four limbs.
- They have tough, dry skin covered by scales.
- They obtain oxygen from air with respiratory organs called lungs.
- Their sensory organs are adapted for sensing on land.
- They lay their eggs, which have shells, on land.

CHECK YOUR READING What characteristics of reptiles are different from the characteristics of amphibians listed on page 167?

Lungs

Reptiles do not get oxygen through their skin the way amphibians do. They are born with lungs that provide their bodies with all the oxygen they need. Lungs are internal organs made up of many small lobes of thin tissue filled with tiny blood vessels. When an animal with lungs inhales, it takes air in through its nostrils or mouth and moves the air into its lungs. There, oxygen is transported across the tissues and into the blood, and carbon dioxide is moved from the blood to the lungs and exhaled.

Reptiles like these garter snakes are covered with scales and breathe through their nostrils.

scales

nostril

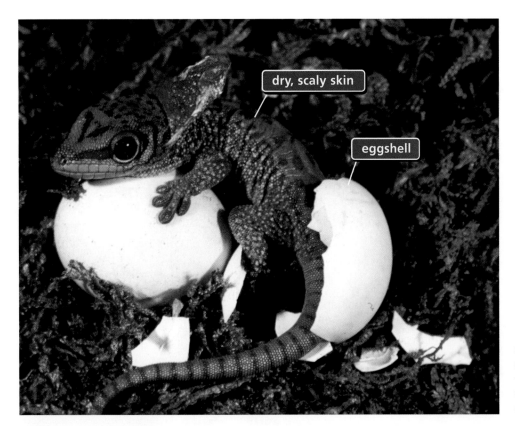

dry, scaly skin

eggshell

CONTRAST How does the egg this gecko hatched from differ from the wood frog eggs shown on page 166?

Dry, Scaly Skin

Reptile skin is hard, dry, and covered with scales made of keratin, a substance much like your fingernails. The thick, waterproof skin of reptiles protects them from the environment and from predators. However, this means that reptiles cannot obtain water through their skin.

Eggs with Shells

The reptile egg is an important adaptation that allows vertebrate animals to survive in hot, dry environments. The eggs of reptiles contain everything an embryo needs: water, nutrients, a system for gas exchange, and a place to store waste. Membranes separate the internal parts of the egg, which is covered by a protective shell.

Reptiles reproduce sexually. The egg cell of the female joins with the sperm cell of the male in the process of fertilization. After fertilization, a protective case, or shell, forms around each egg while it is still inside the female's body. The female selects a place to lay the eggs on land. Many species of reptiles build or dig nests. Some female reptiles, including alligators, guard their nests and care for their offspring after they hatch. Most reptiles, however, leave soon after the eggs are laid. As you can see in the photograph above, when young reptiles hatch, they look like small adults.

RESOURCE CENTER
CLASSZONE.COM

Find out more about reptiles.

INVESTIGATE Eggs

What are some of the characteristics of eggs?

PROCEDURE

1. Carefully examine the outside of the hard-boiled egg. Try to notice as many details as you can. Write your observations in your notebook.

2. Gently crack the eggshell and remove it. Try to keep the shell in large pieces and the egg whole. Set the egg aside, and examine the pieces of shell. Look for details you could not see before. Write your observations in your notebook.

3. Examine the outside of the egg. Make notes about what you see. Include a sketch.

4. Use the knife to cut the egg in half. Take one half apart carefully, trying to notice as many parts as you can. Use the other half for comparison. Write up your observations.

WHAT DO YOU THINK?

- Reptiles, like birds, have eggs with hard shells. What structures does an egg with a shell contain?

- What might the function of each structure be?

CHALLENGE How might the egg's structures support a developing embryo?

The body temperatures of amphibians and reptiles change with the environment.

Amphibians and reptiles are **ectotherms,** animals whose body temperatures change with environmental conditions. You are not an ectotherm. Whether the air temperature of your environment is −4°C (25°F) or 43°C (110°F), your body temperature remains around 37°C (99°F). A tortoise's body temperature changes with the temperature of the air or water surrounding it. On a cool day, a tortoise's body will be cooler than it is on a hot one.

Many ectothermic animals can move and respond more quickly when their bodies are warm. Many ectotherms warm themselves in sunlight. You may have seen turtles or snakes sunning themselves. Ectothermic animals transform most of the food they consume directly into energy. Some ectotherms, even large ones such as alligators, or the Galápagos tortoise in the photograph, can survive for a long time without consuming much food.

This sand-diving lizard can reduce the amount of heat that transfers from the sand into its body by standing on two feet.

Although amphibians and reptiles do not have a constant body temperature, their bodies stop functioning well if they become too hot or too cold. Most amphibians and reptiles live in environments where the temperature of the surrounding air or water does not change too much. Others, like wood frogs and painted turtles, have adaptations that allow them to slow their body processes during the winter.

Amphibians and reptiles also have behaviors that allow them to adjust their body temperature in less extreme ways. The sand-diving lizard in the photograph above is able to control how much heat enters its body through the sand by standing on just two of its four feet. Many amphibians and reptiles live near water and use it to cool off their bodies.

5.2 Review

KEY CONCEPTS

1. What are three adaptations that allowed the first amphibians to survive on land?

2. What are two adaptations reptiles have that allow them to live their whole life on land?

3. A crocodile has been lying in the sun for hours. When it slides into the cool river, how will its body temperature change? Why?

CRITICAL THINKING

4. **Compare and Contrast** Make a diagram to show how amphibians and reptiles are different and how they are similar.

5. **Infer** Some reptiles, like sea turtles, live almost their whole lives in water. What differences would you expect to see between the bodies of a sea turtle and a land turtle?

⬥ CHALLENGE

6. **Hypothesize** For many millions of years, reptiles were the most diverse and successful vertebrate animals on land. Now many of these ancient reptiles are extinct. Give some reasons that might explain the extinction of these reptiles.

Sticky Feet

Imagine having the ability to walk up a polished glass window, across ceiling tiles, and down a mirror—without using suction or glue. Small tropical lizards called geckos have this unique ability, and scientists are beginning to understand what makes these animals stick.

A gecko's foot is covered with billions of tiny hairs. Each hair branches into hundreds of smaller hairs called spatulae, and the atoms in these spatulae are attracted to atoms in the surfaces the geckos walk on.

All atoms contain particles called electrons, which constantly move around. When two atoms get very close, the motion of their electrons can change, attracting the two atoms to one another.

Gecko toes

Spatulae 595 ×

Spatulae are over 200 times narrower than human hair. Because they are so small, many spatulae can get close enough to the surfaces geckoes walk on for their atoms to stick together.

Billions of these tiny atom-level forces combine with enough strength to suspend a gecko's body weight. Scientists call this property dry adhesion and have applied what they've learned from the soles of these small lizards to manufacturing renewable tape that never loses its ability to stick.

EXPLORE

1. **CONNECT** What are some other animals that can walk up walls or across ceilings? How do you think they do this?

2. **CHALLENGE** Do you think geckos would be able to walk up wet surfaces as easily as dry ones? Why or why not?

Shown life-size, the gecko is a reptile with tiny sticky hairs on its feet. Why are chemists and engineers interested in this adaptation?

5.3 Birds meet their needs on land, in water, and in the air.

◀ **BEFORE, you learned**

- Vertebrate animals have endoskeletons with backbones
- Amphibians and reptiles have adaptations for life on land
- Ectotherms do not maintain a constant body temperature

▶ **NOW, you will learn**

- About birds as endotherms
- How the adaptations of birds allow them to live in many environments
- About adaptations for flight

VOCABULARY

endotherm p. 174
incubation p. 179

EXPLORE Feathers

How do feathers differ?

PROCEDURE

MATERIALS
assorted feathers

1. Examine several feathers.

2. Make a list of ways some of your feathers differ from others.

3. Make a diagram of each feather, showing the characteristics you listed.

4. Compare your list and your diagram with those of your classmates.

WHAT DO YOU THINK?

- Of all the characteristics of feathers that you and your classmates listed, which do you think are the most important? Why?
- On the basis of your observations, what are some functions of feathers for birds?

Bird species live in most environments.

NOTETAKING STRATEGY
Be sure to take notes on the main idea, *Bird species live in most environments.* Choose an earlier strategy or one of your own.

Penguins live in Antarctica, and parrots inhabit the tropics. Pelicans scoop their food from the water, while cardinals crack open seeds and eat the insides. Swallows skim insects from above the surface of a pond. A soaring hawk swoops down, and a smaller animal becomes its prey. There are over 10,000 species of the vertebrate animals called birds. Their adaptations allow them to live all over the world.

Some bird species, such as pigeons, are adapted to live in a wide range of environments, while others have adaptations that limit them to living in one place. Many birds travel long distances during their lives. Some migrate as the seasons change, and others cover long distances while searching for food.

It probably seems easy for you to recognize which animals are birds. Birds are distinguished by these characteristics:

- They have feathers and a beak.
- They have four limbs: a pair of scaly legs and a pair of wings.
- Their eggs have hard shells.

Birds can maintain body temperature.

In the last section, you learned that the body temperature of ectotherms, such as amphibians and reptiles, changes with their environment. Birds are **endotherms,** or animals that maintain a constant body temperature. Maintaining temperature allows endotherms to live in some places where frogs, turtles, and alligators cannot.

This chickadee is an endotherm. This means its body remains warm, even in very cold weather.

When an ectothermic animal's body is cool, its systems slow down and it becomes less active. A less active animal consumes little or no food and is unlikely to reproduce. It moves slowly or not at all and breathes less often. Its nervous system becomes less responsive, and its heart pumps more slowly. An ectothermic animal that stays cool for too long will die. Even if it has enough food, its body lacks the energy needed to digest the food.

All animals are affected by the air temperature of their environment and will die if they become too cold. However, birds and other endotherms can stay active in colder climates than ectotherms can. This is because endothermic animals have adaptations for generating more body heat and keeping it near their bodies.

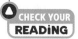 How can endotherms stay alive in colder climates than ectotherms?

Generating Heat

The energy birds produce as body heat comes from food. This means that birds and other endotherms need to eat a lot. An ectotherm such as a frog might be able to survive for days on the energy it gets from just one worm, while a bird on the same diet might starve. Also, the amount of food an endotherm needs is affected by climate. House sparrows and other birds that do not migrate need to eat more food and produce more energy to survive in winter than they do during warmer seasons.

Insulating with Down

Just as warm air trapped between down feathers helps keep geese warm, feathers in a jacket keep a student warm.

Down Feathers

Controlling Body Temperature

Birds have soft feathers, called down, that keep warm air close to their bodies. If you have ever slept with a down comforter or worn a down jacket, you know that these feathers are good insulation, even though they are not very heavy. Other feathers, called contour feathers, cover the down on birds. In most species, contour feathers are water-resistant and protect birds from getting wet.

Birds shiver when they are cold, and this muscular movement generates heat. They also have ways of cooling their bodies down when the weather is hot. Birds do not sweat, but they can fluff their feathers out to release heat. Birds, like other animals, have behaviors for maintaining body temperature, such as resting in a shady place during the hottest part of a summer day.

Most birds can fly.

Of all the animals on Earth today, only three groups have evolved adaptations for flight: insects, bats, and birds. Fossil evidence suggests that the first birds appeared on Earth about 150 million years ago and that they were reptiles with adaptations for flight. Scientists think that all birds are descended from these flying ancestors, even modern species such as ostriches and penguins, which cannot fly.

Adaptations for Flight

To lift its body into the air and fly, an animal's body has to be very strong, but also light. Many adaptations and many millions of years were needed before birds' body plans and systems became capable of flight. With these adaptations, birds lost the ability to do some things that other vertebrates can. As you read about birds' adaptations for flight, match the numbers with the diagram on the next page.

READING TiP

As you read the numbered text on this page, find the matching number on page 177.

1 Endoskeleton Some of the bones in a bird's body are fused, or connected without joints. This makes those parts of a bird's skeleton light and strong, but not as flexible. A specialized bone supports the bird's powerful flight muscles.

2 Wings and Feathers Birds do not have hands or paws on their wings. Contour feathers along the wing are called flight feathers, and are specialized for lifting and gliding. Feathers are a strong and adjustable surface for pushing against air.

3 Specialized Respiratory System Flying takes a lot of energy, so birds need a lot of oxygen. They breathe using a system of air sacs and lungs. Air follows a path through this system that allows oxygen to move constantly through a bird's body.

4 Hollow Bones Many of the bones in a bird's skeleton are hollow. Inside, crisscrossing structures provide strength without adding much weight.

Other body systems within birds are more suited for flight than systems in other invertebrates. Instead of heavy jaws and teeth, an internal organ called a gizzard grinds up food. This adaptation makes a bird lighter in weight and makes flight easier. Birds also have highly developed senses of hearing and vision, senses which are important for flight. Their senses of taste and smell are not as well developed.

 CHECK YOUR READING Give two examples of things that birds cannot do that relate to their adaptations for flight.

Benefits of Flight

Flight allows animals to get food from places where animals living on land or in water cannot. For example, some species of birds spend most of their lives flying over the ocean, hunting for fish. Also, a flying bird can search a large area for food more effectively than it could if it walked, ran, or swam.

For many species of birds, flight makes migration possible. In Chapter 2, you learned that some animals migrate to different living places in different seasons. Most migratory birds have two living places, one for the summer and one for the winter.

Adaptations for Flight

This diagram shows some of the adaptations that make flight possible for most birds.

① Endoskeleton

A bird's skeleton is strong and light. Some bones are fused, or connected without joints.

② Wings and Feathers

A bird's wings are specialized arm bones that support its flight feathers.

vertebrae

lungs

air sac

③ Respiratory Structures

lung

air sacs

A bird's connected system of air sacs and lungs keeps oxygen moving through its body.

④ Hollow Bones

Air fills the inside of a bird's bones.

READING VISUALS Do you think any one of these adaptations is more important than the rest?

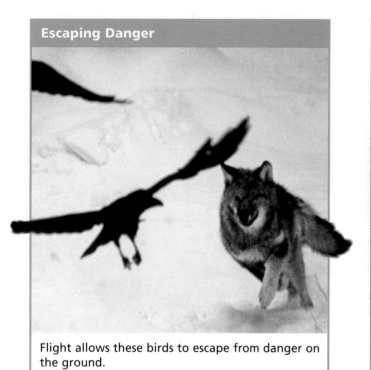

Flight allows these birds to escape from danger on the ground.

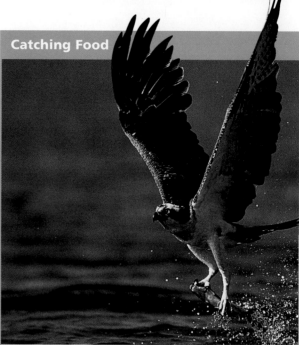

Flight allows this osprey to hunt for fish in bodies of water.

Some birds migrate very long distances. Ruby-throated hummingbirds, for example, migrate from Canada and the United States to Mexico and Central America each winter, flying nonstop 700 kilometers across the Gulf of Mexico.

By flying, birds can escape danger on the ground. Many species of birds are able to lay their eggs and raise their young in places that are difficult for predators to reach. Fossil evidence suggests that birds were the first vertebrate animal species to live on many of Earth's islands. Like the first organisms that adapted to live on land, birds that were the first vertebrates on an island usually had little competition for food, water, and living space.

 CHECK YOUR READING How does flight benefit birds? Give three examples.

Birds lay eggs with hard shells.

Birds reproduce sexually. Many species of birds have distinctive ways of trying to attract mates. Some species sing, and others develop colorful feathers during mating season. Wild turkeys fight each other, bowerbirds construct elaborate nests, and woodcocks fly high in the air and then zig-zag back down. In most bird species, the male animals display and the female selects her mate.

The reproduction process for birds is similar to that of reptiles. After internal fertilization, a shell forms around each fertilized egg while it is still inside the female's body. Reptiles' eggs usually have flexible shells, but the shells of birds' eggs are hard.

Usually the female bird chooses where to lay the eggs. Often this is a nest. In some bird species either the male or the female builds the nest, while in others, mated birds build a nest together. Bird eggs have to be kept at a constant, warm temperature or they will not develop. Nearly all birds use their body heat to keep the eggs warm. They sit on the eggs, which can support the adult bird's weight because the shells are hard. This process is called **incubation**. When the eggs hatch, the young birds are not yet able to fly. They must be cared for until they can meet their own needs.

These 3- to 8-day-old tanagers are being fed by both of their parents.

Most birds take care of their offspring.

In some bird species, male and female mates care for their offspring together. This is often the case for birds, such as the tanagers in the top photograph, whose young hatch before their eyes open or their feathers grow. It takes two adult birds to provide them with enough food, warmth, and protection.

The offspring of some species, like the ducks in the bottom photograph, hatch at a later state of development, with open eyes. They are already covered with down feathers and able to walk. In such species it's common for just one adult, usually the female, to incubate the eggs and care for the young.

These 7-day-old ducklings are able to find their own food while their mother watches over them.

5.3 Review

KEY CONCEPTS

1. What does an endothermic animal need to do in order to generate body heat?

2. What are two types of feathers, and what are their functions?

3. Describe three adaptations that make flight possible for birds.

CRITICAL THINKING

4. **Compare and Contrast** How is reproduction in birds similar to reproduction in reptiles? How does it different?

5. **Synthesize** Some flightless birds live on islands or in remote places where there are few predators. Explain why, in such an environment, flying birds' bodies might have adapted and become flightless.

○ CHALLENGE

6. **Hypothesize** Many species of birds begin migration while food is still plentiful in their current environment. Understanding what triggers migration in birds is an active area of scientific research. Develop a hypothesis about migration triggers in one species of bird. Describe how to test your hypothesis.

CHAPTER INVESTIGATION

Bird Beak Adaptations

OVERVIEW AND PURPOSE The beaks of most birds are adapted for eating particular types of food. In this lab you will

- use models to simulate how different types of beaks function
- infer how the shape of a bird's beak might affect the food a bird eats

▶ Question

For this lab, you will use a tool as a model of a specialized bird beak. You will try to obtain food with your beak at several different feeding stations. Each station will have a different type of food. Examine the tools that will be used for this lab, as well as the feeding stations. Then write a question about how beak shape might affect the food a bird eats. Your question should begin with *Which, How, When, Why,* or *What*. Keep in mind that you will be asked to answer this question at the end of the lab.

▶ Procedure

1. Make a data table like the one shown on page 181.

2. Complete the title of your data table by writing in the name of the tool you will be using.

3. Before you start collecting food at one of the feeding stations, write a prediction in your data table. Predict how well you think the tool will function and why.

MATERIALS
- tweezers
- eyedropper
- slotted spoon
- pliers
- test tubes in rack
- water
- dried pasta
- millet seeds
- jar of rubber bands
- empty containers
- stopwatch

4. See how much food you can collect in one minute. To collect food, you must move it from the feeding station into a different container, and you may only touch the food with the tool.

step 4

5. Describe your results in your data table.

6. Return the food you collected to the feeding station. Try to make it look just like it did when you started.

7. Repeat steps 3–6 at each of the other feeding stations.

Observe and Analyze
Write It Up

1. **INTERPRET DATA** At which feeding station did you have the best results? Why? Explain your answer.

2. **EVALUATE** How accurate were the predictions you made?

3. **APPLY** If you could visit each feeding station again, how would you change the way you used the tool to collect food? Explain your answer.

Conclude
Write It Up

1. **INFER** What answers do you have for the question you wrote at the beginning of this lab?

2. **INFER** In what ways do you think the experience you had during this lab is similar to the ways real birds obtain food?

3. **IDENTIFY LIMITATIONS** What unexpected factors or problems might have affected your results?

4. **SYNTHESIZE** What environmental and physical factors can a bird actually control when it is getting food?

5. **APPLY** Examine the beaks of the birds in the photographs below. Write a brief description of the shape of each bird's beak. Then, for each bird, name one type of food its beak might be suited for and one type of food each bird would probably not be able to eat.

INVESTIGATE Further

CHALLENGE How are other parts of birds' bodies specialized for the environments where they live? Investigate the feet of the following birds: ostrich, heron, woodpecker, pelican, and owl.

Bird Beak Adaptations

Question:

Table 1. Collecting Food with _____

Station	Prediction	Results
Water in test tubes		
Dried pasta		
Millet seeds		
Rubber bands in jar		

5.4 Mammals live in many environments.

◀ BEFORE, you learned	▶ NOW, you will learn
• Endotherms can stay active in cold environments	• About mammals as endotherms
• Many bird adaptations are related to flight	• About the diversity of adaptations in mammals
• Birds lay hard-shelled eggs and usually take care of their young	• That mammals produce milk, which is food for their young

VOCABULARY

mammal p. 183
placenta p. 186
gestation p. 186

THINK ABOUT

How diverse are mammals?

Mammals have adapted to survive in many environments and come in many shapes and sizes. Whales live in the ocean, and goats may live near mountain peaks. Some monkeys live in tropical forests, and polar bears survive in frozen areas. An elephant might not fit in your classroom, but the tiny shrew shown here could fit on your finger. As you read this chapter, think about the characteristics of mammals that help them to survive in such a variety of ways.

Mammals are a diverse group.

NOTETAKING STRATEGY
Using a strategy of your choice, take notes on the idea that mammals are a diverse group. Be sure to include mammal characteristics.

The group of vertebrates called mammals includes many familiar animals. Mice are mammals, and so are cows, elephants, and chimpanzees. You are a mammal, too. Bats are mammals that can fly. Some mammals, including whales, live in water.

Some mammal species, such as raccoons and skunks, have adapted to live in many sorts of environments, including cities. Others, such as cheetahs and polar bears, have adaptations for meeting their needs in just a few environments.

Mammals are a diverse animal group. Although there are less than 5000 species of mammals on Earth, mammal species come in many shapes and sizes, and have many different ways of moving, finding food, and eating. These are some of the characteristics that distinguish **mammals** from other animals:

RESOURCE CENTER
CLASSZONE.COM

Learn more about mammals.

- All mammals have hair during some part of their lives.
- Most mammal species have teeth specialized for consuming particular kinds of food.
- All mammal species produce milk, with which they feed their young.

Mammals are endotherms.

You have learned that endothermic animals are able to stay active in cold environments. This is because endotherms maintain a constant body temperature. Mammals are endotherms. This means that they use some of the food they consume to generate body heat. Mammals also have adaptations for controlling body temperature.

Hair

Many species of mammals have bodies covered with hair. Like birds' feathers, hair is an adaptation that allows mammals to have some control over the warmth or coldness of their bodies. Mammals that live in cold regions, like polar bears, have hair that keeps them warm. Desert mammals, such as camels, have hair that protects them from extreme heat.

Most mammals have at least two types of hair. Soft, fluffy underhairs keep heat close to their bodies, like the down feathers of birds. Water-resistant guard hairs cover the under-hairs and give the animal's fur its color.

Some species of mammals also have specialized hairs. A specialized structure is one that performs a particular function. For example, whiskers are sensory hairs that are part of an animal's sense of touch. Porcupines' quills are hairs that function in self defense.

 CHECK YOUR READING What are three functions of hair?

whiskers

Colored guard hairs give this tiger its stripes. Its whiskers are specialized sensory hairs. It also has underhairs, which you cannot see.

quills

This porcupine's quills are specialized guard hairs.

Body Fat

Some mammal species that live in water, such as dolphins, have very little hair. These mammals have a layer of fat, called blubber, that plays an important role in maintaining body temperature. The blubber is located between the animal's skin and muscles, and provides its organs with insulation from heat and cold.

Body fat can also be a storage place for energy. When a mammal consumes more food than it needs, the extra energy may be stored in its fat cells. Later, if the animal needs energy but cannot find food, it can use the energy stored in the fat.

For example, animals that hibernate, such as woodchucks, may eat a lot more than they need to survive at times when plenty of food is available. This makes them fat. Then, while they are hibernating, they do not have to eat, because their body fat provides them with the energy they need.

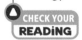 **CHECK YOUR READING** What are two ways that body fat functions in mammals?

INVESTIGATE How Body Fat Insulates

How well does fat keep a mammal warm?

A layer of body fat between the muscles and the skin allows some mammals to survive in very cold places. In this investigation, you will experience how well that adaptation works by making a blubber glove model.

PROCEDURE

1. Half fill one large, zip-lip plastic bag with vegetable shortening. Turn another bag inside out and place it inside the bag with the shortening. Zip the edges of the two bags together so that the shortening is sealed between them.

2. Place one hand inside this "blubber glove." Place the other hand inside the third bag. Then submerge both hands in a tub of ice water. Which hand stays warmer? For how long? Record your observations.

WHAT DO YOU THINK?

How well did the blubber glove insulate your hand?

CHALLENGE Would you expect an animal that lives in a very hot environment to have a thick layer of body fat?

SKILL FOCUS
Making models

MATERIALS
- 3 zip-lip plastic bags, 1/2-gallon size
- can of vegetable shortening
- bowl of ice water

TIME
15 minutes

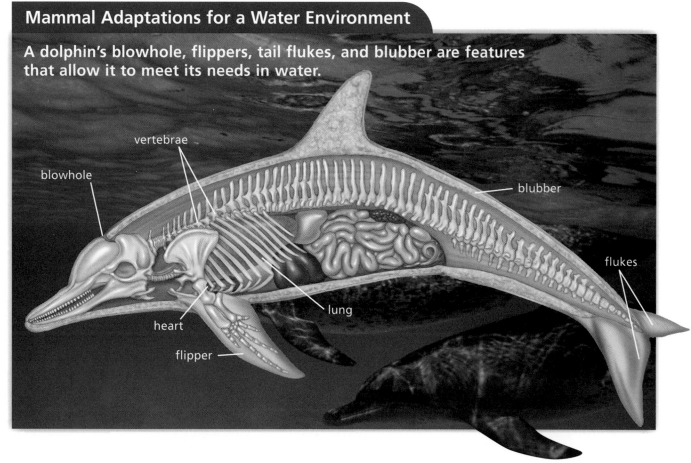

Mammal Adaptations for a Water Environment

A dolphin's blowhole, flippers, tail flukes, and blubber are features that allow it to meet its needs in water.

vertebrae

blowhole

blubber

flukes

lung

heart

flipper

Mammals have adapted to many environments.

Scientists think mammals appeared on Earth about 200 million years ago. Fossil evidence suggests that the first mammals were small land vertebrates with four limbs, a tail, and specialized teeth. They probably had fur and were most active at night.

Over millions of years, those early mammals adapted to live in many different environments and became the diverse group of species they are today. Moles, for example, live almost entirely underground. They have strong limbs for digging and organs specialized for sensing invertebrate prey in the dark. Spider monkeys, on the other hand, live mostly in trees. A spider monkey can use all four of its long limbs and its flexible, grasping tail to move through a forest without touching the ground.

The first mammals lived on land, but over time some species adapted to live in watery environments. Some of them, such as otters and walruses, live mostly in water but can also be found on land. Others, such as dolphins and whales, have bodies so completely adapted for life in the water that they no longer have a way of moving on land. If you look carefully at the diagram above, however, you will see that a dolphin's body plan differs in some important ways from that of a fish.

Mammals have reproductive adaptations.

Mammals reproduce sexually. Before a mammal can produce offspring, it finds a mate. Some mammals, such as lions, live in groups that include both males and females. However, most mammals live alone most of the time. They find a mate when they are ready to reproduce. Some mammal species breed only at certain times of the year. Others can reproduce throughout the year.

Development Before Birth

VOCABULARY
Remember to make a word magnet for the terms *placenta* and *gestation.*

Fertilization occurs internally in mammals. In almost every species of mammal, the offspring develop inside the female's body. Many mammals have a special organ called a **placenta** that transports nutrients, water, and oxygen from the mother's blood to the developing embryo. The embryo's waste materials leave through the placenta and are transported out of the mother's body along with her waste.

The time when a mammal is developing inside its mother is called **gestation**. As you can see in the diagram, the length of the gestation period is different for different species. Gestation ends when the young animal's body has grown and developed enough for it to survive outside the mother. Then it is born.

CHECK YOUR READING Where do the offspring of most mammals develop before they are born?

Length of Gestation

The length of gestation varies greatly in placental mammals.

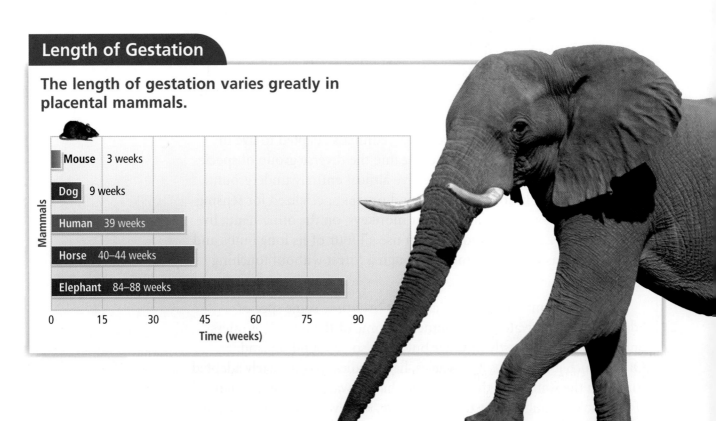

Mammals	Time (weeks)
Mouse	3 weeks
Dog	9 weeks
Human	39 weeks
Horse	40–44 weeks
Elephant	84–88 weeks

Not all mammals fully develop inside their mothers. The duck-billed platypus and two species of spiny anteaters have young that hatch from eggs. Mammals in a group called the marsupials (mahr-SOO-pee-uhlz), which includes kangaroos, develop inside the mother at first but are born when they are still extremely small. Right after birth, a young marsupial climbs across its mother to a special pouch on the outside of her body. It completes its development there. Only one marsupial, the opossum, lives in North America.

Raising Young

Milk, a high-energy liquid food full of proteins, fats, sugars, and other nutrients, is the first food young mammals consume. Each species' milk has a different combination of these ingredients.

Mammals' bodies have special glands for producing milk, called mammary glands. In almost all mammal species, only females' mammary glands function. This means that only female mammals can feed the young with milk. In most mammal species, females gestate and care for the offspring alone. However, in some mammal species, the male helps raise the young.

This dog is feeding her puppies with milk.

Different species of mammals are born at varying stages of development. Most mice are helpless, blind, and naked at birth, while giraffes can walk soon after they are born. The length of time a young mammal needs care from an adult varies. Some seals nurse their young for less than a month before leaving them to survive on their own. Some whales live alongside their young for a much longer time. However, humans may be the mammal species that takes care of their offspring for the longest time of all.

5.4 Review

KEY CONCEPTS

1. Why is a bat classified as a mammal instead of a bird? Why are whales classified as mammals and not fish?

2. Name two adaptations that allow mammals to have control over body temperature.

3. How does the way that mammals feed their young differ from the ways other animals feed their young?

CRITICAL THINKING

4. **Apply** One day on your way home from school, you see an animal that you have never seen before. What clues would you look for to tell you what type of animal it is?

5. **Synthesize** Make a Venn diagram that shows how the vertebrate animal groups you learned about in this chapter are similar and different.

○ CHALLENGE

6. **Evaluate** This section begins with the statement "mammals are a diverse group." Explain what this means and why it is a true statement. How does the diversity of mammals compare to the diversity of other living things, such as bacteria, plants, arthropods, or fish?

Chapter Review

the BIG idea

Vertebrate animals live in most of Earth's environments.

CONTENT REVIEW
CLASSZONE.COM

KEY CONCEPTS SUMMARY

5.1 Vertebrates are animals with endoskeletons.

All **vertebrate** animals have an **endoskeleton** which includes vertebrae, or backbones.

Most vertebrates are fish. Fish are adapted for life in a water environment.

vertebrae

VOCABULARY
vertebrate p. 157
endoskeleton p. 157
scale p. 161

5.2 Amphibians and reptiles are adapted for life on land.

Amphibians and **reptiles** have adaptations for moving, getting food, and breathing on land.

Most amphibians live in moist places.

Many reptiles live in hot, dry places.

VOCABULARY
ectotherm p. 170
amphibian p. 167
reptile p. 168

5.3 Birds meet their needs on land, in water, and in the air.

Birds have adaptations that allow them to survive in many environments. Many of the features and behaviors of birds relate to flight.

VOCABULARY
endotherm p. 174
incubation p. 179

5.4 Mammals live in many environments.

Mammal species live in many environments. Mammals have adaptations that allow them to survive in cold places. They also have distinctive reproductive adaptations.

VOCABULARY
mammal p. 183
placenta p. 186
gestation p. 186

Reviewing Vocabulary

Place each vocabulary term listed below at the center of a description wheel diagram. Write some words describing it on the spokes.

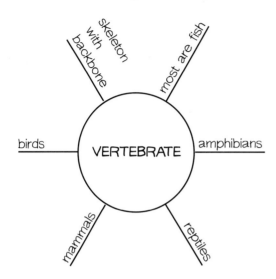

skeleton with backbone
most are fish
birds
VERTEBRATE
amphibians
mammals
reptiles

1. endotherm
2. migration
3. ectotherm
4. scale
5. incubation
6. gestation

Reviewing Key Concepts

Multiple Choice *Choose the letter of the best response.*

7. The vertebrate endoskeleton differs from an arthopod's exoskeleton because it
   a. supports muscles
   b. protects organs
   c. is inside the animal's body
   d. has joints

8. Most vertebrate species are
   a. fish   c. birds
   b. amphibians   d. mammals

9. Fish obtain oxygen from water with structures called
   a. vertebrae   c. lungs
   b. fins   d. gills

10. Down feathers provide insulation for a bird's body because they
    a. trap warm air between them
    b. are waterproof
    c. overlap each other
    d. are slightly oily

11. Which organ do both fish and amphibians have?
    a. lateral line
    b. lungs
    c. gills
    d. scaly skin

12. Mammals differ from other vertebrates because mammals
    a. can lay eggs
    b. can produce milk
    c. are endotherms
    d. are able to swim

13. The two types of vertebrates that lay their eggs in water are
    a. amphibians and birds
    b. reptiles and fish
    c. fish and amphibians
    d. mollusks and fish

14. Which statement is true?
    a. All birds are ectotherms.
    b. All birds can fly.
    c. All birds have two wings and two legs.
    d. All birds have teeth and beaks.

15. The organ that transports materials between a female mammal and the offspring developing inside her body is called a
    a. yolk   c. blubber
    b. placenta   d. vertebrae

Short Answer *Write a short answer to the questions below.*

16. Describe how you would determine if an animal was a salamander or a lizard.

17. Why do bird eggs have to be incubated?

18. **PREDICT** Imagine that you live in Mexico and you have a pen pal who lives in Iceland. Both of you want to know about animals in the other person's country. Which of you will be more likely to have seen wild reptiles? Why?

19. **APPLY** Polar bears live in an arctic environment. Jaguars live in a rain forest environment. Which animal would you expect to have more body fat? Explain.

Refer to diagram below as you answer parts of the next two questions.

20. **COMPARE** Birds, like all vertebrates, have internal skeletons. What functions does a bird's skeleton have in common with all other vertebrates?

21. **INFER** This diagram shows only some of a bird's body systems. Name two systems that are not shown here, including organs that belong to them and their functions.

22. **HYPOTHESIZE** Not all birds migrate. Some birds, such as pigeons and house sparrows, stay in one living place through the winter. What do you think you would find if you compared the diets of birds that migrate with those of birds that do not?

23. **MATH AND SCIENCE** Scientists studying an endangered species of rainforest salamanders estimated that only 875 of these animals were still living in 2002. If this salamander population decreases by 50 animals per year, in what year will it become extinct? Explain how you found your answer.

24. **CLASSIFY** Imagine that you move to a new place and spend a year watching nearby animals. Read each description and identify each animal described below as a fish, amphibian, reptile, bird, or mammal.

   a. A scaly animal warms itself on your sidewalk when the sun is out. It has dry skin, four legs, and a tail.

   b. Small animals swim in a pond near your home. They have no legs, but they do have tails. As they grow older, their tails shrink and they develop four limbs. Then they disappear from the pond.

   c. A furry animal chews a hole under your porch and seems to be living there. You later see it with smaller animals that appear to be its young.

   d. A pair of flying, feathered animals collect objects and carry them into an opening under the gutter of your neighbor's house. At first you see them carrying twigs and grass, but later it looks as if they are carrying worms.

the BIG idea

25. **DRAW CONCLUSIONS** Look again at the picture on pages 154–155. What do penguins and seals have in common? What adaptations do some species of birds and mammals have that allow them to survive in cold environments like Antarctica?

26. **PROVIDE EXAMPLES** Think of an example of a species from each of the vertebrate animal groups you've learned about, and describe an adaptation that suits each to the environment where it lives. Explain your answers.

UNIT PROJECTS

Evaluate all the data, results, and information from your project folder. Prepare to present your project. Be ready to answer questions posed by your classmates about your results.

Analyzing Diagrams

Read the text and study the diagram, and then choose the best response for the questions that follow.

Vertebrates, such as birds, fish, and mammals, have endoskeletons. This internal skeleton is made up of a system of bones that extends throughout the body. Muscles can attach directly to the bones, around joints—the place where two bones meet. As shown in the generalized diagram below, at least two muscles are needed to produce movement. One of the muscles contracts, or shortens, pulling on the bone, while the other muscle extends, or is stretched.

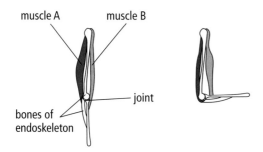

muscle A   muscle B

joint

bones of
endoskeleton

1. Endoskeletons are made up of
  a. contracting muscles
  b. extending muscles
  c. internal bones
  d. external bones

2. A muscle produces movement by
  a. pulling
  b. relaxing
  c. extending
  d. rotating

3. A joint is where
  a. one muscle connects to another
  b. one bone connects to another
  c. a muscle connects to a bone
  d. the bone ends

4. The leg in the diagram bends when
  a. muscle A contracts
  b. muscle A relaxes
  c. muscle B contracts
  d. muscles A and B contract

5. What is the main point of the diagram and the text above?
  a. Two muscles are needed to produce movement in vertebrates.
  b. Vertebrates have internal skeletons.
  c. When one muscle shortens, another muscle gets longer.
  d. Movement in vertebrates is the result of the interaction of muscles and bones.

Extended Response

Use terms from the word box to answer the next question. Underline each term you use in your answer.

6. Many fish go forward by moving their tails from side to side. Describe the action of the muscles on each side of the fish as the tail moves from one side to the other.

contract	pull
extend	muscle

7. Using what you know about joints and muscles and the diagram, describe what happens to muscles and bones as you bend your leg at the knee.

Today's Scientist at Work

Name: Dijanna Figueroa	
Degree: PhD, Biology, University of California, Santa Barbara	
Profession: Marine Biologist	
Location: Santa Barbara, CA	

© Matthew Simmons/Getty Images

Dijanna Figueroa has wanted to be a marine biologist for as long as she can remember. On most days, there is nothing surprising about what she does. Like many scientists, she wears a white lab coat and goggles. She can spend up to 12 hours a day in the lab. There, she studies the metabolisms of creatures that live in extreme environments. They live more than two miles below the ocean's surface. No sunlight reaches their habitats. The water pressure is so great that it would crush a human being. These creatures, therefore, must produce food in ways that were unknown until only recently. How did Dijanna get these animals into her lab? She went down and got them.

You may have seen her face before. Dijanna was one of the scientists in the IMAX film *Aliens of the Deep.* The film shows footage of expeditions down to what may be the harshest place on the planet to live: deep-sea ocean vents. The submarine that took them there is called *Alvin. Alvin* is about eight feet across and holds three people. The complete trip takes about eight hours. The five hours they spend on the ocean floor is not nearly long enough to see everything. They prepared for months to take a few samples back with them. These creatures are what Dijanna now studies in the lab.

Dijanna thinks it's important that her entire life is not just spent in the lab or even under the ocean. Of course, she does a lot of reading. But she also enjoys ballroom dancing with her husband and having breakfast with friends.

Dijanna Figueroa studies thermal vent creatures like the giant tube worm shown here.

©Peter Batson, DeepSeaPhotography.com

Student Resource Handbooks

Making Observations

An **observation** is an act of noting and recording an event, characteristic, behavior, or anything else detected with an instrument or with the senses.

Observations allow you to make informed hypotheses and to gather data for experiments. Careful observations often lead to ideas for new experiments. There are two categories of observations:

- **Quantitative observations** can be expressed in numbers and include records of time, temperature, mass, distance, and volume.

- **Qualitative observations** include descriptions of sights, sounds, smells, and textures.

EXAMPLE

A student dissolved 30 grams of Epsom salts in water, poured the solution into a dish, and let the dish sit out uncovered overnight. The next day, she made the following observations of the Epsom salt crystals that grew in the dish.

Table 1. Observations of Epsom Salt Crystals

Quantitative Observations	Qualitative Observations
• mass = 30 g • mean crystal length = 0.5 cm • longest crystal length = 2 cm	• Crystals are clear. • Crystals are long, thin, and rectangular. • White crust has formed around edge of dish.

> To determine the mass, the student found the mass of the dish before and after growing the crystals and then used subtraction to find the difference.

> The student measured several crystals and calculated the mean length. (To learn how to calculate the mean of a data set, see page R36.)

> Photographs or sketches are useful for recording qualitative observations.

 Epsom salt crystals

MORE ABOUT OBSERVING

- Make quantitative observations whenever possible. That way, others will know exactly what you observed and be able to compare their results with yours.

- It is always a good idea to make qualitative observations too. You never know when you might observe something unexpected.

Predicting and Hypothesizing

A **prediction** is an expectation of what will be observed or what will happen. A **hypothesis** is a tentative explanation for an observation or scientific problem that can be tested by further investigation.

EXAMPLE

Suppose you have made two paper airplanes and you wonder why one of them tends to glide farther than the other one.

1. Start by asking a question.

2. Make an educated guess. After examination, you notice that the wings of the airplane that flies farther are slightly larger than the wings of the other airplane.

3. Write a prediction based upon your educated guess, in the form of an "If . . . , then . . ." statement. Write the independent variable after the word *if,* and the dependent variable after the word *then.*

4. To make a hypothesis, explain why you think what you predicted will occur. Write the explanation after the word *because.*

1. Why does one of the paper airplanes glide farther than the other?

2. The size of an airplane's wings may affect how far the airplane will glide.

3. Prediction: If I make a paper airplane with larger wings, then the airplane will glide farther.

> To read about independent and dependent variables, see page R30.

4. Hypothesis: If I make a paper airplane with larger wings, then the airplane will glide farther, because the additional surface area of the wing will produce more lift.

> Notice that the part of the hypothesis after *because* adds an explanation of why the airplane will glide farther.

MORE ABOUT HYPOTHESES

- The results of an experiment cannot prove that a hypothesis is correct. Rather, the results either support or do not support the hypothesis.

- Valuable information is gained even when your hypothesis is not supported by your results. For example, it would be an important discovery to find that wing size is not related to how far an airplane glides.

- In science, a hypothesis is supported only after many scientists have conducted many experiments and produced consistent results.

Inferring

An **inference** is a logical conclusion drawn from the available evidence and prior knowledge. Inferences are often made from observations.

EXAMPLE

A student observing a set of acorns noticed something unexpected about one of them. He noticed a white, soft-bodied insect eating its way out of the acorn.

The student recorded these observations.

Observations

- There is a hole in the acorn, about 0.5 cm in diameter, where the insect crawled out.
- There is a second hole, which is about the size of a pinhole, on the other side of the acorn.
- The inside of the acorn is hollow.

Here are some inferences that can be made on the basis of the observations.

Inferences

- The insect formed from the material inside the acorn, grew to its present size, and ate its way out of the acorn.
- The insect crawled through the smaller hole, ate the inside of the acorn, grew to its present size, and ate its way out of the acorn.
- An egg was laid in the acorn through the smaller hole. The egg hatched into a larva that ate the inside of the acorn, grew to its present size, and ate its way out of the acorn.

When you make inferences, be sure to look at all of the evidence available and combine it with what you already know.

MORE ABOUT INFERENCES

Inferences depend both on observations and on the knowledge of the people making the inferences. Ancient people who did not know that organisms are produced only by similar organisms might have made an inference like the first one. A student today might look at the same observations and make the second inference. A third student might have knowledge about this particular insect and know that it is never small enough to fit through the smaller hole, leading her to the third inference.

Identifying Cause and Effect

In a **cause-and-effect relationship,** one event or characteristic is the result of another. Usually an effect follows its cause in time.

There are many examples of cause-and-effect relationships in everyday life.

Cause	Effect
Turn off a light.	Room gets dark.
Drop a glass.	Glass breaks.
Blow a whistle.	Sound is heard.

Scientists must be careful not to infer a cause-and-effect relationship just because one event happens after another event. When one event occurs after another, you cannot infer a cause-and-effect relationship on the basis of that information alone. You also cannot conclude that one event caused another if there are alternative ways to explain the second event. A scientist must demonstrate through experimentation or continued observation that an event was truly caused by another event.

EXAMPLE

Make an Observation

Suppose you have a few plants growing outside. When the weather starts getting colder, you bring one of the plants indoors. You notice that the plant you brought indoors is growing faster than the others are growing. You cannot conclude from your observation that the change in temperature was the cause of the increased plant growth, because there are alternative explanations for the observation. Some possible explanations are given below.

- The humidity indoors caused the plant to grow faster.

- The level of sunlight indoors caused the plant to grow faster.

- The indoor plant's being noticed more often and watered more often than the outdoor plants caused it to grow faster.

- The plant that was brought indoors was healthier than the other plants to begin with.

To determine which of these factors, if any, caused the indoor plant to grow faster than the outdoor plants, you would need to design and conduct an experiment.

See pages R28–R35 for information about designing experiments.

Recognizing Bias

Television, newspapers, and the Internet are full of experts claiming to have scientific evidence to back up their claims. How do you know whether the claims are really backed up by good science?

Bias is a slanted point of view, or personal prejudice. The goal of scientists is to be as objective as possible and to base their findings on facts instead of opinions. However, bias often affects the conclusions of researchers, and it is important to learn to recognize bias.

When scientific results are reported, you should consider the source of the information as well as the information itself. It is important to critically analyze the information that you see and read.

SOURCES OF BIAS

There are several ways in which a report of scientific information may be biased. Here are some questions that you can ask yourself:

1. Who is sponsoring the research?

Sometimes, the results of an investigation are biased because an organization paying for the research is looking for a specific answer. This type of bias can affect how data are gathered and interpreted.

2. Is the research sample large enough?

Sometimes research does not include enough data. The larger the sample size, the more likely that the results are accurate, assuming a truly random sample.

3. In a survey, who is answering the questions?

The results of a survey or poll can be biased. The people taking part in the survey may have been specifically chosen because of how they would answer. They may have the same ideas or lifestyles. A survey or poll should make use of a random sample of people.

4. Are the people who take part in a survey biased?

People who take part in surveys sometimes try to answer the questions the way they think the researcher wants them to answer. Also, in surveys or polls that ask for personal information, people may be unwilling to answer questions truthfully.

SCIENTIFIC BIAS

It is also important to realize that scientists have their own biases because of the types of research they do and because of their scientific viewpoints. Two scientists may look at the same set of data and come to completely different conclusions because of these biases. However, such disagreements are not necessarily bad. In fact, a critical analysis of disagreements is often responsible for moving science forward.

Identifying Faulty Reasoning

Faulty reasoning is wrong or incorrect thinking. It leads to mistakes and to wrong conclusions. Scientists are careful not to draw unreasonable conclusions from experimental data. Without such caution, the results of scientific investigations may be misleading.

EXAMPLE

Scientists try to make generalizations based on their data to explain as much about nature as possible. If only a small sample of data is looked at, however, a conclusion may be faulty. Suppose a scientist has studied the effects of the El Niño and La Niña weather patterns on flood damage in California from 1989 to 1995. The scientist organized the data in the bar graph below.

The scientist drew the following conclusions:

1. The La Niña weather pattern has no effect on flooding in California.

2. When neither weather pattern occurs, there is almost no flood damage.

3. A weak or moderate El Niño produces a small or moderate amount of flooding.

4. A strong El Niño produces a lot of flooding.

Flood and Storm Damage in California

Estimated damage (millions of dollars)

Legend:
- Weak–moderate El Niño
- Strong El Niño

Starting year of season
(July 1–June 30)

SOURCE: *Governor's Office of Emergency Services, California*

For the six-year period of the scientist's investigation, these conclusions may seem to be reasonable. However, a six-year study of weather patterns may be too small of a sample for the conclusions to be supported. Consider the following graph, which shows information that was gathered from 1949 to 1997.

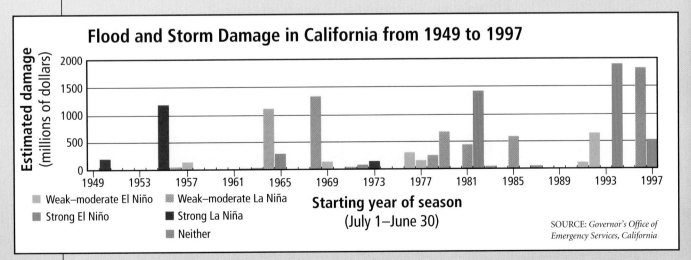

Flood and Storm Damage in California from 1949 to 1997

Estimated damage (millions of dollars)

Legend:
- Weak–moderate El Niño
- Strong El Niño
- Weak–moderate La Niña
- Strong La Niña
- Neither

Starting year of season
(July 1–June 30)

SOURCE: *Governor's Office of Emergency Services, California*

The only one of the conclusions that all of this information supports is number 3: a weak or moderate El Niño produces a small or moderate amount of flooding. By collecting more data, scientists can be more certain of their conclusions and can avoid faulty reasoning.

Analyzing Statements

To **analyze** a statement is to examine its parts carefully. Scientific findings are often reported through media such as television or the Internet. A report that is made public often focuses on only a small part of research. As a result, it is important to question the sources of information.

Evaluate Media Claims

To **evaluate** a statement is to judge it on the basis of criteria you've established. Sometimes evaluating means deciding whether a statement is true.

Reports of scientific research and findings in the media may be misleading or incomplete. When you are exposed to this information, you should ask yourself some questions so that you can make informed judgments about the information.

1. Does the information come from a credible source?

   Suppose you learn about a new product and it is stated that scientific evidence proves that the product works. A report from a respected news source may be more believable than an advertisement paid for by the product's manufacturer.

2. How much evidence supports the claim?

   Often, it may seem that there is new evidence every day of something in the world that either causes or cures an illness. However, information that is the result of several years of work by several different scientists is more credible than an advertisement that does not even cite the subjects of the experiment.

3. How much information is being presented?

   Science cannot solve all questions, and scientific experiments often have flaws. A report that discusses problems in a scientific study may be more believable than a report that addresses only positive experimental findings.

4. Is scientific evidence being presented by a specific source?

   Sometimes scientific findings are reported by people who are called experts or leaders in a scientific field. But if their names are not given or their scientific credentials are not reported, their statements may be less credible than those of recognized experts.

Differentiate Between Fact and Opinion

Sometimes information is presented as a fact when it may be an opinion. When scientific conclusions are reported, it is important to recognize whether they are based on solid evidence. Again, you may find it helpful to ask yourself some questions.

1. **What is the difference between a fact and an opinion?**

   A **fact** is a piece of information that can be strictly defined and proved true. An **opinion** is a statement that expresses a belief, value, or feeling. An opinion cannot be proved true or false. For example, a person's age is a fact, but if someone is asked how old they feel, it is impossible to prove the person's answer to be true or false.

2. **Can opinions be measured?**

   Yes, opinions can be measured. In fact, surveys often ask for people's opinions on a topic. But there is no way to know whether or not an opinion is the truth.

HOW TO DIFFERENTIATE FACT FROM OPINION

Human Activities and the Environment

Unfortunately, human use of fossil fuels is one of the most significant developments of the past few centuries. Humans rely on fossil fuels, a non-renewable energy resource, for more than 90 percent of their energy needs.

This careless misuse of our planet's resources has resulted in pollution, global warming, and the destruction of fragile ecosystems. For example, oil pipelines carry more than one million barrels of oil each day across tundra regions. Transporting oil across such areas can only result in oil spills that poison the land for decades.

Opinions

Notice words or phrases that express beliefs or feelings. The words *unfortunately* and *careless* show that opinions are being expressed.

Opinion

Look for statements that speculate about events. These statements are opinions, because they cannot be proved.

Facts

Statements that contain statistics tend to be facts. Writers often use facts to support their opinions.

Lab Handbook

Safety Rules

Before you work in the laboratory, read these safety rules twice. Ask your teacher to explain any rules that you do not completely understand. Refer to these rules later on if you have questions about safety in the science classroom.

Directions

- Read all directions and make sure that you understand them before starting an investigation or lab activity. If you do not understand how to do a procedure or how to use a piece of equipment, ask your teacher.
- Do not begin any investigation or touch any equipment until your teacher has told you to start.
- Never experiment on your own. If you want to try a procedure that the directions do not call for, ask your teacher for permission first.
- If you are hurt or injured in any way, tell your teacher immediately.

Dress Code

goggles

apron

gloves

- Wear goggles when
  - — using glassware, sharp objects, or chemicals
  - — heating an object
  - — working with anything that can easily fly up into the air and hurt someone's eye
- Tie back long hair or hair that hangs in front of your eyes.
- Remove any article of clothing—such as a loose sweater or a scarf—that hangs down and may touch a flame, chemical, or piece of equipment.
- Observe all safety icons calling for the wearing of eye protection, gloves, and aprons.

Heating and Fire Safety

fire safety

heating safety

- Keep your work area neat, clean, and free of extra materials.
- Never reach over a flame or heat source.
- Point objects being heated away from you and others.
- Never heat a substance or an object in a closed container.
- Never touch an object that has been heated. If you are unsure whether something is hot, treat it as though it is. Use oven mitts, clamps, tongs, or a test-tube holder.
- Know where the fire extinguisher and fire blanket are kept in your classroom.
- Do not throw hot substances into the trash. Wait for them to cool or use the container your teacher puts out for disposal.

Electrical Safety

electrical
safety

- Never use lamps or other electrical equipment with frayed cords.
- Make sure no cord is lying on the floor where someone can trip over it.
- Do not let a cord hang over the side of a counter or table so that the equipment can easily be pulled or knocked to the floor.
- Never let cords hang into sinks or other places where water can be found.
- Never try to fix electrical problems. Inform your teacher of any problems immediately.
- Unplug an electrical cord by pulling on the plug, not the cord.

Chemical Safety

chemical
safety

poison

fumes

- If you spill a chemical or get one on your skin or in your eyes, tell your teacher right away.
- Never touch, taste, or sniff any chemicals in the lab. If you need to determine odor, waft. Wafting consists of holding the chemical in its container 15 centimeters (6 in.) away from your nose, and using your fingers to bring fumes from the container to your nose.
- Keep lids on all chemicals you are not using.
- Never put unused chemicals back into the original containers. Throw away extra chemicals where your teacher tells you to.
- Pour chemicals over a sink or your work area, not over the floor.
- If you get a chemical in your eye, use the eyewash right away.
- Always wash your hands after handling chemicals, plants, or soil.

Wafting

Glassware and Sharp-Object Safety

sharp
objects

- If you break glassware, tell your teacher right away.
- Do not use broken or chipped glassware. Give these to your teacher.
- Use knives and other cutting instruments carefully. Always wear eye protection and cut away from you.

Animal Safety

- Never hurt an animal.
- Touch animals only when necessary. Follow your teacher's instructions for handling animals.
- Always wash your hands after working with animals.

Cleanup

disposal

- Follow your teacher's instructions for throwing away or putting away supplies.
- Clean your work area and pick up anything that has dropped to the floor.
- Wash your hands.

Using Lab Equipment

Different experiments require different types of equipment. But even though experiments differ, the ways in which the equipment is used are the same.

Beakers

- Use beakers for holding and pouring liquids.
- Do not use a beaker to measure the volume of a liquid. Use a graduated cylinder instead. (See page R16.)
- Use a beaker that holds about twice as much liquid as you need. For example, if you need 100 milliliters of water, you should use a 200- or 250-milliliter beaker.

Test Tubes

- Use test tubes to hold small amounts of substances.
- Do not use a test tube to measure the volume of a liquid.
- Use a test tube when heating a substance over a flame. Aim the mouth of the tube away from yourself and other people.
- Liquids easily spill or splash from test tubes, so it is important to use only small amounts of liquids.

Test-Tube Holder

- Use a test-tube holder when heating a substance in a test tube.
- Use a test-tube holder if the substance in a test tube is dangerous to touch.
- Make sure the test-tube holder tightly grips the test tube so that the test tube will not slide out of the holder.
- Make sure that the test-tube holder is above the surface of the substance in the test tube so that you can observe the substance.

Test-Tube Rack

- Use a test-tube rack to organize test tubes before, during, and after an experiment.

- Use a test-tube rack to keep test tubes upright so that they do not fall over and spill their contents.

- Use a test-tube rack that is the correct size for the test tubes that you are using. If the rack is too small, a test tube may become stuck. If the rack is too large, a test tube may lean over, and some of its contents may spill or splash.

Forceps

- Use forceps when you need to pick up or hold a very small object that should not be touched with your hands.

- Do not use forceps to hold anything over a flame, because forceps are not long enough to keep your hand safely away from the flame. Plastic forceps will melt, and metal forceps will conduct heat and burn your hand.

Hot Plate

- Use a hot plate when a substance needs to be kept warmer than room temperature for a long period of time.

- Use a hot plate instead of a Bunsen burner or a candle when you need to carefully control temperature.

- Do not use a hot plate when a substance needs to be burned in an experiment.

- Always use "hot hands" safety mitts or oven mitts when handling anything that has been heated on a hot plate.

Microscope

Scientists use microscopes to see very small objects that cannot easily be seen with the eye alone. A microscope magnifies the image of an object so that small details may be observed. A microscope that you may use can magnify an object 400 times—the object will appear 400 times larger than its actual size.

Eyepiece Objects are viewed through the eyepiece. The eyepiece contains a lens that commonly magnifies an image 10 times.

Coarse Adjustment This knob is used to focus the image of an object when it is viewed through the low-power lens.

Fine Adjustment This knob is used to focus the image of an object when it is viewed through the high-power lens.

Low-Power Objective Lens This is the smallest lens on the nosepiece. It magnifies an image approximately 10 times.

Arm The arm supports the body above the stage. Always carry a microscope by the arm and base.

Stage Clip The stage clip holds a slide in place on the stage.

Base The base supports the microscope.

Body The body separates the lens in the eyepiece from the objective lenses below.

Nosepiece The nosepiece holds the objective lenses above the stage and rotates so that all lenses may be used.

High-Power Objective Lens This is the largest lens on the nosepiece. It magnifies an image approximately 40 times.

Stage The stage supports the object being viewed.

Diaphragm The diaphragm is used to adjust the amount of light passing through the slide and into an objective lens.

Mirror or Light Source Some microscopes use light that is reflected through the stage by a mirror. Other microscopes have their own light sources.

VIEWING AN OBJECT

1. Use the coarse adjustment knob to raise the body tube.

2. Adjust the diaphragm so that you can see a bright circle of light through the eyepiece.

3. Place the object or slide on the stage. Be sure that it is centered over the hole in the stage.

4. Turn the nosepiece to click the low-power lens into place.

5. Using the coarse adjustment knob, slowly lower the lens and focus on the specimen being viewed. Be sure not to touch the slide or object with the lens.

6. When switching from the low-power lens to the high-power lens, first raise the body tube with the coarse adjustment knob so that the high-power lens will not hit the slide.

7. Turn the nosepiece to click the high-power lens into place.

8. Use the fine adjustment knob to focus on the specimen being viewed. Again, be sure not to touch the slide or object with the lens.

MAKING A SLIDE, OR WET MOUNT

1 Place the specimen in the center of a clean slide.

2 Place a drop of water on the specimen.

3 Place a cover slip on the slide. Put one edge of the cover slip into the drop of water and slowly lower it over the specimen.

4 Remove any air bubbles from under the cover slip by gently tapping the cover slip.

5 Dry any excess water before placing the slide on the microscope stage for viewing.

Spring Scale (Force Meter)

- Use a spring scale to measure a force pulling on the scale.
- Use a spring scale to measure the force of gravity exerted on an object by Earth.
- To measure a force accurately, a spring scale must be zeroed before it is used. The scale is zeroed when no weight is attached and the indicator is positioned at zero.
- Do not attach a weight that is either too heavy or too light to a spring scale. A weight that is too heavy could break the scale or exert too great a force for the scale to measure. A weight that is too light may not exert enough force to be measured accurately.

Graduated Cylinder

- Use a graduated cylinder to measure the volume of a liquid.
- Be sure that the graduated cylinder is on a flat surface so that your measurement will be accurate.
- When reading the scale on a graduated cylinder, be sure to have your eyes at the level of the surface of the liquid.
- The surface of the liquid will be curved in the graduated cylinder. Read the volume of the liquid at the bottom of the curve, or meniscus (muh-NIHS-kuhs).
- You can use a graduated cylinder to find the volume of a solid object by measuring the increase in a liquid's level after you add the object to the cylinder.

meniscus

Read the volume at the bottom of the meniscus. The volume is 96 mL.

Metric Rulers

- Use metric rulers or meter sticks to measure objects' lengths.

- Do not measure an object from the end of a metric ruler or meter stick, because the end is often imperfect. Instead, measure from the 1-centimeter mark, but remember to subtract a centimeter from the apparent measurement.

- Estimate any lengths that extend between marked units. For example, if a meter stick shows centimeters but not millimeters, you can estimate the length that an object extends between centimeter marks to measure it to the nearest millimeter.

- **Controlling Variables** If you are taking repeated measurements, always measure from the same point each time. For example, if you're measuring how high two different balls bounce when dropped from the same height, measure both bounces at the same point on the balls—either the top or the bottom. Do not measure at the top of one ball and the bottom of the other.

EXAMPLE

How to Measure a Leaf

1. Lay a ruler flat on top of the leaf so that the 1-centimeter mark lines up with one end. Make sure the ruler and the leaf do not move between the time you line them up and the time you take the measurement.

2. Look straight down on the ruler so that you can see exactly how the marks line up with the other end of the leaf.

3. Estimate the length by which the leaf extends beyond a marking. For example, the leaf below extends about halfway between the 4.2-centimeter and 4.3-centimeter marks, so the apparent measurement is about 4.25 centimeters.

4. Remember to subtract 1 centimeter from your apparent measurement, since you started at the 1-centimeter mark on the ruler and not at the end. The leaf is about 3.25 centimeters long (4.25 cm – 1 cm = 3.25 cm).

Triple-Beam Balance

This balance has a pan and three beams with sliding masses, called riders. At one end of the beams is a pointer that indicates whether the mass on the pan is equal to the masses shown on the beams.

1. Make sure the balance is zeroed before measuring the mass of an object. The balance is zeroed if the pointer is at zero when nothing is on the pan and the riders are at their zero points. Use the adjustment knob at the base of the balance to zero it.

2. Place the object to be measured on the pan.

3. Move the riders one notch at a time away from the pan. Begin with the largest rider. If moving the largest rider one notch brings the pointer below zero, begin measuring the mass of the object with the next smaller rider.

4. Change the positions of the riders until they balance the mass on the pan and the pointer is at zero. Then add the readings from the three beams to determine the mass of the object.

300 g	position of largest rider
90 g	position of middle rider
+ 3 g	position of smallest rider
393 g	mass of beaker

pan

beams

largest rider (300 g)

middle rider (90 g)

smallest rider (3 g)

Double-Pan Balance

This type of balance has two pans. Between the pans is a pointer that indicates whether the masses on the pans are equal.

1. Make sure the balance is zeroed before measuring the mass of an object. The balance is zeroed if the pointer is at zero when there is nothing on either of the pans. Many double-pan balances have sliding knobs that can be used to zero them.

2. Place the object to be measured on one of the pans.

3. Begin adding standard masses to the other pan. Begin with the largest standard mass. If this adds too much mass to the balance, begin measuring the mass of the object with the next smaller standard mass.

4. Add standard masses until the masses on both pans are balanced and the pointer is at zero. Then add the standard masses together to determine the mass of the object being measured.

LAB HANDBOOK

```
        200 g
        100 g
         50 g
         20 g
         20 g
          2 g
      +   1 g
      ─────────
        393 g  mass of beaker
```

Never place chemicals or liquids directly on a pan. Instead, use the following procedure:

1. Determine the mass of an empty container, such as a beaker.

2. Pour the substance into the container, and measure the total mass of the substance and the container.

3. Subtract the mass of the empty container from the total mass to find the mass of the substance.

The Metric System and SI Units

Scientists use International System (SI) units for measurements of distance, volume, mass, and temperature. The International System is based on multiples of ten and the metric system of measurement.

Basic SI Units		
Property	**Name**	**Symbol**
length	meter	m
volume	liter	L
mass	kilogram	kg
temperature	kelvin	K

SI Prefixes		
Prefix	**Symbol**	**Multiple of 10**
kilo-	k	1000
hecto-	h	100
deca-	da	10
deci-	d	$0.1 \left(\frac{1}{10}\right)$
centi-	c	$0.01 \left(\frac{1}{100}\right)$
milli-	m	$0.001 \left(\frac{1}{1000}\right)$

Changing Metric Units

You can change from one unit to another in the metric system by multiplying or dividing by a power of 10.

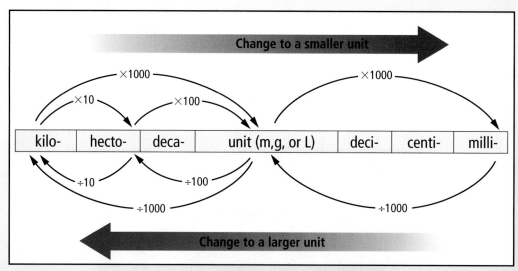

Example

Change 0.64 liters to milliliters.

(1) Decide whether to multiply or divide.

(2) Select the power of 10.

ANSWER 0.64 L = 640 mL

Change to a smaller unit by multiplying.

L ——— × 1000 ———→ mL

0.64 × 1000 = 640.

Example

Change 23.6 grams to kilograms.

(1) Decide whether to multiply or divide.

(2) Select the power of 10.

ANSWER 23.6 g = 0.0236 kg

Change to a larger unit by dividing.

kg ←——— ÷ 1000 ——— g

23.6 ÷ 1000 = 0.0236

Temperature Conversions

Even though the kelvin is the SI base unit of temperature, the degree Celsius will be the unit you use most often in your science studies. The formulas below show the relationships between temperatures in degrees Fahrenheit (°F), degrees Celsius (°C), and kelvins (K).

$$°C = \frac{5}{9}(°F - 32)$$

$$°F = \frac{9}{5}°C + 32$$

$$K = °C + 273$$

See page R42 for help with using formulas.

Examples of Temperature Conversions		
Condition	Degrees Celsius	Degrees Fahrenheit
Freezing point of water	0	32
Cool day	10	50
Mild day	20	68
Warm day	30	86
Normal body temperature	37	98.6
Very hot day	40	104
Boiling point of water	100	212

Converting Between SI and U.S. Customary Units

Use the chart below when you need to convert between SI units and U.S. customary units.

SI Unit	From SI to U.S. Customary			From U.S. Customary to SI		
Length	When you know	multiply by	to find	When you know	multiply by	to find
kilometer (km) = 1000 m	kilometers	0.62	miles	miles	1.61	kilometers
meter (m) = 100 cm	meters	3.28	feet	feet	0.3048	meters
centimeter (cm) = 10 mm	centimeters	0.39	inches	inches	2.54	centimeters
millimeter (mm) = 0.1 cm	millimeters	0.04	inches	inches	25.4	millimeters
Area	When you know	multiply by	to find	When you know	multiply by	to find
square kilometer (km^2)	square kilometers	0.39	square miles	square miles	2.59	square kilometers
square meter (m^2)	square meters	1.2	square yards	square yards	0.84	square meters
square centimeter (cm^2)	square centimeters	0.155	square inches	square inches	6.45	square centimeters
Volume	When you know	multiply by	to find	When you know	multiply by	to find
liter (L) = 1000 mL	liters	1.06	quarts	quarts	0.95	liters
	liters	0.26	gallons	gallons	3.79	liters
	liters	4.23	cups	cups	0.24	liters
	liters	2.12	pints	pints	0.47	liters
milliliter (mL) = 0.001 L	milliliters	0.20	teaspoons	teaspoons	4.93	milliliters
	milliliters	0.07	tablespoons	tablespoons	14.79	milliliters
	milliliters	0.03	fluid ounces	fluid ounces	29.57	milliliters
Mass	When you know	multiply by	to find	When you know	multiply by	to find
kilogram (kg) = 1000 g	kilograms	2.2	pounds	pounds	0.45	kilograms
gram (g) = 1000 mg	grams	0.035	ounces	ounces	28.35	grams

Precision and Accuracy

When you do an experiment, it is important that your methods, observations, and data be both precise and accurate.

low precision

precision, but not accuracy

precision and accuracy

Precision

In science, **precision** is the exactness and consistency of measurements. For example, measurements made with a ruler that has both centimeter and millimeter markings would be more precise than measurements made with a ruler that has only centimeter markings. Another indicator of precision is the care taken to make sure that methods and observations are as exact and consistent as possible. Every time a particular experiment is done, the same procedure should be used. Precision is necessary because experiments are repeated several times and if the procedure changes, the results will change.

EXAMPLE

Suppose you are measuring temperatures over a two-week period. Your precision will be greater if you measure each temperature at the same place, at the same time of day, and with the same thermometer than if you change any of these factors from one day to the next.

Accuracy

In science, it is possible to be precise but not accurate. **Accuracy** depends on the difference between a measurement and an actual value. The smaller the difference, the more accurate the measurement.

EXAMPLE

Suppose you look at a stream and estimate that it is about 1 meter wide at a particular place. You decide to check your estimate by measuring the stream with a meter stick, and you determine that the stream is 1.32 meters wide. However, because it is hard to measure the width of a stream with a meter stick, it turns out that you didn't do a very good job. The stream is actually 1.14 meters wide. Therefore, even though your estimate was less precise than your measurement, your estimate was actually more accurate.

Making Data Tables and Graphs

Data tables and graphs are useful tools for both recording and communicating scientific data.

Making Data Tables

You can use a **data table** to organize and record the measurements that you make. Some examples of information that might be recorded in data tables are frequencies, times, and amounts.

EXAMPLE

Suppose you are investigating photosynthesis in two elodea plants. One sits in direct sunlight, and the other sits in a dimly lit room. You measure the rate of photosynthesis by counting the number of bubbles in the jar every ten minutes.

1. Title and number your data table.
2. Decide how you will organize the table into columns and rows.
3. Any units, such as seconds or degrees, should be included in column headings, not in the individual cells.

Table 1. Number of Bubbles from Elodea

Time (min)	Sunlight	Dim Light
0	0	0
10	15	5
20	25	8
30	32	7
40	41	10
50	47	9
60	42	9

◀ Always number and title data tables.

The data in the table above could also be organized in a different way.

Table 1. Number of Bubbles from Elodea

Light Condition	Time (min)						
	0	10	20	30	40	50	60
Sunlight	0	15	25	32	41	47	42
Dim light	0	5	8	7	10	9	9

◀ Put units in column heading.

Making Line Graphs

You can use a **line graph** to show a relationship between variables. Line graphs are particularly useful for showing changes in variables over time.

EXAMPLE

Suppose you are interested in graphing temperature data that you collected over the course of a day.

Table 1. Outside Temperature During the Day on March 7

	Time of Day						
	7:00 A.M.	9:00 A.M.	11:00 A.M.	1:00 P.M.	3:00 P.M.	5:00 P.M.	7:00 P.M.
Temp (°C)	8	9	11	14	12	10	6

1. Use the vertical axis of your line graph for the variable that you are measuring—temperature.

2. Choose scales for both the horizontal axis and the vertical axis of the graph. You should have two points more than you need on the vertical axis, and the horizontal axis should be long enough for all of the data points to fit.

3. Draw and label each axis.

4. Graph each value. First find the appropriate point on the scale of the horizontal axis. Imagine a line that rises vertically from that place on the scale. Then find the corresponding value on the vertical axis, and imagine a line that moves horizontally from that value. The point where these two imaginary lines intersect is where the value should be plotted.

5. Connect the points with straight lines.

Be sure to add a number and a title to your graph.

Figure 1. Outside Temperature During the Day on March 7

vertical axis

horizontal axis

Making Circle Graphs

You can use a **circle graph,** sometimes called a pie chart, to represent data as parts of a circle. Circle graphs are used only when the data can be expressed as percentages of a whole. The entire circle shown in a circle graph is equal to 100 percent of the data.

EXAMPLE

Suppose you identified the species of each mature tree growing in a small wooded area. You organized your data in a table, but you also want to show the data in a circle graph.

1. To begin, find the total number of mature trees.

    $56 + 34 + 22 + 10 + 28 = 150$

2. To find the degree measure for each sector of the circle, write a fraction comparing the number of each tree species with the total number of trees. Then multiply the fraction by 360°.

    Oak: $\frac{56}{150} \times 360° = 134.4°$

3. Draw a circle. Use a protractor to draw the angle for each sector of the graph.

4. Color and label each sector of the graph.

5. Give the graph a number and title.

Table 1. Tree Species in Wooded Area

Species	Number of Specimens
Oak	56
Maple	34
Birch	22
Willow	10
Pine	28

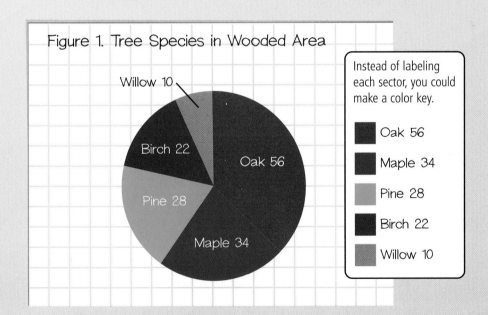

Figure 1. Tree Species in Wooded Area

Willow 10
Birch 22
Pine 28
Oak 56
Maple 34

Instead of labeling each sector, you could make a color key.

Oak 56
Maple 34
Pine 28
Birch 22
Willow 10

Bar Graph

A **bar graph** is a type of graph in which the lengths of the bars are used to represent and compare data. A numerical scale is used to determine the lengths of the bars.

EXAMPLE

To determine the effect of water on seed sprouting, three cups were filled with sand, and ten seeds were planted in each. Different amounts of water were added to each cup over a three-day period.

Table 1. Effect of Water on Seed Sprouting

Daily Amount of Water (mL)	Number of Seeds That Sprouted After 3 Days in Sand
0	1
10	4
20	8

1. Choose a numerical scale. The greatest value is 8, so the end of the scale should have a value greater than 8, such as 10. Use equal increments along the scale, such as increments of 2.

2. Draw and label the axes. Mark intervals on the vertical axis according to the scale you chose.

3. Draw a bar for each data value. Use the scale to decide how long to make each bar.

Figure 1. Effect of Water on Seed Sprouting

Be sure to add a number and a title.

Number of sprouting seeds

Water added each day (mL)

Label the scale.

Label each bar.

Double Bar Graph

A **double bar graph** is a bar graph that shows two sets of data. The two bars for each measurement are drawn next to each other.

EXAMPLE

The seed-sprouting experiment was done using both sand and potting soil. The data for sand and potting soil can be plotted on one graph.

1. Draw one set of bars, using the data for sand, as shown below.

2. Draw bars for the potting-soil data next to the bars for the sand data. Shade them a different color. Add a key.

Table 2. Effect of Water and Soil on Seed Sprouting

Daily Amount of Water (mL)	Number of Seeds That Sprouted After 3 Days in Sand	Number of Seeds That Sprouted After 3 Days in Potting Soil
0	1	2
10	4	5
20	8	9

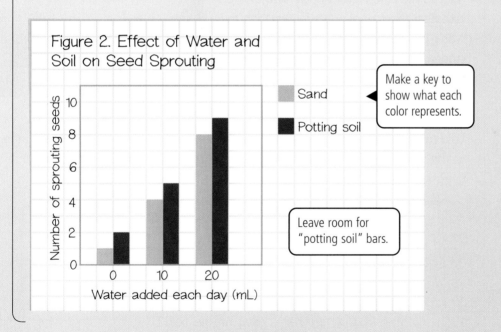

Figure 2. Effect of Water and Soil on Seed Sprouting

Make a key to show what each color represents.

Leave room for "potting soil" bars.

Designing an Experiment

Use this section when designing or conducting an experiment.

Determining a Purpose

You can find a purpose for an experiment by doing research, by examining the results of a previous experiment, or by observing the world around you. An **experiment** is an organized procedure to study something under controlled conditions.

1. Write the purpose of your experiment as a question or problem that you want to investigate.
2. Write down research questions and begin searching for information that will help you design an experiment. Consult the library, the Internet, and other people as you conduct your research.

> Don't forget to learn as much as possible about your topic before you begin.

EXAMPLE

Middle school students observed an odor near the lake by their school. They also noticed that the water on the side of the lake near the school was greener than the water on the other side of the lake. The students did some research to learn more about their observations. They discovered that the odor and green color in the lake came from algae. They also discovered that a new fertilizer was being used on a field nearby. The students inferred that the use of the fertilizer might be related to the presence of the algae and designed a controlled experiment to find out whether they were right.

Problem

How does fertilizer affect the presence of algae in a lake?

Research Questions

- Have other experiments been done on this problem? If so, what did those experiments show?
- What kind of fertilizer is used on the field? How much?
- How do algae grow?
- How do people measure algae?
- Can fertilizer and algae be used safely in a lab? How?

> **Research**
> As you research, you may find a topic that is more interesting to you than your original topic, or learn that a procedure you wanted to use is not practical or safe. It is OK to change your purpose as you research.

Writing a Hypothesis

A **hypothesis** is a tentative explanation for an observation or scientific problem that can be tested by further investigation. You can write your hypothesis in the form of an "If . . . , then . . . , because . . ." statement.

Hypothesis

If the amount of fertilizer in lake water is increased, then the amount of algae will also increase, because fertilizers provide nutrients that algae need to grow.

Hypotheses
For help with hypotheses, refer to page R3.

Determining Materials

Make a list of all the materials you will need to do your experiment. Be specific, especially if someone else is helping you obtain the materials. Try to think of everything you will need.

Materials

- 1 large jar or container
- 4 identical smaller containers
- rubber gloves that also cover the arms
- sample of fertilizer-and-water solution
- eyedropper
- clear plastic wrap
- scissors
- masking tape
- marker
- ruler

Determining Variables and Constants

EXPERIMENTAL GROUP AND CONTROL GROUP

An experiment to determine how two factors are related always has two groups—a control group and an experimental group.

1. Design an experimental group. Include as many trials as possible in the experimental group in order to obtain reliable results.

2. Design a control group that is the same as the experimental group in every way possible, except for the factor you wish to test.

Experimental Group: two containers of lake water with one drop of fertilizer solution added to each

Control Group: two containers of lake water with no fertilizer solution added

Go back to your materials list and make sure you have enough items listed to cover both your experimental group and your control group.

VARIABLES AND CONSTANTS

Identify the variables and constants in your experiment. In a controlled experiment, a **variable** is any factor that can change. **Constants** are all of the factors that are the same in both the experimental group and the control group.

1. Read your hypothesis. The **independent variable** is the factor that you wish to test and that is manipulated or changed so that it can be tested. The independent variable is expressed in your hypothesis after the word *if*. Identify the independent variable in your laboratory report.

2. The **dependent variable** is the factor that you measure to gather results. It is expressed in your hypothesis after the word *then*. Identify the dependent variable in your laboratory report.

Hypothesis
If the amount of fertilizer in lake water is increased, then the amount of algae will also increase, because fertilizers provide nutrients that algae need to grow.

Table 1. Variables and Constants in Algae Experiment

Independent Variable	Dependent Variable	Constants
Amount of fertilizer in lake water	Amount of algae that grow	• Where the lake water is obtained • Type of container used • Light and temperature conditions where water will be stored

Set up your experiment so that you will test only one variable.

MEASURING THE DEPENDENT VARIABLE

Before starting your experiment, you need to define how you will measure the dependent variable. An **operational definition** is a description of the one particular way in which you will measure the dependent variable.

Your operational definition is important for several reasons. First, in any experiment there are several ways in which a dependent variable can be measured. Second, the procedure of the experiment depends on how you decide to measure the dependent variable. Third, your operational definition makes it possible for other people to evaluate and build on your experiment.

EXAMPLE 1

An operational definition of a dependent variable can be qualitative. That is, your measurement of the dependent variable can simply be an observation of whether a change occurs as a result of a change in the independent variable. This type of operational definition can be thought of as a "yes or no" measurement.

Table 2. Qualitative Operational Definition of Algae Growth

Independent Variable	Dependent Variable	Operational Definition
Amount of fertilizer in lake water	Amount of algae that grow	Algae grow in lake water

A qualitative measurement of a dependent variable is often easy to make and record. However, this type of information does not provide a great deal of detail in your experimental results.

EXAMPLE 2

An operational definition of a dependent variable can be quantitative. That is, your measurement of the dependent variable can be a number that shows how much change occurs as a result of a change in the independent variable.

Table 3. Quantitative Operational Definition of Algae Growth

Independent Variable	Dependent Variable	Operational Definition
Amount of fertilizer in lake water	Amount of algae that grow	Diameter of largest algal growth (in mm)

A quantitative measurement of a dependent variable can be more difficult to make and analyze than a qualitative measurement. However, this type of data provides much more information about your experiment and is often more useful.

Writing a Procedure

Write each step of your procedure. Start each step with a verb, or action word, and keep the steps short. Your procedure should be clear enough for someone else to use as instructions for repeating your experiment.

> If necessary, go back to your materials list and add any materials that you left out.

Controlling Variables
The same amount of fertilizer solution must be added to two of the four containers.

Controlling Variables
All four containers must receive the same amount of light.

Procedure

1. Put on your gloves. Use the large container to obtain a sample of lake water.

2. Divide the sample of lake water equally among the four smaller containers.

3. Use the eyedropper to add one drop of fertilizer solution to two of the containers.

4. Use the masking tape and the marker to label the containers with your initials, the date, and the identifiers "Jar 1 with Fertilizer," "Jar 2 with Fertilizer," "Jar 1 without Fertilizer," and "Jar 2 without Fertilizer."

5. Cover the containers with clear plastic wrap. Use the scissors to punch ten holes in each of the covers.

6. Place all four containers on a window ledge. Make sure that they all receive the same amount of light.

7. Observe the containers every day for one week.

8. Use the ruler to measure the diameter of the largest clump of algae in each container, and record your measurements daily.

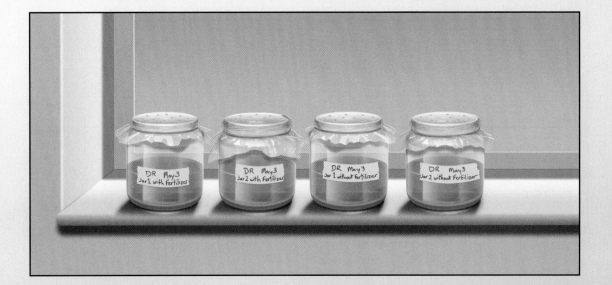

Recording Observations

Once you have obtained all of your materials and your procedure has been approved, you can begin making experimental observations. Gather both quantitative and qualitative data. If something goes wrong during your procedure, make sure you record that too.

Observations
For help with making qualitative and quantitative observations, refer to page R2.

For more examples of data tables, see page R23.

Table 4. Fertilizer and Algae Growth

	Experimental Group		Control Group		
Date and Time	Jar 1 with Fertilizer (diameter of algae in mm)	Jar 2 with Fertilizer (diameter of algae in mm)	Jar 1 without Fertilizer (diameter of algae in mm)	Jar 2 without Fertilizer (diameter of algae in mm)	Observations
5/3 4:00 P.M.	0	0	0	0	condensation in all containers
5/4 4:00 P.M.	0	3	0	0	tiny green blobs in jar 2 with fertilizer
5/5 4:15 P.M.	4	5	0	3	green blobs in jars 1 and 2 with fertilizer and jar 2 without fertilizer
5/6 4:00 P.M.	5	6	0	4	water light green in jar 2 with fertilizer
5/7 4:00 P.M.	8	10	0	6	water light green in jars 1 and 2 with fertilizer and in jar 2 without fertilizer
5/8 3:30 P.M.	10	18	0	6	cover off jar 2 with fertilizer
5/9 3:30 P.M.	14	23	0	8	drew sketches of each container

Notice that on the sixth day, the observer found that the cover was off one of the containers. It is important to record observations of unintended factors because they might affect the results of the experiment.

Use technology, such as a microscope, to help you make observations when possible.

Drawings of Samples Viewed Under Microscope on 5/9 at 100x

Jar 1 with Fertilizer

Jar 2 with Fertilizer

Jar 1 without Fertilizer

Jar 2 without Fertilizer

Summarizing Results

To summarize your data, look at all of your observations together. Look for meaningful ways to present your observations. For example, you might average your data or make a graph to look for patterns. When possible, use spreadsheet software to help you analyze and present your data. The two graphs below show the same data.

EXAMPLE 1

Figure 1. Fertilizer and Algae Growth

> Always include a number and a title with a graph.

> Line graphs are useful for showing changes over time. For help with line graphs, refer to page R24.

> Bar graphs are useful for comparing different data sets. This bar graph has four bars for each day. Another way to present the data would be to calculate averages for the tests and the controls, and to show one test bar and one control bar for each day.

EXAMPLE 2

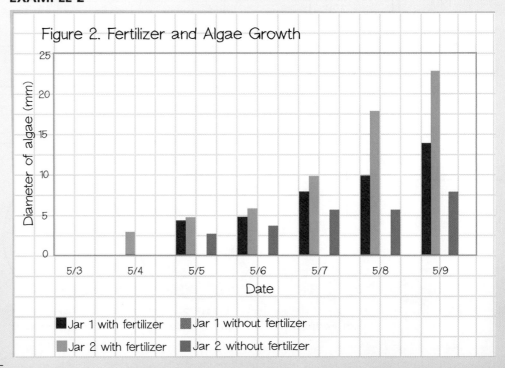

Figure 2. Fertilizer and Algae Growth

Drawing Conclusions

RESULTS AND INFERENCES

To draw conclusions from your experiment, first write your results. Then compare your results with your hypothesis. Do your results support your hypothesis? Be careful not to make inferences about factors that you did not test.

For help with making inferences, see page R4.

Results and Inferences

The results of my experiment show that more algae grew in lake water to which fertilizer had been added than in lake water to which no fertilizer had been added. My hypothesis was supported. I infer that it is possible that the growth of algae in the lake was caused by the fertilizer used on the field.

Notice that you cannot conclude from this experiment that the presence of algae in the lake was due only to the fertilizer.

QUESTIONS FOR FURTHER RESEARCH

Write a list of questions for further research and investigation. Your ideas may lead you to new experiments and discoveries.

Questions for Further Research

• What is the connection between the amount of fertilizer and algae growth?
• How do different brands of fertilizer affect algae growth?
• How would algae growth in the lake be affected if no fertilizer were used on the field?
• How do algae affect the lake and the other life in and around it?
• How does fertilizer affect the lake and the life in and around it?
• If fertilizer is getting into the lake, how is it getting there?

Math Handbook

Describing a Set of Data

Means, medians, modes, and ranges are important math tools for describing data sets such as the following widths of fossilized clamshells.

13 mm   25 mm   14 mm   21 mm   16 mm   23 mm   14 mm

Mean

The **mean** of a data set is the sum of the values divided by the number of values.

> **Example**
>
> To find the mean of the clamshell data, add the values and then divide the sum by the number of values.
>
> $$\frac{13\text{ mm} + 25\text{ mm} + 14\text{ mm} + 21\text{ mm} + 16\text{ mm} + 23\text{ mm} + 14\text{ mm}}{7} = \frac{126\text{ mm}}{7} = 18\text{ mm}$$
>
> **ANSWER** The mean is 18 mm.

Median

The **median** of a data set is the middle value when the values are written in numerical order. If a data set has an even number of values, the median is the mean of the two middle values.

> **Example**
>
> To find the median of the clamshell data, arrange the values in order from least to greatest. The median is the middle value.
>
> 13 mm   14 mm   14 mm   16 mm   21 mm   23 mm   25 mm
>
> **ANSWER** The median is 16 mm.

Mode

The **mode** of a data set is the value that occurs most often.

Example

To find the mode of the clamshell data, arrange the values in order from least to greatest and determine the value that occurs most often.

13 mm   14 mm   14 mm   16 mm   21 mm   23 mm   25 mm

ANSWER The mode is 14 mm.

A data set can have more than one mode or no mode. For example, the following data set has modes of 2 mm and 4 mm:

2 mm   2 mm   3 mm   4 mm   4 mm

The data set below has no mode, because no value occurs more often than any other.

2 mm   3 mm   4 mm   5 mm

Range

The **range** of a data set is the difference between the greatest value and the least value.

Example

To find the range of the clamshell data, arrange the values in order from least to greatest.

13 mm   14 mm   14 mm   16 mm   21 mm   23 mm   25 mm

Subtract the least value from the greatest value.

13 mm is the least value.
25 mm is the greatest value.

25 mm − 13 mm = 12 mm

ANSWER The range is 12 mm.

Using Ratios, Rates, and Proportions

You can use ratios and rates to compare values in data sets. You can use proportions to find unknown values.

Ratios

A **ratio** uses division to compare two values. The ratio of a value a to a nonzero value b can be written as $\frac{a}{b}$.

Example

The height of one plant is 8 centimeters. The height of another plant is 6 centimeters. To find the ratio of the height of the first plant to the height of the second plant, write a fraction and simplify it.

$$\frac{8 \text{ cm}}{6 \text{ cm}} = \frac{4 \times \overset{1}{\cancel{2}}}{3 \times \underset{1}{\cancel{2}}} = \frac{4}{3}$$

ANSWER The ratio of the plant heights is $\frac{4}{3}$.

You can also write the ratio $\frac{a}{b}$ as "a to b" or as $a:b$. For example, you can write the ratio of the plant heights as "4 to 3" or as $4:3$.

Rates

A **rate** is a ratio of two values expressed in different units. A unit rate is a rate with a denominator of 1 unit.

Example

A plant grew 6 centimeters in 2 days. The plant's rate of growth was $\frac{6 \text{ cm}}{2 \text{ days}}$. To describe the plant's growth in centimeters per day, write a unit rate.

Divide numerator and denominator by 2: $\quad \frac{6 \text{ cm}}{2 \text{ days}} = \frac{6 \text{ cm} \div 2}{2 \text{ days} \div 2}$ ◀ You divide 2 days by 2 to get 1 day, so divide 6 cm by 2 also.

Simplify: $\quad = \frac{3 \text{ cm}}{1 \text{ day}}$

ANSWER The plant's rate of growth is 3 centimeters per day.

Proportions

A **proportion** is an equation stating that two ratios are equivalent. To solve for an unknown value in a proportion, you can use cross products.

Example

If a plant grew 6 centimeters in 2 days, how many centimeters would it grow in 3 days (if its rate of growth is constant)?

$$\text{Write a proportion:} \qquad \frac{6 \text{ cm}}{2 \text{ days}} = \frac{x}{3 \text{ days}}$$

$$\text{Set cross products:} \qquad 6 \text{ cm} \cdot 3 = 2x$$

$$\text{Multiply 6 and 3:} \qquad 18 \text{ cm} = 2x$$

$$\text{Divide each side by 2:} \qquad \frac{18 \text{ cm}}{2} = \frac{2x}{2}$$

$$\text{Simplify:} \qquad 9 \text{ cm} = x$$

ANSWER The plant would grow 9 centimeters in 3 days.

Using Decimals, Fractions, and Percents

Decimals, fractions, and percentages are all ways of recording and representing data.

Decimals

A **decimal** is a number that is written in the base-ten place value system, in which a decimal point separates the ones and tenths digits. The values of each place is ten times that of the place to its right.

Example

A caterpillar traveled from point A to point C along the path shown.

A   **36.9 cm**   B   **52.4 cm**   C

ADDING DECIMALS To find the total distance traveled by the caterpillar, add the distance from A to B and the distance from B to C. Begin by lining up the decimal points. Then add the figures as you would whole numbers and bring down the decimal point.

$$
\begin{array}{r}
36.9 \text{ cm} \\
+ \ 52.4 \text{ cm} \\
\hline
89.3 \text{ cm}
\end{array}
$$

ANSWER The caterpillar traveled a total distance of 89.3 centimeters.

Example continued

SUBTRACTING DECIMALS To find how much farther the caterpillar traveled on the second leg of the journey, subtract the distance from *A* to *B* from the distance from *B* to *C*.

$$
\begin{array}{r}
52.4 \text{ cm} \\
- \ 36.9 \text{ cm} \\
\hline
15.5 \text{ cm}
\end{array}
$$

ANSWER The caterpillar traveled 15.5 centimeters farther on the second leg of the journey.

Example

A caterpillar is traveling from point *D* to point *F* along the path shown. The caterpillar travels at a speed of 9.6 centimeters per minute.

MULTIPLYING DECIMALS You can multiply decimals as you would whole numbers. The number of decimal places in the product is equal to the sum of the number of decimal places in the factors.

For instance, suppose it takes the caterpillar 1.5 minutes to go from *D* to *E*. To find the distance from *D* to *E*, multiply the caterpillar's speed by the time it took.

Align as shown.

$$
\begin{array}{r}
9.6 \quad\quad 1 \quad \text{decimal place} \\
\times \ 1.5 \quad\quad + 1 \quad \text{decimal place} \\
\hline
480 \\
96 \quad\quad\quad\quad\quad\quad\quad\quad \\
\hline
14.40 \quad\quad 2 \quad \text{decimal places}
\end{array}
$$

ANSWER The distance from *D* to *E* is 14.4 centimeters.

DIVIDING DECIMALS When you divide by a decimal, move the decimal points the same number of places in the divisor and the dividend to make the divisor a whole number.

For instance, to find the time it will take the caterpillar to travel from *E* to *F*, divide the distance from *E* to *F* by the caterpillar's speed.

$$
9.6 \overline{)33.6}
$$

Move each decimal point one place to the right.

$$
\begin{array}{r}
3.5 \\
96 \overline{)336.} \\
\underline{288} \\
480 \\
\underline{480} \\
0
\end{array}
$$

Line up decimal points.

ANSWER The caterpillar will travel from *E* to *F* in 3.5 minutes.

Fractions

A **fraction** is a number in the form $\frac{a}{b}$, where b is not equal to 0. A fraction is in **simplest form** if its numerator and denominator have a greatest common factor (GCF) of 1. To simplify a fraction, divide its numerator and denominator by their GCF.

Example

A caterpillar is 40 millimeters long. The head of the caterpillar is 6 millimeters long. To compare the length of the caterpillar's head with the caterpillar's total length, you can write and simplify a fraction that expresses the ratio of the two lengths.

Write the ratio of the two lengths: $\dfrac{\text{Length of head}}{\text{Total length}} = \dfrac{6 \text{ mm}}{40 \text{ mm}}$

Write numerator and denominator as products of numbers and the GCF: $= \dfrac{3 \times 2}{20 \times 2}$

Divide numerator and denominator by the GCF: $= \dfrac{3 \times \overset{1}{\cancel{2}}}{20 \times \underset{1}{\cancel{2}}}$

Simplify: $= \dfrac{3}{20}$

ANSWER In simplest form, the ratio of the lengths is $\dfrac{3}{20}$.

Percents

A **percent** is a ratio that compares a number to 100. The word *percent* means "per hundred" or "out of 100." The symbol for *percent* is %.

For instance, suppose 43 out of 100 caterpillars are female. You can represent this ratio as a percent, a decimal, or a fraction.

Percent	Decimal	Fraction
43%	0.43	$\dfrac{43}{100}$

Example

In the preceding example, the ratio of the length of the caterpillar's head to the caterpillar's total length is $\dfrac{3}{20}$. To write this ratio as a percent, write an equivalent fraction that has a denominator of 100.

Multiply numerator and denominator by 5: $\dfrac{3}{20} = \dfrac{3 \times 5}{20 \times 5}$

$= \dfrac{15}{100}$

Write as a percent: $= 15\%$

ANSWER The caterpillar's head represents 15 percent of its total length.

Using Formulas

A **formula** is an equation that shows the general relationship between two or more quantities.

The term *variable* is also used in science to refer to a factor that can change during an experiment.

In science, a formula often has a word form and a symbolic form. The formula below expresses Ohm's law.

Word Form

$$\text{Current} = \frac{\text{voltage}}{\text{resistance}}$$

Symbolic Form

$$I = \frac{V}{R}$$

In this formula, I, V, and R are variables. A mathematical **variable** is a symbol or letter that is used to represent one or more numbers.

Example

Suppose that you measure a voltage of 1.5 volts and a resistance of 15 ohms. You can use the formula for Ohm's law to find the current in amperes.

Write the formula for Ohm's law: $I = \dfrac{V}{R}$

Substitute 1.5 volts for V and 15 ohms for R: $I = \dfrac{1.5 \text{ volts}}{15 \text{ ohms}}$

Simplify: $I = 0.1 \text{ amp}$

ANSWER The current is 0.1 ampere.

If you know the values of all variables but one in a formula, you can solve for the value of the unknown variable. For instance, Ohm's law can be used to find a voltage if you know the current and the resistance.

Example

Suppose that you know that a current is 0.2 amperes and the resistance is 18 ohms. Use the formula for Ohm's law to find the voltage in volts.

Write the formula for Ohm's law: $I = \dfrac{V}{R}$

Substitute 0.2 amp for I and 18 ohms for R: $0.2 \text{ amp} = \dfrac{V}{18 \text{ ohms}}$

Multiply both sides by 18 ohms: $0.2 \text{ amp} \cdot 18 \text{ ohms} = V$

Simplify: $3.6 \text{ volts} = V$

ANSWER The voltage is 3.6 volts.

Finding Areas

The area of a figure is the amount of surface the figure covers.

Area is measured in square units, such as square meters (m²) or square centimeters (cm²). Formulas for the areas of three common geometric figures are shown below.

Area = (side length)²
$A = s^2$

Area = length × width
$A = lw$

Area = $\frac{1}{2}$ × base × height
$A = \frac{1}{2} bh$

Example

Each face of a halite crystal is a square like the one shown. You can find the area of the square by using the steps below.

3 mm

3 mm

Write the formula for the area of a square: $A = s^2$

Substitute 3 mm for s: = (3 mm)²

Simplify: = 9 mm²

ANSWER The area of the square is 9 square millimeters.

Finding Volumes

The volume of a solid is the amount of space contained by the solid.

Volume is measured in cubic units, such as cubic meters (m³) or cubic centimeters (cm³). The volume of a rectangular prism is given by the formula shown below.

Volume = length × width × height
$V = lwh$

Example

A topaz crystal is a rectangular prism like the one shown. You can find the volume of the prism by using the steps below.

10 mm

12 mm

20 mm

Write the formula for the volume of a rectangular prism: $V = lwh$

Substitute dimensions: = 20 mm × 12 mm × 10 mm

Simplify: = 2400 mm³

ANSWER The volume of the rectangular prism is 2400 cubic millimeters.

Using Significant Figures

The **significant figures** in a decimal are the digits that are warranted by the accuracy of a measuring device.

When you perform a calculation with measurements, the number of significant figures to include in the result depends in part on the number of significant figures in the measurements. When you multiply or divide measurements, your answer should have only as many significant figures as the measurement with the fewest significant figures.

Example

Using a balance and a graduated cylinder filled with water, you determined that a marble has a mass of 8.0 grams and a volume of 3.5 cubic centimeters. To calculate the density of the marble, divide the mass by the volume.

Write the formula for density: Density $= \dfrac{\text{mass}}{\text{Volume}}$

Substitute measurements: $= \dfrac{8.0 \text{ g}}{3.5 \text{ cm}^3}$

Use a calculator to divide: $\approx 2.285714286 \text{ g/cm}^3$

ANSWER Because the mass and the volume have two significant figures each, give the density to two significant figures. The marble has a density of 2.3 grams per cubic centimeter.

Using Scientific Notation

Scientific notation is a shorthand way to write very large or very small numbers. For example, 73,500,000,000,000,000,000,000 kg is the mass of the Moon. In scientific notation, it is 7.35×10^{22} kg.

Example

You can convert from standard form to scientific notation.

Standard Form	Scientific Notation
720,000	7.2×10^5
5 decimal places left	Exponent is 5.
0.000291	2.91×10^{-4}
4 decimal places right	Exponent is −4.

You can convert from scientific notation to standard form.

Scientific Notation	Standard Form
4.63×10^7	46,300,000
Exponent is 7.	7 decimal places right
1.08×10^{-6}	0.00000108
Exponent is −6.	6 decimal places left

Note-Taking Handbook

Note-Taking Strategies

Taking notes as you read helps you understand the information. The notes you take can also be used as a study guide for later review. This handbook presents several ways to organize your notes.

Content Frame

1. Make a chart in which each column represents a category.
2. Give each column a heading.
3. Write details under the headings.

NAME	GROUP	CHARACTERISTICS	DRAWING
snail	mollusks	mantle, shell	
ant	arthropods	six legs, exoskeleton	
earthworm	segmented worms	segmented body, circulatory and digestive systems	
heartworm	roundworms	digestive system	
sea star	echinoderms	spiny skin, tube feet	
jellyfish	cnidarians	stinging cells	

categories

details

Combination Notes

1. For each new idea or concept, write an informal outline of the information.
2. Make a sketch to illustrate the concept, and label it.

NOTES

Types of forces
- contact force
- gravity
- friction

informal outline

forces on a box being pushed

sketch with labels

contact force

gravity

friction

Make flash cards to help you study for a test. Write a concept on one side of each card and draw the sketch that goes with it on the other side. Use the cards to review concepts with a friend.

Main Idea and Detail Notes

1. In the left-hand column of a two-column chart, list main ideas. The blue headings express main ideas throughout this textbook.

2. In the right-hand column, write details that expand on each main idea.

You can shorten the headings in your chart. Be sure to use the most important words.

When studying for tests, cover up the detail notes column with a sheet of paper. Then use each main idea to form a question—such as "How does latitude affect climate?" Answer the question, and then uncover the detail notes column to check your answer.

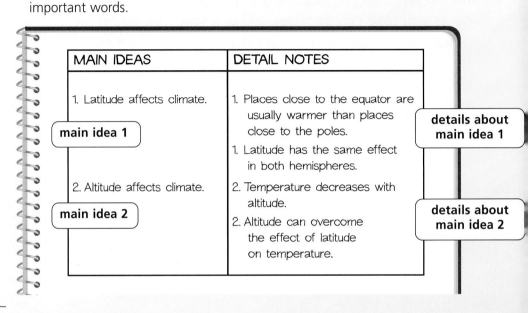

MAIN IDEAS	DETAIL NOTES
1. Latitude affects climate. **main idea 1**	1. Places close to the equator are usually warmer than places close to the poles. 1. Latitude has the same effect in both hemispheres.
2. Altitude affects climate. **main idea 2**	2. Temperature decreases with altitude. 2. Altitude can overcome the effect of latitude on temperature.

details about main idea 1

details about main idea 2

Main Idea Web

1. Write a main idea in a box.

2. Add boxes around it with related vocabulary terms and important details.

You can find definitions near highlighted terms.

definition of *work*
Work is the use of force to move an object.

formula
Work = force · distance

main idea   Force is necessary to do work.

The joule is the unit used to measure work.
definition of *joule*

Work depends on the size of a force.
important detail

NOTE-TAKING HANDBOOK

Mind Map

1. Write a main idea in the center.

2. Add details that relate to one another and to the main idea.

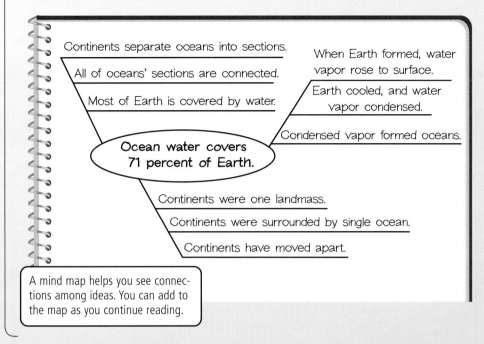

Continents separate oceans into sections.

All of oceans' sections are connected.

Most of Earth is covered by water.

When Earth formed, water vapor rose to surface.

Earth cooled, and water vapor condensed.

Condensed vapor formed oceans.

Ocean water covers 71 percent of Earth.

Continents were one landmass.

Continents were surrounded by single ocean.

Continents have moved apart.

A mind map helps you see connections among ideas. You can add to the map as you continue reading.

Supporting Main Ideas

1. Write a main idea in a box.

2. Add boxes underneath with information—such as reasons, explanations, and examples—that supports the main idea.

main idea

Electromagnetic waves have unique properties.

You can use the headings in blue type as main ideas.

EM waves are disturbances in a field rather than in a material medium.

EM waves can travel through a vacuum.

EM waves travel at the speed of light.

Outline

1. Copy the chapter title and headings from the book in the form of an outline.

2. Add notes that summarize in your own words what you read.

Cell Processes

I. Cells capture and release energy. — **1st key idea**

   A. All cells need energy. — **1st subpoint of I**

   B. Some cells capture light energy. — **2nd subpoint of I**

      1. Process of photosynthesis — **1st detail about B**

      2. Chloroplasts (site of photosynthesis) — **2nd detail about B**

      3. Carbon dioxide and water as raw materials

      4. Glucose and oxygen as products

   C. All cells release energy.

      1. Process of cellular respiration

      2. Fermentation of sugar to carbon dioxide

      3. Bacteria that carry out fermentation

II. Cells transport materials through membranes.

   A. Some materials move by diffusion.

      1. Particle movement from higher to lower concentrations

      2. Movement of water through membrane (osmosis)

   B. Some transport requires energy.

      1. Active transport

      2. Examples of active transport

Correct Outline Form

Include a title.

Arrange key ideas, subpoints, and details as shown.

Indent the divisions of the outline as shown.

Use the same grammatical form for items of the same rank. For example, if A is a sentence, B must also be a sentence.

You must have at least two main ideas or subpoints. That is, every A must be followed by a B, and every 1 must be followed by a 2.

Concept Map

1. Write an important concept in a large oval.
2. Add details related to the concept in smaller ovals.
3. Write linking words on arrows that connect the ovals.

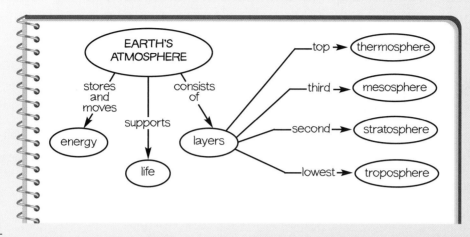

The main ideas or concepts can often be found in the blue headings. An example is "The atmosphere stores and moves energy." Use nouns from these concepts in the ovals, and use the verb or verbs on the lines.

Venn Diagram

1. Draw two overlapping circles, one for each item that you are comparing.
2. In the overlapping section, list the characteristics that are shared by both items.
3. In the outer sections, list the characteristics that are peculiar to each item.
4. Write a summary that describes the information in the Venn diagram.

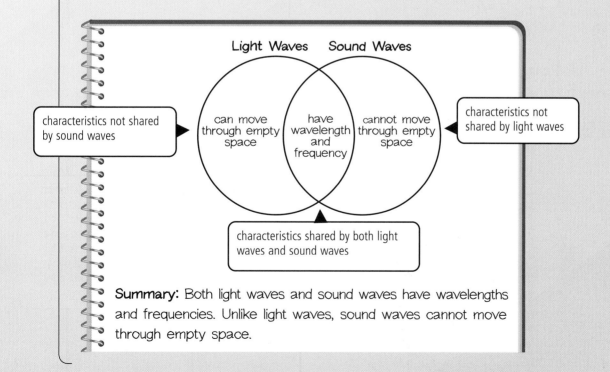

Summary: Both light waves and sound waves have wavelengths and frequencies. Unlike light waves, sound waves cannot move through empty space.

Vocabulary Strategies

Important terms are highlighted in this book. A definition of each term can be found in the sentence or paragraph where the term appears. You can also find definitions in the Glossary. Taking notes about vocabulary terms helps you understand and remember what you read.

Description Wheel

1. Write a term inside a circle.
2. Write words that describe the term on "spokes" attached to the circle.

When studying for a test with a friend, read the phrases on the spokes one at a time until your friend identifies the correct term.

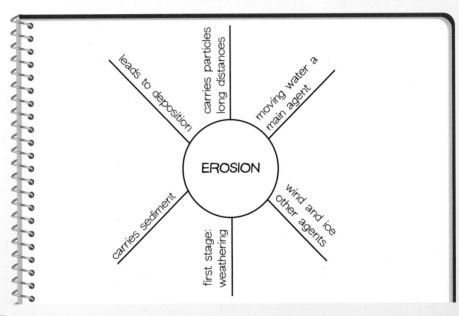

Four Square

1. Write a term in the center.
2. Write details in the four areas around the term.

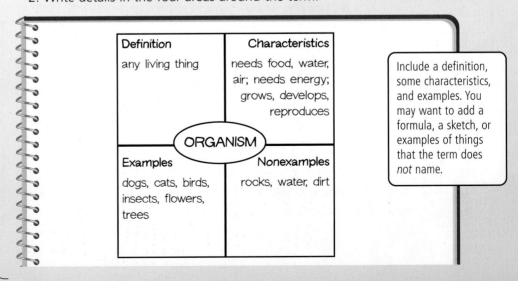

Include a definition, some characteristics, and examples. You may want to add a formula, a sketch, or examples of things that the term does *not* name.

NOTE-TAKING HANDBOOK

Frame Game

1. Write a term in the center.
2. Frame the term with details.

Include examples, descriptions, sketches, or sentences that use the term in context. Change the frame to fit each new term.

Magnet Word

1. Write a term on the magnet.
2. On the lines, add details related to the term.

You can also use phrases or sentences on the lines.

Word Triangle

1. Write a term and its definition in the bottom section.
2. In the middle section, write a sentence in which the term is used correctly.
3. In the top section, draw a small picture to illustrate the term.

Appendix

Classification of Living Things

Living things are classified into three domains. These domains are further divided into kingdoms, and then phyla. Major phyla are described in the table below, along with important features that are used to distinguish each group.

Classification of Living Things			
Domain	Kingdom	Phylum	Common Name and Description
Archaea	**Archaea**		Single-celled, with no nucleus. Live in some of Earth's most extreme environments, including salty, hot, and acid environments, and the deep ocean.
Bacteria	**Bacteria**		Single-celled, with no nucleus, but chemically different from Archaea. Live in all types of environments, including the human body; reproduce by dividing from one cell into two. Includes blue-green bacteria (cyanobacteria), *Streptococcus,* and *Bacillus.*
Eukarya			Cells are larger than archaea or bacteria and are eukaryotic (have a nucleus containing DNA). Single-celled or multicellular.
	Protista		Usually single-celled, but sometimes multicellular. DNA contained in a nucleus. Many phyla resemble plants, fungi, or animals but are usually smaller or simpler in structure.
	Animal-like protists	Ciliophora	Ciliates; have many short, hairlike extensions called cilia, which they use for feeding and movement. Includes paramecium.
		Zoomastigina	Zooflagellates; have usually one or two long, hairlike extensions called flagella.
		Sporozoa	Cause diseases in animals such as birds, fish, and humans. Includes *Plasmodium,* which causes malaria.
		Sarcodina	Use footlike extensions to move and feed. Includes foraminifers and amoebas. Sometimes called Rhizopoda.
	Plantlike protists	Euglenozoa	Single-celled, with one flagellum. Some have chloroplasts that carry out photosynthesis. Includes euglenas and *Trypanosoma,* which causes African sleeping sickness.
		Dinoflagellata	Dinoflagellates; usually single-celled; usually have chloroplasts and flagellum. In great numbers, some species can cause red tides along coastlines.

Classification of Living Things (cont.)

Domain	Kingdom	Phylum	Common Name and Description
		Chrysophyta	Yellow algae, golden-brown algae, and diatoms; single-celled; named for the yellow pigments in their chloroplasts (*chrysophyte,* in Greek, means "golden plant").
		Chlorophyceae	Green algae; have chloroplasts and are chemically similar to land plants. Unicellular or forms simple colonies of cells. Includes *Chlamydomonas, Ulva* (sea lettuce), and *Volvox.*
		Phaeophyta	Brown seaweed; contain a special brown pigment that gives these organisms their color. Multicellular, live mainly in salt water; includes kelp.
		Rhodophyta	Red algae; contain a red pigment that makes these organisms red, purple, or reddish-black. Multicellular, live in salt water.
	Funguslike protists	Acrasiomycota	Cellular slime molds; live partly as free-living single-celled organisms, then fuse together to form a many-celled mass. Live in damp, nutrient-rich environments; decomposers.
		Myxomycota	Acellular slime molds; form large, slimy masses made of many nuclei but technically a single cell.
		Oomycota	Water molds and downy mildews; produce thin, cottonlike extensions called hyphae. Feed off of dead or decaying material, often in water.
	Fungi		Usually multicellular; eukaryotic; cells have a thick cell wall. Obtain nutrients through absorption; often function as decomposers.
		Chytridiomycota	Oldest and simplest fungi; usually aquatic (fresh water or brackish water); single-celled or multicellular.
		Basidiomycota	Multicellular; reproduce with a club-shaped structure that is commonly seen on forest floors. Includes mushrooms, puffballs, rusts, and smuts.
		Zygomycota	Mostly disease-causing molds; often parasitic.
		Ascomycota	Includes single-celled yeasts and multicellular sac fungi. Includes *Penicillium.*

Classification of Living Things (cont.)

Domain	Kingdom	Phylum	Common Name and Description
	Plantae		Multicellular and eukaryotic; make sugars using energy from sunlight. Cells have a thick cell wall of cellulose.
		Bryophyta	Mosses; small, grasslike plants that live in moist, cool environments. Includes sphagnum (peat) moss. Seedless, nonvascular plants.
		Hepatophyta	Liverworts; named for the liver-shaped structure of one part of the plant's life cycle. Live in moist environments. Seedless, nonvascular plants.
		Anthoceratophyta	Hornworts; named for the visible hornlike structures with which they reproduce. Live on forest floors and other moist, cool environments. Seedless, nonvascular plants.
		Psilotophyta	Simple plant, just two types. Includes whisk ferns found in tropical areas, a common greenhouse weed. Seedless, vascular plants.
		Lycophyta	Club mosses and quillworts; look like miniature pine trees; live in moist, wooded environments. Includes *Lycopodium* (ground pine). Seedless vascular plants.
		Sphenophyta	Plants with simple leaves, stems, and roots. Grow about a meter tall, usually in moist areas. Includes *Equisetum* (scouring rush). Seedless, vascular plants.
		Pterophyta	Ferns; fringed-leaf plants that grow in cool, wooded environments. Includes many species. Seedless, vascular plants.
		Cycadophyta	Cycads; slow-growing palmlike plants that grow in tropical environments. Reproduce with seeds.
		Ginkgophyta	Includes only one species: *Ginkgo biloba,* a tree that is often planted in urban environments. Reproduce with seeds in cones.
		Gnetophyta	Small group includes desert-dwelling and tropical species. Includes *Ephedra* (Mormon tea) and *Welwitschia,* which grows in African deserts. Reproduce with seeds.
		Coniferophyta	Conifers, including pines, spruces, firs, sequoias. Usually evergreen trees; tend to grow in cold, dry environments; reproduce with seeds produced in cones.

Classification of Living Things (cont.)

Domain	Kingdom	Phylum	Common Name and Description
		Anthophyta	Flowering plants; includes grasses and flowering trees and shrubs. Reproduce with seeds produced in flowers, becoming fruit.
	Animalia		Multicellular and eukaryotic; obtain energy by consuming food. Usually able to move around.
		Porifera	Sponges; spend most of their lives fixed to the ocean floor. Feed by filtering water (containing nutrients and small organisms) through their body.
		Cnidaria	Aquatic animals with a radial (spokelike) body shape; named for their stinging cells (cnidocytes). Includes jellyfish, hydras, sea anemones, and corals.
		Ctenophora	Comb jellies; named for the comblike rows of cilia (hairlike extensions) that are used for movement.
		Platyhelminthes	Flatworms; thin, flattened worms with simple tissues and sensory organs. Includes planaria and tapeworms, which cause diseases in humans and other hosts.
		Nematoda	Roundworms; small, round worms; many species are parasites, causing diseases in humans, such as trichinosis and elephantiasis.
		Annelida	Segmented worms; body is made of many similar segments. Includes earthworms, leeches, and many marine worms.
		Mollusca	Soft-bodied, aquatic animals that usually have an outer shell. Includes snails, mussels, clams, octopus, and squid.
		Arthropoda	Animals with an outer skeleton (exoskeleton) and jointed appendages (for example, legs or wings). Very large group that includes insects, spiders and ticks, centipedes, millipedes, and crustaceans.
		Echinodermata	Marine animals with a radial (spokelike) body shape. Includes feather stars, sea stars (starfish), sea urchins, sand dollars, and sea cucumbers.
		Chordata	Mostly vertebrates (animals with backbones) that share important stages of early development. Includes tunicates (sea squirts), fish, sharks, amphibians, reptiles, birds, and mammals.

Plant and Animal Cells

Plants and animals are eukaryotes, that is, their cells contain a nucleus and other membrane-bound structures called organelles. The diagrams on page R57 show the different structures that can be found in plant and animal cells. The table below lists the functions of the structures.

Cell Structures and Their Functions	Plant Cell	Animal Cell
Nucleus	✔	✔
stores genetic material that enables a cell to function and divide		
Cell Membrane	✔	✔
controls what comes into and goes out of a cell		
Cell wall	✔	
tough outer covering provides support		
Ribosome	✔	✔
uses genetic material to assemble materials needed to make proteins		
Endoplasmic reticulum	✔	✔
manufactures proteins and other materials a cell needs to function		
Golgi apparatus	✔	✔
finishes processing proteins and transports them		
Vesicle	✔	✔
stores and transports materials and wastes		
Mitochondrion	✔	✔
releases chemical energy stored in sugars		
Chloroplast	✔	
uses energy from sunlight to make sugars		
Lysosome		✔
breaks down food particles and wastes		

Plant Cell

Found in plant cells, not animal cells:

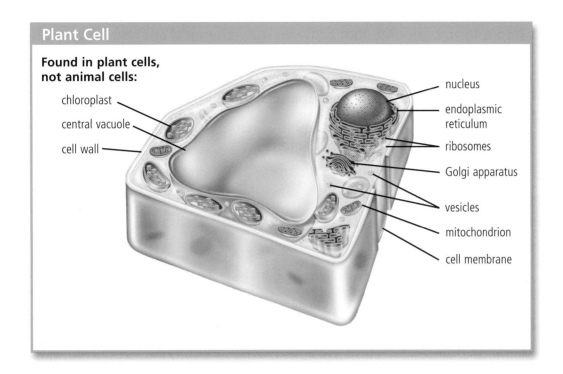

- chloroplast
- central vacuole
- cell wall
- nucleus
- endoplasmic reticulum
- ribosomes
- Golgi apparatus
- vesicles
- mitochondrion
- cell membrane

Animal Cell

Found in animal cells, not plant cells:

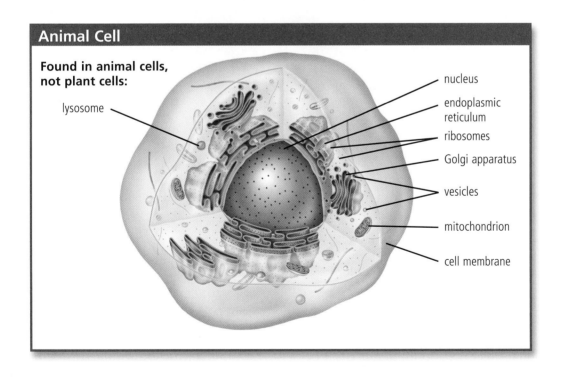

- lysosome
- nucleus
- endoplasmic reticulum
- ribosomes
- Golgi apparatus
- vesicles
- mitochondrion
- cell membrane

Photosynthesis and Cellular Respiration

The source of energy for almost all organisms is the Sun. Plants and other photosynthetic organisms such as algae change the energy in sunlight into a form of energy that cells can use—chemical energy. Photosynthesis is the process that changes the energy from sunlight into chemical energy and produces glucose, an energy-rich sugar. The process takes place in cellular structures called chloroplasts, found in the cytoplasm.

All cells must have energy to function. Glucose and other sugars and starches store energy, as well as serve as a source of material for cells.

Photosynthesis

1 **The starting materials** Carbon dioxide from the air and water from the soil enter the chloroplasts.

2 **The process** Inside the chloroplasts, chlorophyll captures energy from sunlight. This energy is used to change starting materials into new products.

3 **The products** Glucose provides energy and materials for the plant; most oxygen is released into the air.

Carbon dioxide ($6CO_2$)

Light Energy

Water ($6H_2O$)

Glucose ($C_6H_{12}O_6$)

Oxygen ($6O_2$)

Chloroplast

Water $6H_2O$	+	Carbon dioxide $6CO_2$	+	Light Energy	→	Glucose $C_6H_{12}O_6$	+	Oxygen $6O_2$

Chemical energy is stored in the bonds of the sugar and starch molecules. Cellular respiration is the process that releases energy from sugars. The process takes place in cellular structures called mitochondria, found in the cytoplasm. In cellular respiration, cells use oxygen to release energy as the molecules are broken down.

Compare the starting materials and products of photosynthesis with those of cellular respiration. The starting materials of one process are the products of the other process.

Cellular Respiration

1. **The starting materials** Glucose and oxygen enter the cell. Glucose is split into smaller molecules.

2. **The process** Inside the mitochondria more chemical bonds are broken in the smaller molecules. Oxygen is needed for this process.

3. **The products** Energy is released, and water and carbon dioxide are produced.

Oxygen $(6O_2)$

Energy

Glucose $(C_6H_{12}O_6)$ → SMALLER MOLECULES

Carbon dioxide $(6CO_2)$

Water $(6H_2O)$

Energy

Mitochondrion

| Glucose $C_6H_{12}O_6$ | + | Oxygen $6O_2$ | → | Chemical Energy | + | Water $6H_2O$ | + | Carbon dioxide $6CO_2$ |

Glossary

A

adaptation
A characteristic, a behavior, or any inherited trait that makes a species able to survive and reproduce in a particular environment. (p. xxi)

adaptación Una característica, un comportamiento o cualquier rasgo heredado que permite a una especie sobrevivir o reproducirse en un medio ambiente determinado.

algae
Protists that live mostly in water and use sunlight as a source of energy. *Algae* is a plural word; the singular is *alga.* (p. 31)

algas Protistas que viven principalmente en el agua y que usan la luz solar como fuente de energía.

amphibian
A cold-blooded vertebrate animal that lives in water and breathes with gills when it is young; as an adult, it moves onto land and breathes air with lungs. (p. 167)

anfibio Un vertebrado de sangre fría que vive en el agua y respira con branquias cuando es juvenil; cuando es adulto, se mueve a la tierra y respire aire con pulmones.

angiosperm (AN-jee-uh-SPURM)
A plant that has flowers and produces seeds enclosed in fruit. (p. 107)

angiosperma Una planta que tiene flores y que produce semillas dentro de frutas.

archaea (AHR-kee-uh)
Single-celled organisms without nuclei that can survive in extreme environments. *Archaea* is a plural word; the singular is *archaean.* (p. 18)

archaea Organismos de una sola célula sin núcleo que pueden sobrevivir en medios ambientes extremosos.

arthropod
An invertebrate animal with an exoskeleton, a segmented body, and jointed legs. (p. 142)

artrópodo Un animal invertebrado con un exoesqueleto, un cuerpo segmentado y patas articuladas.

atom
The smallest particle of an element that has the chemical properties of that element.

átomo La partícula más pequeña de un elemento que tiene las propiedades químicas de ese elemento.

autotroph (AW-tuh-TRAHF)
An organism that captures energy from sunlight and uses it to produce energy-rich carbon compounds, usually through the process of photosynthesis. (p. 52)

autótrofo Un organismo que capta energía de la luz solar y la usa para producir compuestos de carbono ricos en energía, usualmente mediante el proceso de fotosíntesis.

B

bacteria (bak-TEER-ee-uh)
A large group of one-celled organisms that sometimes cause disease. *Bacteria* is a plural word; the singular is *bacterium.* (p. 16)

bacterias Un grupo grande de organismos unicelulares que algunas veces causan enfermedades.

behavior
An organism's action in response to a stimulus. (p. 62)

comportamiento La acción de un organismo en respuesta a un estímulo.

binary fission
A form of asexual reproduction by which some single-celled organisms reproduce. The genetic material is copied, and one cell divides into two independent cells that are each a copy of the original cell. Prokaryotes such as bacteria reproduce by binary fission. (p. 12)

fisión binaria Una forma asexual de reproducción mediante la cual algunos organismos unicelulares se reproducen. El material genético se copia y una célula se divide en dos células independientes las cuales son copias de la célula original. Los organismos procariotas, tales como las bacterias, se reproducen mediante fisión binaria.

biodiversity
The number and variety of living things found on Earth or within an ecosystem. (p. xxi)

> **biodiversidad** La cantidad y variedad de organismos vivos que se encuentran en la Tierra o dentro de un ecosistema.

blubber
A layer of fat in some sea mammals that lies beneath the skin. It insulates the animal from cold and stores reserve energy. (p. 184)

> **grasa de ballena** Una capa de tejido graso en algunos mamíferos marinos que yace bajo la piel. Aísla al animal del frió y almacena energía de reserva.

C

cell
The smallest unit that is able to perform the basic functions of life. (p. xv)

> **célula** La unidad más pequeña capaz de realizar las functiones básicas de la vida.

cellular respiration
A process in which cells use oxygen to release energy stored in sugars. (p. 53)

> **respiración celular** Un proceso en el cual las células usan oxígeno para liberar energía almacenada en las azúcares.

classification
The systematic grouping of different types of organisms by their shared characteristics.

> **clasificación** La agrupación sistemática de diferentes tipos de organismos en base a las características que comparten.

cnidarian (ny-DAIR-ee-uhn)
An invertebrate animal such as a jellyfish that has a body with radial symmetry, tentacles with stinging cells, and a central internal cavity. (p. 128)

> **cnidario** Un animal invertebrado tal como una medusa que tiene un cuerpo con simetría radial, tentáculos con células urticantes y una cavidad central interna.

compound
A substance made up of two or more different types of atoms bonded together.

> **compuesto** Una sustancia formada por dos o más diferentes tipos de átomos enlazados.

consumer
A living thing that gets its energy by eating other living things in a food chain; consumers are also called heterotrophs. (p. 58)

> **consumidor** Un organismo vivo que obtiene su energía alimentándose de otros organismos vivos en una cadena alimentaria; los consumidores también son llamados heterótrofos.

cycle
n. A series of events or actions that repeat themselves regularly; a physical and/or chemical process in which one material continually changes locations and/or forms. Examples include the water cycle, the carbon cycle, and the rock cycle.

v. To move through a repeating series of events or actions.

> **ciclo** Una serie de eventos o acciones que se repiten regularmente; un proceso físico y/o químico en el cual un material cambia continuamente de lugar y/o forma. Ejemplos: el ciclo del agua, el ciclo del carbono y el ciclo de las rocas.

D

data
Information gathered by observation or experimentation that can be used in calculating or reasoning. *Data* is a plural word; the singular is *datum.*

> **datos** Información reunida mediante observación o experimentación y que se puede usar para calcular o para razonar.

decomposer
An organism that feeds on and breaks down dead plant or animal matter. (p. 19)

> **descomponedor** Un organismo que se alimenta de y degrada materia vegetal o animal.

density
A property of matter representing the mass per unit volume.

> **densidad** Una propiedad de la materia que representa la masa por unidad de volumen.

DNA
The genetic material found in all living cells that contains the information needed for an organism to grow, maintain itself, and reproduce. Deoxyribonucleic acid (dee-AHK-see-RY-boh-noo-KLEE-ihk).

> **ADN** El material genético que se encuentra en todas las céulas vivas y que contiene la información necesaria para que un organismo crezca, se mantenga a sí mismo y se reproduzca. Ácido desoxiribunucleico.

E

echinoderm
An invertebrate sea animal with a spiny skeleton, a water vascular system, and tube feet. (p. 139)

equinodermo Un animal invertebrado marino con esqueleto espinoso, sistema vascular acuífero y pies ambulacrales.

ectotherm
An animal whose body temperature changes with environmental conditions. (p. 170)

poiquilotermo o poiquilotérmico Un animal cuya temperatura corporal cambia con las condiciones del medio ambiente.

element
A substance that cannot be broken down into a simpler substance by ordinary chemical changes. An element consists of atoms of only one type.

elemento Una sustancia que no puede descomponerse en otra sustancia más simple por medio de cambios químicos normales. Un elemento consta de átomos de un solo tipo.

embryo (EHM-bree-OH)
A multicellular organism, plant or animal, in its earliest stages of development. (p. 98)

embrión Una planta o un animal en su estadio mas temprano de desarrollo.

endoskeleton
An internal support system; such a skeleton made of bone tissue is a distinguishing characteristic of vertebrate animals. (p. 157)

endoesqueleto Un sistema de soporte interno, como un esqueleto formado de tejido óseo es una característica distintiva de los animales vertebrados.

endotherm
An animal that maintains a constant body temperature. (p. 174)

homeotermo o endotermo Un animal que mantiene una temperatura corporal constante.

energy
The ability to do work or to cause a change. For example, the energy of a moving bowling ball knocks over pins; energy from food allows animals to move and to grow; and energy from the Sun heats Earth's surface and atmosphere, which causes air to move.

energía La capacidad para trabajar o causar un cambio. Por ejemplo, la energía de una bola de boliche en movimiento tumba los pinos; la energía proveniente de su alimento permite a los animales moverse y crecer; la energía del Sol calienta la superficie y la atmósfera de la Tierra, lo que ocasiona que el aire se mueva.

environment
Everything that surrounds a living thing. An environment is made up of both living and nonliving factors. (p. xix)

medio ambiente Todo lo que rodea a un organismo vivo. Un medio ambiente está compuesto de factores vivos y factores sin vida.

exoskeleton
The strong, flexible outer covering of some invertebrate animals, such as arthropods. (p. 143)

exoesqueleto La cubierta exterior fuerte y flexible de algunos animales invertebrados, como los artrópodos.

experiment
An organized procedure to study something under controlled conditions. (p. xxiv)

experimento Un procedimiento organizado para estudiar algo bajo condiciones controladas.

extinction
The permanent disappearance of a species. (p. xxi)

extinción La desaparición permanente de una especie.

F

fertilization
Part of the process of sexual reproduction in which a male reproductive cell and a female reproductive cell combine to make a new cell that can develop into a new organism. (p. 48)

fertilización El proceso mediante el cual una célula reproductiva masculina y una célula reproductiva femenina se combinan para formar una nueva célula que puede convertirse en un organismo nuevo.

flower
The reproductive structure of an angiosperm, containing male and female parts. (p. 108)

flor La estructura reproductiva de una angiosperma, contiene las partes masculinas y femeninas.

fruit

The ripened ovary of a flowering plant that contains the seeds. (p. 108)

fruta El ovario maduro de una planta floreciente que contiene las semillas.

G

genetic material

The nucleic acid DNA, which is present in all living cells and contains the information for a cell's growth, maintenance, and reproduction.

material genético El ácido nucleico ADN, ue esta presente en todas las células vivas y que contiene la información necesaria para el crecimiento, el mantenimiento y la reproducción celular.

germination (JUR-muh-NAY-shuhn)

The beginning of growth of a new plant from a spore or a seed. (p. 99)

germinación El inicio del crecimiento de una nueva planta a partir de una espora o una semilla.

gestation

In mammals, the period of time spent by a developing offspring inside the mother's body. (p. 186)

gestación En los mamíferos, el periodo de tiempo que pasa una cría en desarrollo dentro del cuerpo de la madre.

gill

A respiratory organ that filters oxgen dissolved in water. (p. 137)

branquia Un órgano respiratorio que filtra oxígeno disuelto en el agua.

gymnosperm (JIHM-nuh-SPURM)

A plant that produces seeds that are not enclosed in flowers or fruit. (p. 102)

Gimnosperma Una planta que produce semillas que no están dentro de las flores o las frutas.

H

heterotroph (HEHT-uhr-uh-TRAWF)

An organism that consumes other organisms to get energy. (p. 58)

heterótrofo Un organismo que consume a otros organismos para obtener energía.

hibernation

A sleeplike state in which certain animals spend the winter. Hibernation reduces an animal's need for food and helps protect it from cold. (p. 64)

hibernación Un estado parecido al de sueño en el cual ciertos animales pasan el invierno. La hibernación reduce la necesidad de alimento de un animal y le ayuda a protegerse del frío.

host cell

A cell that a virus infects and uses to make copies of itself. (p. 26)

célula hospedera Una célula que un virus infecta y usa para hacer copias de sí mismo.

hyphae

Threadlike tubes that form the structural parts of the body of a fungus. *Hyphae* is a plural word; the singular is *hypha.* (p. 67)

hifas Los tubos, similares a hilos, que forman las partes estructurales del cuerpo de un hongo.

hypothesis

A tentative explanation for an observation or phenomenon. A hypothesis is used to make testable predictions. (p. xxiv)

hipótesis Una explicación provisional de una observación o de un fenómeno. Una hipótesis se usa para hacer predicciones que se pueden probar.

I, J

incubation

The process of keeping eggs warm by bodily heat until they hatch. (p. 179)

incubación El proceso de mantener huevos cálidos por medio de calor corporal hasta que eclosionen.

insect

An arthropod with three body segments, six legs, two antennae, and compound eyes. (p. 145)

insecto Un artrópodo con tres segmentos corporales, seis patas, dos antenas y ojos compuestos.

interaction

The condition of acting or having an influence upon something. Living things in an ecosystem interact with both the living and nonliving parts of their environment. (p. xix)

interacción La condición de actuar o influir sobre algo. Los organismos vivos en un ecosistema interactúan con las partes vivas y las partes sin vida de su medio ambiente.

invertebrate

An animal that has no backbone. (p. 123)

invertebrado Un animal que no tiene columna vertebral.

K

kingdom

One of six large groupings of living things that have common characteristics. The kingdoms are Plantae, Animalia, Fungi, Protista, Archaea, and Bacteria. (p. 11)

reino Uno de los seis grandes grupos de organismos vivos que tienen características en común. Los reinos son Plantae, Animalia, Fungi, Protista, Archae y Bacteria.

L

larva

A free-living early form of a developing organism that is very different from its adult form. (p. 126)

larva Una etapa temprana de vida libre de un organismo en desarrollo que es muy diferente a su etapa adulta.

law

In science, a rule or principle describing a physical relationship that always works in the same way under the same conditions. The law of conservation of energy is an example.

ley En las ciencias, una regla o un principio que describe una relación física que siempre funciona de la misma manera bajo las mismas condiciones. La ley de la conservación de la energía es un ejemplo.

lichen (LY-kuhn)

An organism that results from a close association between single-celled algae and fungi. (p. 70)

liquen Un organismo que resulta de una asociación cercana entre algas unicelulares y hongos.

lung

A respiratory organ that absorbs oxygen from the air. (p. 137)

pulmón Un órgano respiratorio que absorbe oxígeno del aire.

M, N

mammal

A warm-blooded vertebrate animal whose young feed on milk produced by the mother's mammary glands. (p. 183)

mamífero Un animal vertebrado de sangre caliente cuyas crías se alimentan de leche producida por las glándulas mamarias de la madre.

mass

A measure of how much matter an object is made of.

masa Una medida de la cantidad de materia de la que está compuesto un objeto.

matter

Anything that has mass and volume. Matter exists ordinarily as a solid, a liquid, or a gas.

materia Todo lo que tiene masa y volumen. Generalmente la materia existe como sólido, líquido o gas.

meiosis (my-OH-sihs)

A part of sexual reproduction in which cells divide to form sperm cells in a male and egg cells in a female. Meiosis occurs only in reproductive cells. (p. 48)

meiosis Una parte de la reproducción sexual en la cual las células se dividen para formar espermatozoides en los machos y óvulos en las hembras. La meiosis sólo ocurre en las células reproductivas.

metamorphosis

The transformation of an animal from its larval form into its adult form. (p. 146)

metamorfosis La transformación de un animal de su forma larvaria a su forma adulta.

microorganism

A very small organism that can be seen only with a microscope. Bacteria are examples of microorganisms. (p. 10)

microorganismo Un organismo muy pequeño que solamente puede verse con un microscopio. Las bacterias son ejemplos de microorganismos.

migration

The movement of animals from one region to another in response to changes in the seasons or the environment. (p. 64)

migración El movimiento de animales de una región a otra en respuesta a cambios en las estaciones o en el medio ambiente.

mobile
Able to move from place to place. (p. 130)

> **móvil** Capaz de moverse de un lugar a otro.

molecule
A group of atoms that are held together by covalent bonds so that they move as a single unit.

> **molécula** Un grupo de átomos que están unidos mediante enlaces covalentes de tal manera que se mueven como una sola unidad.

mollusk
An invertebrate animal with a soft body, a muscular foot, and a mantle. Many mollusks have a hard outer shell. (p. 136)

> **molusco** Un animal invertebrado con cuerpo blando, un pie muscular y un manto. Muchos moluscos tienen una concha exterior dura.

molting
The process of an arthropod shedding its exoskeleton to allow for growth. (p. 143)

> **muda** El proceso mediante el cual un artrópodo se despoja de su exoesqueleto para poder crecer.

organ
A structure in a plant or animal that is made up of different tissues working together to perform a particular function. (p. 44)

> **órgano** Una estructura en un plato o en un animal compuesta de diferentes tejidos que trabajan juntos para realizar una función determinada.

organism
An individual living thing, made up of one or many cells, that is capable of growing and reproducing.

> **organismo** Un individuo vivo, compuesto de una o muchas células, que es capaz de crecer y reproducirse.

P, Q

parasite
An organism that absorbs nutrients from the body of another organism, often harming it in the process. (p. 19)

> **parásito** Un organismo que absorbe nutrientes del cuerpo de otro organismo, a menudo causándole daño en el proceso.

photosynthesis (FOH-toh-SIHN-thih-sihs)
The process by which green plants and other producers use simple compounds and energy from light to make sugar, an energy-rich compound. (p. 52)

> **fotosíntesis** El proceso mediante el cual las plantas verdes y otros productores usan compuestos simples y energía de la luz para producir azúcares, compuestos ricos en energía.

placenta
An organ that transports materials between a pregnant female mammal and the offspring developing inside her body. (p. 186)

> **placenta** Un órgano que transporta sustancias entre un mamífero hembra preñado y la cría que se está desarrollando dentro de su cuerpo.

plankton
Mostly microscopic organisms that drift in great numbers through bodies of water. (p. 33)

> **plancton** Organismos, en su mayoría microscópicos, que se mueven a la deriva en grandes números por cuerpos de agua.

pollen
Tiny multicellular grains that contain the undeveloped sperm cells of a plant. (p. 100)

> **polen** Los diminutos granos multicelulares que contienen las células espermáticas sin desarrollar de una planta.

predator
An animal that hunts other animals and eats them. (p. 63)

> **predador** Un animal que caza otros animales y se los come.

prey
An animal that other animals hunt and eat. (p. 63)

> **presa** Un animal que otros animales cazan y se comen.

producer
An organism that captures energy from sunlight and transforms it into chemical energy that is stored in energy-rich carbon compounds. Producers are a source of food for other organisms. (p. 19)

> **productor** Un organismo que capta energía de la luz solar y la transforma a energía química que se almacena en compuestos de carbono ricos en energía. Los productores son una fuente de alimento para otros organismos.

protozoa

Animal-like protists that eat other organisms or decaying parts of other organisms. *Protozoa* is a plural word; the singular is *protozoan.* (p. 34)

protozoarios Protistas parecidos a los animales que comen otros organismos o partes en descomposición de otros organismos.

R

reptile

A cold-blooded vertebrate that has skin covered with scales or horny plates and has lungs. (p. 168)

reptil Un vertebrado de sangre fría que tiene la piel cubierta de escamas o placas callosas y que tiene pulmones.

S

scale

One of the thin, small, overlapping plates that cover most fish and reptiles and some other animals. (p. 161)

escama Una de las pequeñas y delgadas placas traslapadas que cubren a la mayoría de los peces y reptiles y algunos otros animales.

seed

A plant embryo that is enclosed in a protective coating and has its own source of nutrients. (p. 98)

semilla El embrión de una planta que esta dentro de una cubierta protectora y que tiene su propia fuente de nutrientes.

sessile (SEHS-eel)

The quality of being attached to one spot; not free-moving. (p. 125)

sésil La cualidad de estar sujeto a un punto; sin libre movimiento.

sexual reproduction

A type of reproduction in which male and female reproductive cells combine to form offspring with genetic material from both cells. (p. 48)

reproducción sexual Un tipo de reproducción en el cual se combinan las células reproductivas femeninas y masculinas para formar una cría con material genético de ambas células.

species

A group of living things that are so closely related that they can breed with one another and produce offspring that can breed as well. (p. xxi)

especie Un grupo de organismos que están tan estrechamente relacionados que pueden aparearse entre sí y producir crías que también pueden aparearse.

sponge

A simple multicellular invertebrate animal that lives attached to one place and filters food from water. (p. 125)

esponja Un animal invertebrado multicelular simple que vive sujeto a un lugar y filtra su alimento del agua.

spore

A single reproductive cell that can grow into a multicellular organism. (p. 67)

espora Una célula reproductiva individual que puede convertirse en un organismo multicelular.

stimulus

Something that causes a response in an organism or a part of the body. (p. 55)

estímulo Algo que causa una respuesta en un organismo o en una parte del cuerpo.

system

A group of objects or phenomena that interact. A system can be as simple as a rope, a pulley, and a mass. It also can be as complex as the interaction of energy and matter in the four parts of the Earth system.

sistema Un grupo de objetos o fenómenos que interactúan. Un sistema puede ser algo tan sencillo como una cuerda, una polea y una masa. También puede ser algo tan complejo como la interacción de la energía y la materia en las cuatro partes del sistema de la Tierra.

T, U

technology

The use of scientific knowledge to solve problems or engineer new products, tools, or processes.

tecnología El uso de conocimientos científicos para resolver problemas o para diseñar nuevos productos, herramientas o procesos.

tentacle
A long, slender, flexible extension of the body of certain animals, such as jellyfish. Tentacles are used to touch, move, or hold. (p. 128)

tentáculo Una extensión larga, delgada y flexible del cuerpo de ciertos animales, como las medusas. Los tentáculos se usan para tocar, mover o sujetar.

theory
In science, a set of widely accepted explanations of observations and phenomena. A theory is a well-tested explanation that is consistent with all available evidence.

teoría En las ciencias, un conjunto de explicaciones de observaciones y fenómenos que es ampliamente aceptado. Una teoría es una explicación bien probada que es consecuente con la evidencia disponible.

tissue
A group of similar cells that together perform a specific function in an organism. (p. 44)

tejido Un grupo de células parecidas que juntas realizan una función específica en un organismo.

transpiration (TRAN-spuh-RAY-shuhn)
The movement of water vapor out of a plant and into the air. (p. 88)

transpiración El movimiento de vapor de agua hacia fuera de una planta y hacia el aire.

V, W, X, Y, Z

variable
Any factor that can change in a controlled experiment, observation, or model. (p. R30)

variable Cualquier factor que puede cambiar en un experimento controlado, en una observación o en un modelo.

vascular system (VAS-kyuh-lur)
Long tubelike tissues in plants through which water and nutrients move from one part of the plant to another. (p. 87)

sistema vascular Tejidos largos en forma de tubo en las plantas a través de los cuales se mueven agua y nutrientes de una parte de la planta a otra.

vertebrate
An animal with an internal backbone. (p. 157)

vertebrado Un animal que tiene columna vertebral interna.

virus
A nonliving disease-causing particle that uses the materials inside cells to make copies of itself. A virus consists of genetic material enclosed in a protein coat. (p. 14)

virus Una particular sin vida, que causa enfermedad y que usa los materiales dentro de las células para reproducirse. Un virus consiste de material genético encerrado en una cubierta proteica.

volume
An amount of three-dimensional space, often used to describe the space that an object takes up.

volumen Una cantidad de espacio tridimensional; a menudo se usa este término para describir el espacio que ocupa un objeto.

Index

Page numbers for definitions are printed in **boldface** type.
Page numbers for illustrations, maps, and charts are printed in *italics.*

diversity, 9–11. *See also* adaptation
    of birds, 173
    and environment, 46
    of fish, 158
    of insects, 145
    of mammals, 182–183, 185
    of mollusks, 139
    of plants, 85–86, *86*
    of protists, 30–32, *32*
    and reproduction, 48–49
    scientific discoveries in, 78–81
division, cellular, 12, *12*
DNA. *See also* genetic material
    in bacteria, *12,* 17
    and binary fission, 12
    and sexual reproduction, 48
    in viruses, 14
dry fruits, 111

E

echinoderms, 124, **139,** 139–140, *140*
ectotherms, **170.** *See also* body temperature
egg cells, 48
eggs. *See also* reproduction
    of birds, 178–179, *179*
    of fish, 161–162
    of reptiles, 169, *169*
embryo, **98,** 98–99, *99*
endoskeleton, **157**
    in birds, 176, *177*
    in mammals, *158, 185*
endotherms, **174.** *See also* body temperature
    birds, 174
    mammals, 183
energy, 13
    for animals, 58–61
    for plants, 51–53, *53*
    plants as source of, 113
    for protists, 32, 33, 34
environment
    and adaptation, 46, *47,* 48
    of amphibians and reptiles, 170–171
    animal interaction with, 62–64
    of archaea, 18
    of bacteria, 16, 19, 20
    of birds, 173–174
    and body temperature, 2–5, 170–171, 183–184
    of fish, 158
    of mammals, 182, 185
    organism response to, 12
    plant adaptation to, 53–54
    plant response to, *55,* 55–57, *56*
    of plants, 85–86, *86*
    of protists, 30–32

euglena, 32, *32*
evaluating, **R8**
    media claims, R8
evidence, collection of, xxiv
exoskeleton, **143,** *143*
experiment, **xxiv.** *See also* labs
    conclusions, drawing, R35
    constants, determining, R30
    controlled, **R28,** R30
    designing, R28–R35
    hypothesis, writing, R29
    materials, determining, R29
    observations, recording, R33
    procedure, writing, R32
    purpose, determining, R28
    results, summarizing, R34
    variables, R30–R31, R32
experimental group, R30

F

fact, **R9**
    different from opinion, R9
fat, body, 184
faulty reasoning, **R7**
feathers
    and body temperature, 175
    and flight, 176, *177*
feeding. *See also* food
    of animals, 59
    of arachnids, 148
    of bivalves, 137
    of crustaceans, 147
    of echinoderms, 139, 140
    of fish, 161
    of insects, 145
    of mammals, 187
    of sponges, 125, *125*
    of worms, 132, 133
ferns, *96*
    adaptation of, 92–93
    reproduction of, 97
    vascular system of, 96, *96*
fertilization, **48.** *See also* reproduction
    of cherry trees, 108, *109*
    of mosses, 95
    of pine trees, 100, *101*
fish, 158–162
    adaptation and development of, 165
    bony, *160,* 161
    cartilaginous, *160,* 161
    characteristics of, 158–159
    jawless, *160, 160*
    reproduction of, 161–162, *162*

INDEX

of animals, 62–64
of plants, 55–57
rod-shaped bacteria, 17, *17*
root systems, 87–90
of ferns, 96
rotovirus, *14*
round-shaped bacteria, 17, *17*
roundworms, 133, *133*

S

safety, R10–R11
animal, R11
chemical, R11
clean up, R11
directions, R10
dress code, R10
electrical, R11
fire, R10
glassware, R11
heating, R10
icons, R10–R11
lab, R10–R11
sharp object, R11
salamanders. *See* amphibians
sand dollars, 139
scales, **161**
scallops, 137, *137*
scavengers, 63
science, nature of, xxii–xxv
Science on the Job
wildlife photographer, 65
scientific notation, **R44**
scientific process, xxiii–xxv
asking questions and, xxiii
determining what is known and, xxiii
interpreting results and, xxv
investigating and, xxiv
sharing results and, xxv
scorpions, 148
SCUBA diving, 80
sea anemones, 128. *See also* cnidarians
sea cucumbers, 139
seasonal changes
adaptation to, 2–5
animal response to, 64
plant response to, 57
sea stars, 128, 139–140, *140,* 141, *141*
sea urchins, 139, *139*
seaweed, 31, 32, *32*
seeds, **98,** 98–103, *99, 101*
compared with spores, 99
and gynmosperms, 102–103
Internet Activity for, 83
and reproductive cycle, 100, *101*

survival of, 106
segmented worms, 132–133, *133*
sepals, 110, *110*
sessile, **125**
sexual reproduction, **48.** *See also* reproduction
and adaptation, 48–49, *49*
of amphibians, *166,* 167
of arthropods, 143
of cnidarians, 130
of ferns, *97*
of fish, 161–162
of fungi, 67–68
of insects, 146–147
of mosses, 95, 95
of reptiles, 169
of sponges, 126
of worms, 133
sharks, *160,* 161
shells, 136–138. *See also* eggs
significant figures, **R44**
single-celled organisms. *See* archaea; bacteria; organisms; protists; yeasts
siphon (cephalopods), 138
SI units. *See* International System of Units
skeletons
of arthropods, 143
of echinoderms, 139
endoskeletons, **157**
exoskeletons, **143**
skin
of amphibians, 167
of reptiles, 169
slides, making, R15, *R15*
slime molds, 31, 35
slugs, 137
smallpox virus, *26*
snails, 137, *137*
snakes. *See* reptiles
social behaviors, 63, *63*
social insects, 145
sperm cells, 48
spicules, 126
spiders, 148, *148*
spines, 139, *139*
spiracles
arachnid, 148
insect, 61, *61*
spiral-shaped bacteria, 17, *17*
sponges, 124, **125,** *125,* 125–126, *126*
spores, **67,** 67–68
compared with seeds, 99
and ferns, 97
and molds, 69, *69*
and mosses, 95, *95*
squids, 138
stamen, 110, *110*

INDEX

Acknowledgments

Photography

Cover © Buddy Mays/Corbis; **iii** Photograph of James Trefil by Evan Cantwell; Photograph of Rita Ann Calvo by Joseph Calvo; Photograph of Kenneth Cutler by Kenneth A. Cutler; Photograph of Douglas Carnine by McDougal Littell; Photograph of Linda Carnine by Amilcar Cifuentes; Photograph of Donald Steely by Marni Stamm; Photograph of Sam Miller by Samuel Miller; Photograph of Vicky Vachon by Redfern Photographics; **vi** © Orion Press/Corbis; **ix** *top* Photograph by Ken O'Donoghue; *bottom (both)* Photographs by Frank Siteman; **xiv, xv** © Mark Hamblin/Age Fotostock; **xvi, xvii** © Georgette Duowma/Taxi/Getty Images; **xviii, xix** © Ron Sanford/Corbis; **xx, xxi** © Nick Vedros & Assoc./Stone/Getty Images; **xxii** *left* © Michael Gadomski/Animals Animals; *right* © Shin Yoshino/Minden Pictures; **xxiii** © Laif Elleringmann/Aurora Photos; **xxiv** © Pascal Goetgheluck/Science Photo Library/Photo Researchers, Inc.; **xxv** *top left* © David Parker/Science Photo Library/Photo Researchers, Inc.; *top right* © James King-Holmes/Science Photo Library/Photo Researchers, Inc.; *bottom* Sinsheimer Labs/University of California, Santa Cruz; **xxvi, xxvii** *background* © Maximillian Stock/Photo Researchers, Inc.; **xxvi** Courtesy, John Lair, Jewish Hospital, University of Louisville; **xxvii** *top* © Brand X Pictures/Alamy; *center* Courtesy, AbioMed; **xxxii** © Chedd-Angier Production Company; **2, 3** *background* Yva Momatiuk/John Eastcott/Minden Pictures; **3** *top* © Pat O'Hara/Corbis; *bottom* © Darrell Gulin/Corbis; **4** *top left* © Bruce Marlin/Cirrus Digital Imaging; *top right* © A.B. Sheldon; *bottom* © Chedd-Angier Production Company; **6, 7** © Science VU/Visuals Unlimited; **7** *top* Photograph by Frank Siteman; *center* Photograph by Ken O'Donoghue; *bottom* © Custom Medical Stock Photo; **9** Photograph by Ken O'Donoghue; **10** *background* © Lynda Richardson/Corbis; *inset* © Astrid & Hanns-Frieder Michler/Photo Researchers, Inc.; **12** © A.B. Dowsett/Science Photo Library/Photo Researchers, Inc.; **13** Photograph by Ken O'Donoghue; **14** *right* © Dr. Gopal Murti/Photo Researchers, Inc.; *left* © K.G. Murti/Visuals Unlimited; **15** © CNRI/ Photo Researchers, Inc.; **16** © Dennis Kunkel/Visuals Unlimited; **17** *left* © Tina Carvalho/Visuals Unlimited; *center* © D.M. Phillips/Visuals Unlimited; *right* © CNRI/Photo Researchers, Inc.; **18** *left* © Grant Heilman/Grant Heilman Photography; *left inset* © Dr. Kari Lounatmaa/Photo Researchers, Inc.; *center* © Roger Tidman/Corbis; *center inset* © Alfred Pasieka/Science Photo Library/Photo Researchers, Inc.; *right* © ML Sinbaldi/Corbis; *right inset* © Wolfgang Baumeister/Photo Researchers, Inc.; **19** *left* © Jack Novak/Photri-Microstock; *left inset* © Dr. Kari Lounatmaa/Photo Researchers, Inc.; *center* © Dennis Flaherty/Photo Researchers, Inc.; *center inset* © Microfield Scientific LTD/Science Photo Library/Photo Researchers, Inc.; *right* © Dr. P. Marazzi/Science Photo Library/Photo Researchers, Inc.; *right inset* © Dr. Kari Lounatmaa/Photo Researchers, Inc.; **20** © *background* Runk/Schoenberger/Grant Heilman Photography; *left inset* © Simko/Visuals Unlimited; *right inset* © Dwight R. Kuhn; **21** © T.A. Zitter/Cornell University; **22** *top* © Adam Hart-Davis, Leeds Public Health Laboraory/Photo Researchers, Inc. ; *bottom (both)* Photographs by Ken O'Donoghue; **24, 25** Photographs by Frank Siteman; **26** © Hans Gelderblom/Visuals Unlimited; **27** *(both)* © Lee D. Simon/Photo Researchers, Inc.; **28** © Bettmann/Corbis; **29** *left* © Judy White/GardenPhotos.com; *right* © Dennis Kunkel Microscopy, Inc.; **30** © Corbis; **31** Photograph by Ken O'Donoghue; **32** *left* © R. Kessel-G. Shih/Visuals Unlimited; *center* © Jan Hinsch/Photo Researchers, Inc.; *right* © Runk/Schoenberger/Grant Heilman Photography; **33** © R. Kessel-C.Y. Shih/Visuals Unlimited; **34** © Andrew Syred/Photo Researchers, Inc.; **35** © Ed Reschke/Peter Arnold, Inc.; **36** *bottom left* © Runk/Schoenberger/Grant Heilman Photography; *bottom center* © Ed Reschke/Peter Arnold, Inc.; *bottom right* © Andrew Syred/Photo Researchers, Inc.; **38** *left* © A.B. Dowsett/Science Photo Library/Photo Researchers, Inc.; *right* © Science VU/Visuals Unlimited; **40, 41** © Orion Press/Corbis; **41** *top, center* Photographs by Ken O'Donoghue; **43** © David G. Massey/AP Wide World Photos; **44** Photograph by Frank Siteman; **45** © Joe McDonald/Bruce Coleman, Inc.; **46** © Michael Doolittle/PictureQuest; **47** *background* © Photospin; *top* © A. Mercieca/Photo Researchers, Inc.; *center* © Jim Brandenburg/Minden Pictures; *center inset* © Yva Momatiuk/John Eastcott/Minden Pictures; *bottom* © Tim Fitzharris/Minden Pictures; **48** © Matt Brown/Corbis; **49** *left* © Joe McDonald/Corbis; *right* © David J. Wrobel/Visuals Unlimited; **50** © Frans Lanting/Minden Pictures; **51, 52** Photographs by Ken O'Donoghue; **53** *top* © Peter Dean/Grant Heilman Photography; *inset* © Pascal Goetgheluck/Science Photo Library/Photo Researchers, Inc.; **54** *(both)* © D. Suzio/Photo Researchers, Inc.; **55** *left* © Joel Arrington/Visuals Unlimited; *right* © Gary W. Carter/Visuals Unlimited; **57** © Josiah Davidson/Picturesque/PictureQuest; **58** © Yva Momatiuk/John Eastcott/Minden Pictures; **59** *left* © Brandon Cole; *right* © Rauschenbach/Premium Stock/PictureQuest ; **60** Photograph by Frank Siteman; **61** *left and left inset* © Dwight R.Kuhn; *center* © Steve Maslowski/Visuals Unlimited; *right* © Belinda Wright/DRK Photo; **62** © J. Sneesby/B. Wilkins/Getty Images; **63** *top* © Shin Yoshino/Minden Pictures; *bottom left* © Charles V. Angelo/Photo Researchers, Inc.; *bottom right* © Fred McConnaughey/Photo Researchers, Inc.; **64** *left* © Ron Austing/Photo Researchers, Inc.; *right* © Kevin Schafer; **65** *left, top right* © Steve Winter/National Geographic Image Collection; *bottom right* © Brian J. Skerry/National Geographic Image Collection; **66** Photograph by Ken O'Donoghue; **68** © IFA/eStock Photography/PictureQuest ; **69** *top* © Andrew Syred/Science Photo Library/Photo Researchers; *bottom* © Simko/Visuals Unlimited; **71** *(both)* © Lennart Nilsson/Albert Bonniers Forlag AB; **72** *top* © Bob Daemmrich/Stock Boston, Inc./PictureQuest; *bottom* Photograph by Ken O'Donoghue; **73** Photograph by Frank Siteman; **74** *top* © Matt Brown/Corbis; *center* © Rauschenbach/ Premium Stock/PictureQuest ; *bottom* © IFA/eStock Photography/PictureQuest; **78** *top* © Academy of Natural Sciences of Philadelphia/Corbis; *bottom* © The Granger Collection, New York; **79** *top left, top right* © The Natural History Museum, London; *bottom left* © Photo Researchers, Inc.; *bottom right* © The Granger Collection, New York; **80** *top left* © B. Boonyaratanakornit & D.S. Clark, G. Vrdoljak/EM Lab, UC Berkeley/Visuals Unlimited, Inc.; *top right* © OAR/National Undersea Research Program; *center* © Terry Erwin/Smithsonian Institution; *bottom* © Emory Kristoff/National Geographic Image Collection; **81** *top left* © Michael Bordelon/Smithsonian Institution; *top right* © East London Museum; **82, 83** © David J. Job/AlaskaStock.com; **83** *(both)* Photographs by Ken O'Donoghue; **85** Photograph by Ken O'Donoghue; **86** *left* © Nick Garbutt/Nature Picture Library; *center* © D. Cavagnaro/Visuals Unlimited; *right* © Hal Horwitz/Corbis; **87** © Andrew Syred/Photo Researchers, Inc.; **88** *(both)* © Dr. Jeremy Burgess/Science Photo Library/Photo Researchers, Inc.; **89** *background* © Donna Disario/Corbis; *top left* ©

Photodisc/Getty Images; **90** © Craig K. Lorenz/Photo Researchers, Inc.; **91** *top* © Delphoto/Premium Stock/PictureQuest; *inset* © Unicorn Stock Photo; **92** Photograph by Frank Siteman; **93** *top* © Ray Simmons/Photo Researchers, Inc.; *bottom* The Field Museum of Natural History, #GEO85637c; **94** Photograph by Frank Siteman; **95** © Dwight R. Kuhn; **96** *left* © Dr. Jeremy Burgess/Science Photo Library/Photo Researchers, Inc.; *inset* School Division, Houghton Mifflin Co.; *right* © Michael & Patricia Fogden/Corbis; **97** *left* © Dwight R. Kuhn; *right* © Sylvester Allred/Fundamental Photographs; **98** © Keren Su/Corbis; **99** © Dwight R. Kuhn; **100** © Martha Cooper/Peter Arnold, Inc.; **101** *background* © Photospin; *top* © Scott Barrow/ImageState; *bottom* © Bryan Mullenix/Getty Images; **102** Photograph by Ken O'Donoghue; **103** © Robert Gustafson/Visuals Unlimited; **104** *top* © Michael J. Doolittle/The Image Works; *bottom right* © James A. Sugar/Corbis; **105** Photograph by Frank Siteman; **106** *left* © Raymond Gehman/Corbis; *top right* © David Sieren/Visuals Unlimited, Inc.; *bottom right* © George Bernard/Science Photo Library; **107** Photograph by Ken O'Donoghue; **109** *background* © John Marshall; *left* © George D. Lepp/Corbis; *center* © Sergio Piumatti; *right* © Gary Braasch/Corbis; **110** © Ed Reschke; **111** *top* Photograph by Ken O'Donoghue; *bottom* © Custom Medical Stock Photo; **112** *left* © Frank Lane Picture Agency/Corbis; *right* © Eastcott/ Momatiuc/Animals Animals; **113** *right* © Craig Aurness/Corbis; *inset* © Michael Newman/PhotoEdit; **114** *background* © Lance Nelson/Corbis; *top, left* National Cotton Council of America; *right* © Mary Kate Denny/PhotoEdit; **115** *left* © Patricia Agre/Photo Researchers, Inc.; *right* © Martin B. Withers, Frank Lane Picture Agency/Corbis; **116** *top* © Hal Horwitz/Corbis; *center left* © Martha Cooper/Peter Arnold, Inc.; *center right* © Dwight R. Kuhn; *bottom left* © Gary Braasch/Corbis; *bottom right* © George D. Lepp/Corbis; **117** *(both)* © Wolfgang Bayer/Bruce Coleman, Inc./PictureQuest ; **120, 121** © Norbert Wu; **121** *top* Photograph by Frank Siteman; *bottom* © Photospin; **123** © Andrew J. Martinez/ Visuals Unlimited; **124** Photograph by Ken O'Donoghue; **125** *background* © Viola's Photo Visions, Inc./Animals Animals; **126** © Marty Snyderman/Visuals Unlimited; **127** *background* © Kevin Schafer/Getty Images; **128** Photograph by Ken O'Donoghue; **129** © Photodisc/Getty Images; **130** *top left, bottom left* © John D. Cunningham/ Visuals Unlimited; **131** *left* © Bob Evans/Peter Arnold, Inc.; *right* © Visuals Unlimited; **132** © Dwight R.Kuhn; **133** *top* © Larry Lipsky/DRK Photo; *center* © A. Flowers & L. Newman/Photo Researchers, Inc.; *bottom* © Richard Kessel/Visuals Unlimited; **134** *top* © Robert Pickett/Corbis; *bottom* Photograph by Ken O'Donoghue; **135** *top* Photograph by Ken O'Donoghue; *bottom* Photograph by Frank Siteman; **136** © Sinclair Stammers/Photo Researchers, Inc.; **137** *top* © Andrew J. Martinez/Photo Researchers, Inc.; *bottom* © Konrad Wothe/Minden Pictures; **138** *top* Photograph by Ken O'Donoghue; *bottom* © Fred Bavendam/Minden Pictures; **139** *top* © Andrew J. Martinez; *bottom* © David Wrobel/Visuals Unlimited; **140** *left* © Fred Winner/Jacana/Photo Researchers, Inc.; *right* © Gerald & Buff Corsi/Visuals Unlimited; **141** *background* © Dwight R. Kuhn; *inset* Thomas Kitchin/Tom Stack & Associates; **142** Photograph by Frank Siteman; **143** *top* © Kelvin Aitken/Peter Arnold, Inc.; *bottom* © Barry Runk/Grant Heilman Photography; **144** *background* © Corbis-Royalty Free; *top* © Tim Davis/Corbis; *center* © Steve Wolper/DRK Photo; *bottom* © George Calef/DRK Photo; **146** Photograph by Ken O'Donoghue; **147** *top (all)* © Dwight R. Kuhn; *bottom* © Frans Lanting/Minden Pictures; **148** *top* © David Scharf/Peter Arnold, Inc.; **148** *bottom* © E.R. Degginger/Color-Pic, Inc.; **149** *left* © Science Photo Library/Photo Researchers, Inc.; *right* © Claus Meyer/Minden Pictures; **150** *top right* © Viola's Photo Visions, Inc./Animals Animals; *center left* © John D. Cunningham/Visuals Unlimited; *bottom left* © Konrad Wothe/Minden Pictures; *bottom right* © Gerald & Buff Corsi/Visuals Unlimited; **154, 155** © Paul A. Souders/Corbis; **155** *top* Photograph by Frank Siteman; *center left* © Steven Frame/Stock Boston Inc./PictureQuest; *center right* © Rod Planck/Photo Researchers, Inc.; **157** Photograph by Frank Siteman; **158** © Corbis-Royalty Free; **159** *background* © SeaLifeStyles Signature Series/Imagin; **160** *background* © Colla - V&W/Bruce Coleman, Inc.; *left* © Norbert Wu; *left inset* © Brandon Cole; *center* © Georgienne E. Bradley & Jay Ireland/Bradley Ireland Productions; *right* © Brandon Cole; **162** © David Doubilet; **163** *left* © Kennan Ward/Corbis; *right* © Frans Lanting/Minden Pictures; **164** *left* © Bianca Lavies/National Geographic Image Collection; *right* Photograph by Frank Siteman; **165** *left* © Dwight R. Kuhn; *right* © Joe McDonald/Bruce Coleman, Inc.; **166** *all* © Dwight R. Kuhn; **168** © Francois Gohier/Photo Researchers, Inc.; **169** © Carmela Leszczynski/Animals Animals; **170** *top* Photograph by Frank Siteman; *bottom* © Tui de Roy/Minden Pictures; **171** © Michael Fogden/Animals Animals; **172** *left* ©Frans Lanting/Minden Pictures; *center* © E.R. Degginger/Color-Pic, Inc.; *right* © Science Photo Library/Photo Researchers, Inc.; **173** Photograph by Ken O'Donoghue; **174** © Michael Quinton/Minden Pictures; **175** *left* © Julie Habel/Corbis; *center* © Randy Faris/Corbis; *right* © David-Young Wolff/PhotoEdit; **177** *background* © Tim Bird/Corbis; **178** *left* © Jim Brandenburg/Minden Pictures; *right* © Fritz Polking/Visuals Unlimited; **179** *top* © Ron Austing/Photo Researchers, Inc.; *bottom* © S. Nielsen/DRK Photo; **180** *top* © DigitalVision/PictureQuest; *bottom* Photograph by Frank Siteman **181** *top* Photograph by Frank Siteman; *bottom left* © Corbis-Royalty Free; *bottom center* © Frans Lemmens/ Getty Images; *bottom right* © Arthur Morris/Corbis; **182** © Carleton Ray/Photo Researchers, Inc.; **183** *top* © Mitsuaki Iwago/Minden Pictures; *bottom* © Don Enger/Animals Animals; **184** Photograph by Frank Siteman; **185** *background* © Stephen Frink/Corbis; **186** *left* © Photodisc/Getty Images; *right* © Frans Lanting/Minden Pictures; **187** © Comstock; **188** *top left* © Dwight R. Kuhn; *top right* © Michael Fogden/Animals Animals; *center right* © Fritz Polking/Visuals Unlimited; *bottom left* © Frans Lanting/Minden Pictures; *bottom right* © Photodisc/Getty Images; **r28** © PhotoDisc/ Getty Images.

Illustration and Maps

Robin Boutell/Wildlife Art Ltd. **132, 150** *(center right)*
Peter Bull/Wildlife Art Ltd. **26, 33, 34**
Myriam Kirkman-Oh/KO Studios **87**
Debbie Maizels **45, 56** *(inset)*, **89, 99, 101, 109, 118, 158**
MapQuest.com, Inc. **47**
Laurie O'Keefe **125, 130, 159, 185**
Mick Posen/Wildlife Art Ltd. **129**
Tony Randazzo/American Artists Rep. Inc. **56** *(background)*
Ian Jackson/Wildlife Art Ltd. **67, 70, 145, 150** *(bottom)*, **177**
Steve Oh/KO Studios **17, 27, 36**
UNEP-WCMC, 2002 World Atlas of Biodiversity **81**
Dan Stuckenschneider/Uhl Studios **R11-R19, R22, R32**